THE POETICS OF EPIPHANY IN THE SPANISH LYRIC OF TODAY

THE POETICS OF EPIPHANY IN THE SPANISH LYRIC OF TODAY

JUDITH NANTELL

Bucknell University | Bucknell University Press

Lewisburg, Pennsylvania

Library of Congress Cataloging-in-Publication Data

Names: Nantell, Judith, author.
Title: The poetics of epiphany in the Spanish lyric of today / Judith Nantell.
Description: Lewisburg, Pennsylvania : Bucknell University Press, [2019] | Includes bibliographical references and index.
Identifiers: LCCN 2019002489 | ISBN 9781684481576 (pbk.)
Subjects: LCSH: Spanish poetry—21st century—History and criticism. | Lyric poetry—History and criticism. | Cognition in literature. | Spanish poetry—21st century.
Classification: LCC PQ6086 .N36 2019 | DDC 861/.040907—dc23
LC record available at https://lccn.loc.gov/2019002489

A British Cataloging-in-Publication record for this book is available from the British Library.

∞ The paper used in this publication meets the requirements of the American National Standard for Information Sciences—Permanence of Paper for Printed Library Materials, ANSI Z39.48–1992.

www.bucknell.edu/UniversityPress
Distributed worldwide by Rutgers University Press

Manufactured in the United States of America

To Chris, with love

CONTENTS

NOTE ON TRANSLATIONS

Unless otherwise noted, translations are mine.

In chapter 1, on Luis Muñoz, many of the translations are from this poet's collection *From behind What Landscape: New and Selected Poems*, trans. Curtis Bauer (Madrid: Vaso Roto Ediciones, 2015).

In chapter 2, on Abraham Gragera, the majority of the translations are by Juan de Dios León Gómez.

In chapter 3, on Josep M. Rodríguez, the English translations by Ben Clark, Monika Izabela Jaworska, and Ester Boldú first appeared in *Radar. Antología bilingüe* (Lucena: El Orden del Mundo, 2017).

In chapter 4, on Ada Salas, the English translations are mine.

In presenting the poetry in Spanish in this book and in English translation I have attempted to reproduce the original spacing of the poetic lines given the limitations of production.

THE POETICS OF EPIPHANY IN THE SPANISH LYRIC OF TODAY

INTRODUCTION

There is a palpable literary vitality in Spain, and the poetry of the poets presented in this study is central to it. These authors exemplify the salient voices energizing the innovative expressivity characterizing the current Spanish lyric. Luis Muñoz, Abraham Gragera, Josep M. Rodríguez, and Ada Salas are representative catalysts, and their superb poetry collections, published from the cusp of the twenty-first century, continue to enliven literary studies and discussions. The first two decades of the new millennium signal this vibrant period that has advanced and enriched the course of Spain's poetry. The works of these poets best embody the invigorating results. Their efforts, as this book will demonstrate, reveal their own unique creative endeavors to engage with the poem as a method of epistemic inquiry. Each poet, in his or her own way, presents an exceptional discourse of discovery articulating the prominent theme inspiring this monograph—the poetics of epiphany.

INQUIRY

Detecting and elucidating the emergence of a sudden realization, of a unique instant of a startling revelation, of that flash of unforeseen and fresh understanding, grounds my study. By exploring selected representative poems, the book illustrates the sophisticated precision with which Muñoz, Gragera, Rodríguez, and Salas inventively shape their unique investigations and epiphanic results. How the poem illuminates an overall new understanding, at times in astounding ways, is the subject of my book. This significant feature of their works has not received the critical attention that it merits, and the present study addresses this matter. My work, however, does not seek to impose the theme of the poetics of epiphany onto all recent Spanish poetry. Instead, I offer an original thematic strategy for scrutinizing, as do each of these poets, both the nature of knowledge and the nature of poetry. Four central chapters provide a close reading of the language of the poems under investigation. Each also sheds light on the evolving process of writing the poem as a means for acquiring new understandings of poetry, reality, being, and epistemic inquiry. With distinctive access points—the instant in the case of Luis Muñoz, the word in the work of Abraham Gragera, the image as conceived and displayed by Josep M. Rodríguez, and the creative process in the poetry and poetics of Ada Salas—each poet elucidates new discoveries.

STRUCTURE

In chapter 1, "The Instant," I examine the propitious present moment in selected works by Luis Muñoz. A master at inspecting the constituents of the instantaneous, Muñoz's precise and meticulously crafted imagery successfully isolates this unique temporal interval and figuratively conveys its essence. In his work, unusual events and surprising situations often both encapsulate and portray unique insights into the instant. Chapter 2, "The Word," uncovers the cognitive potential of metaphor in the poetry of Abraham Gragera. The works that I study solidly demonstrate Gragera's desire to invent a new poetic discourse. To do so he infuses the word with a fresh referential capacity and transformative metaphoric energy. For Abraham Gragera, the genesis of the word is a revelatory transaction that makes the unknown known in approaching the world as if newly created. In chapter 3, "The Image," I investigate this figure in the poetry of Josep M. Rodríguez. The most salient feature of his remarkable work is his conception of the image as an exact and invaluable poetic instrument for cultivating an original discourse of analogy. With a refined and condensed expressivity, Rodríguez excels at divulging various instructive and epiphanic elucidations concerning ways in which to come to know, to experience, and to comprehend the complex aspects of human existence. Chapter 4, "Poetry and Poetics," examines this intimate interconnected relationship in the works of Ada Salas. Her keen mindfulness in pursuing the precise word coupled with her concentrated and introspective self-attentiveness to the linguistic identity of the poet characterize her current lyric. Ada Salas's poetry is in constant intertextual dialogue with her pensive and penetrating prose poetics. The chapter examines this innovative intersection and demonstrates that Salas's excavations into the potential expressivity of the word define the activity of artistic creation. Both her exquisitely chiseled poems and her elucidating prose poetics manifest writing as a sustained epistemic endeavor.

I selected the poets because of the quality of their poetry and the different and exciting ways in which their innovative works manifest aspects of the overall thematic matter central to my monograph. Throughout, I make no attempt to compare or contrast the poets and their poetry because each individual author presents crucial facets of the book's essential theme in his or her own singularly distinguished way. Structurally, the book does not adhere to a chronological ordering of the poets or to the poetic works examined in each chapter. This stance sets my work apart from the more general and historical investigations surveying Spain's contemporary poetry in a linear manner during the final decades of the twentieth century. Such studies are notable because their authors establish temporal considerations regarding the evolution of Spanish poetry from a point in time. My study takes these time-based studies into full consideration.[1] I ground my thematic study, however, in an analytical and thematic approach to the poems of the selected poets in my book.

UNIQUE FEATURES

My book displays innovative and multifaceted features not usually found in traditional scholarly monographs. The four poets whose works I examine have been involved in my book during its development. This was accomplished in various ways: personal conversations with each, e-mail correspondences, meetings to discuss the progress of the book manuscript, and intellectual discussions that constantly renewed and bolstered the evolution of an investigative research project that I had begun as early as 2012–2013. Their contributions are evident from the outset. There are four central chapters each of which concerns the work of a specific poet. At the beginning of each chapter, a personal biographical account is provided, written by the poet at my request. The first endnote in each chapter introduces the poet to the reader by first presenting relevant bibliographical contributions since the turn of the new century. In the previous section, "Note on Translations," specific sources are provided by chapter. This deviation from a standard introduction to the poet allowed each the opportunity to sketch an original and individualized self-portrait from a personalized perspective. Captivatingly honest, humble, and epiphanic, these self-representations spotlight unanticipated and, at times enticing, revelations. They bring to light many new discoveries, many of which were unknown to me. Their own biographical contributions to my study provide entryways to the chapters. My only prerequisite was the length of the personal biography, nothing more.

Each chapter concludes with another novel aspect to the book. The final section of each chapter features a poem that the poet selected as exemplifying his or her poetics of epiphany. Each of these poems is followed by an interpretive analysis written by the poet for inclusion in the book. The explications are personal, inimitable, exquisite, and epistemic. These poetics of epiphany have not been published before and, thus, are unique to my book. Again, these analyses also were written at my request for a debut in my study. I provided no guidelines, asking only that the explication conform to a certain length and/or word count range. The poem selection was left entirely to each poet, and it did not matter to me if the work was new, old, or examined in my book.

Both participatory events on the part of each of the poets distinguish and enhance my study in ways in which I had not anticipated. Each appreciated the opportunity to choose and present features of their life and their work in a personalized discourse. The self-reflective poem analysis crafted by each of the poets provides the reader with insights into poetry as an epiphanic process from an individualized poetic perspective.

Three other facets of the monograph are worthy of note. Throughout, my book presents translations into English of the material quoted in Spanish.[2] In this way the study invites an international readership. Also, after each of the poet's chapters, my monograph also provides an exclusive section presenting the poems examined in the chapter in their full context. Each poem appears first in Spanish and then is followed by an English translation. Having the poems appear in full with translations at the end of each chapter allows the reader to interact with the text and to engage more fully in the analyses I offer in the relevant chapter. Lastly, each poet, at my request, has provided a recent photograph for inclusion in my book. The photograph was to be in black and white. Each poet considered their own photograph as forming a part of the chapter introducing their personal biography and works.

RECONSTRUCTING RECENT SPANISH POETRY

The aim of my monograph is not to establish the most recent history of the development of Spanish poetry. Nonetheless, the poetry I examine did not emerge in a vacuum, and the poets I include did not develop in isolation. Each of them, however, comprehends that one of the defining characteristics of poetry is that it is dynamic and not static, that its *modus operandi* is one of constant movement and continuing change. Luis Muñoz indicates in an early poetics in 1999, "La poesía está obligada a moverse, como un pueblo nómada. Y en el trasiego, en las paradas de ese camino, que tantas veces tiene el carácter de una huida, y de un agotamiento, paradójicamente se vigoriza, se tonifica" (*La generación del 1999*, 253). [Poetry is compelled to shift, like a nomadic people. And in this passage, in the stopovers along the way, which so often display the feature of flight, and exhaustion, paradoxically, it is energized, reinvigorated.]

In looking back, the era of the 1980s and 1990s in Spanish poetry was one of intense debate. Factions arose arguing for or against poetry written in a specific style and with certain aims. In a portion of his 2005 "Transición," which served as the introductory poetics for his recompilation of his poetry published prior to that date, titled *Limpiar pescado. Poesía reunida (1991–2005)*, Muñoz surveys these decades and offers firsthand insight into Spanish poetry of that era and its effects on his evolution as a poet.[3] He explains that certain "schools of Spanish poetry" advocated for explicit ideas and aesthetic concepts.[4] He found that these had little to do with his way of "understanding poetry." He also discovered that his approaches to and self-reflections concerning his own poetic enterprise as a new poet in that same era did not necessarily "coincide with" the thoughts and practices being advanced by the "opposing groups" ("Transición," 11). Although he admired "some of the poets of the time," he was not able "to assimilate the debates" (*From behind What Landscape*, 135, 137). Focusing on a turning point for the strategic approaches that he would use in becoming a poet and in writing his poetry, Muñoz explains, in this same poetics, the impact of the work of the Italian author Giuseppe Ungaretti,[5] indicating,

> La lectura de los poemas de Ungaretti y de sus ensayos y declaraciones sobre la naturaleza de la poesía me sirvieron para observar con cierta perspectiva este cruce de consignas y para intentar construirme un diálogo con las distintas formas de entender la poesía y sobre todo para formular mis propias preguntas en torno a ella. La concepción que Ungaretti tuvo de su obra como la de alguien que ha reflexionado sobre el sentido de la poesía en profundidad, pero cuya preocupación mayor era encontrar un modo de expresión que se correspondiera íntegramente con su vida de hombre, que es lo que dice en el arranque de *Ragioni di una poesia*, me sirvió para entender que la tarea es solitaria y debe ir, como también dijo Ungaretti, a reafirmar "la integridad, la autonomía y la dignidad de la persona." ("Transición," 12–13)
>
> [The reading of Ungaretti's poems and his essays and declarations about the nature of poetry helped me observe with a certain perspective this intersection of slogans in order to construct for myself a dialogue with different ways of understanding poetry and, most of all, to formulate my own questions around it. Ungaretti's conception of his own work as that of someone who has reflected deeply on poetic rhetoric but whose major concern was to find a mode of expression that would correspond entirely with his life as a man, which is what he says at the beginning of *Ragioni di una poesia*, helped me understand that the task is solitary and must work, as Ungaretti also said, to reaffirm "the integrity, autonomy, and dignity of the individual."] (*From behind What Landscape*, 137)

Earlier, and from a different point of view, Ignacio Elguero explains in the introduction to his 2002 *Inéditos 11 poetas*, "Ahora posiblemente asistamos a un nuevo cambio, a otro giro, a otra saludable evolución propiciada por la libertad que permite no tener que escribir como o para alguien, la libertad de las individualidades."[6] [Perchance now we may be witnessing a new change, another shift, another healthy evolution made possible by freedom that allows for not having to write like or for someone, the freedom of individualities.] Diana Cullell offers important insight explaining the following: "The young poets of the twenty-first century were not interested in the earlier altercations between poetic factions and tendencies. [. . .] Distancing themselves from such debates, they strived to achieve something new without adhering to established precepts or previous groups. [. . .] The rejection and dismissal of factions and poetic groups that had polarized the previous decade and a half allowed a much richer map of poetic aesthetics to emerge, together with significant poetic creativity" ("Introduction," *Spanish Contemporary Poetry*, 22).

The personal biographies that I have included in my book for the poets whose works I study exhibit this sense of personal identity and individuality. However, these two traits are most evident when the poems and their analyses of their own poem are taken into consideration. Muñoz, Gragera, Rodríguez, and Salas are first and foremost poets. They take their "oficio" seriously, and they always have. My conversations with these poets have enlightened my views concerning their engaging in their own creative activity of writing regardless of schools, camps, and slogans that developed or even could be developing in Spain. Ada Salas indicates in her most recent poetics from 2016, which I quote toward the end of my chapter 4 on her work, that she cannot imagine living without writing. To do so would be, for her, to renounce life. These poets write and will continue to write. As they engage in their future poetry, each will do so in his or her own way according to personal intuitions, insights, expectations, and needs to express. Their poetry contributes to the ongoing "conversation" that Andújar perceptively describes in 2008, "La poesía debe cambiar continuamente de conversación. Si no lo hace, está perdida."[7] [Poetry should continuously change its conversation. If it doesn't, it is lost.]

POETRY UNDER CONSTRUCTION

In today's poetry published in Spain, there are significant avenues worthy of exploration. Various thematic matters and stylistic manifestations surface. Several of these thoughtfully have been disclosed and studied by literary critics who, in some cases, also are poets. There are many diverse and worthwhile entry points. I indicate the contributions of important anthologies, listed here by author/editor and by chronological date of publication, to provide an overview surveying current Spanish scholarship on this lively era of the lyric. This enumeration is not exhaustive, but it does situate significant works by, for example, Luis Antonio de Villena (2003, 2010), Rafael Morales Barba (2006), María Rosal (2006), Juan Carlos Abril (2008), Ángel L. Prieto de Paula (2010), Luis Bagué Quílez (2012), Remedios Sánchez García and Anthony Geist (2015), and Vicente Luis Mora (2016).[8] Very noteworthy literary criticism, new investigative approaches, and additional introductions—in some cases, to anthological works—also are significant portals through which to begin to review a productive era in Spanish poetry. I offer here the works of Antonio Jiménez Millán (2006), Alberto Santamaría (2006), Domingo Sánchez-Mesa Martínez (2014), José Andújar Almansa (2007, 2008, 2014), Juan Carlos Abril (2008, 2011, 2013), Luis Bagué Quílez (2008, 2012, 2013, 2014), José-Carlos Mainer (2009), Ángel L. Prieto de Paula (2009, 2010, 2014), Diana Cullell (2014), Araceli Iravedra (2014), and Juan José Lanz (2014).[9] Of importance is the seminal special issue on contemporary Spanish poetry published by *Ínsula. Revista de letras y ciencias humanas* in 2014,[10] which I shall discuss shortly and where I shall indicate the several literary critics contributing to this groundbreaking publication and the titles of their illustrative articles. All the works mentioned above, as well as those I shall refer to from the 2014 *Ínsula* special issue greatly inform the critical inquiry underlying my book.

The current Spanish lyric is constantly involved in its own invigorating construction and as such it provides innumerable possibilities for other explorations. New poets emerge. Innovative books of poetry are published. Fresh critical approaches offer additional ideas. Poetics are reformulated. Innovative insights are revealed. Today in Spain, two approaches to examining the lyric are evident, and my study better converges with these. On the part of several of the poets, there is a tendency to see themselves as individuals and their works as unique. During this self-examination process, they demonstrate the view of being active participants in a more global poetry stretching beyond the confines of linguistic, geographic, and/or past conventional territories. Nonetheless, recent poets do not denounce the Spanish literary tradition or any other poetic tradition. Most firmly believe that their own work is intimately connected with it. Josep M. Rodríguez, for example, offers insights. He explains in 2001, "Cada autor debe bucear en la tradición, trazar su propia ruta de acceso a la poesía."[11] [Each author should dive into the tradition, chart his own access route to poetry.] This poet articulates in 2003 another formative aspect of today's poet that also is worthy of consideration, "En la actualidad, la poesía española se enriquece con el diálogo entre generaciones."[12] [At the moment, the dialogue among generations enhances Spanish poetry.] He further affirms in 2008, "Cada poeta establece su propio árbol genealógico, ya sea en función de sus gustos, de sus prejuicios, de sus intenciones o del azar. [. . .] Creo en una tradición lo más plural y abierta posible."[13] [Each poet establishes his own family tree, it may be a function of his tastes, biases, intentions, or chance. (. . .) I believe in the most plural and the most open possible tradition.] These attitudes are shared by others. The poet Juan Carlos Abril maintains that he and his contemporaries are attentive to continuing a "search for other traditions" (*Campos magnéticos*, 14). Poet Martín López-Vega believes that he and others foster "a universal poetic tradition" (2011).[14] The plurality of protagonists, experiences, and styles and the embracing of a rich and multicultural literary tradition reflect, in the opinion of Sánchez-Mesa, their work as translators (*Cambio de siglo*, 41) and their voracious readings of poetry, past and present, from countries other than Spain, as Andújar indicates in 2008 ("El paisaje de la poesía última," 32–33). On the part of a few critics, among them Abril, Andújar, Bagué, Morales Barba, and Sánchez-Mesa, their own tendency to avoid the term "generation" underscores their view that the poets of today display a multiplicity of voices and wide-ranging, varied, and international influences without borders. Bagué, himself a poet, observes in 2014 when surveying current Spanish poetry that the traditional denominations no longer adequately characterize "a creative process that is under construction." He finds "una suerte de desconfianza endémica hacia las definiciones colectivas por parte de los poetas actuales" (5) [a kind of defensive uneasiness with identificational groupings on the part of the present-day poets]. And in looking back, Bagué further reports, "Lo cierto es que ni unos (los nacidos en los sesenta) ni otros (los nacidos en los setenta) se dejan atrapar fácilmente por los alfileres de la taxonomía" ("La poesía bajo el efecto," 2014, 5). [What is certain is that neither some (those born in the sixties) nor others (those born in the seventies) allow themselves to get easily pinned down by taxonomy.]

NOMENCLATURES

My book deviates from the more traditional method advanced in Spain for investigating poets and their works within the classification of a literary "generation." My decision was deliberate and liberating. The generational approach usually is determined by an interval of fifteen years where an assemblage of poets demonstrates a similarity in birthdates and/or in publishing a first significant work and/or in sharing common aesthetic pursuits, as Luis Antonio de Villena indicates (*La inteligencia y el hacha*, 7–8). The principally time-sensitive limitations of the generational method, in my view, confine poets and their poetry within a rubric that has been superimposed by critics. My book illustrates, instead, a perspective voiced in 2013 by a current poet and essayist, Juan Carlos Abril, who argues the following:

> Cuando hablamos de "generación" sabemos las imprecisiones que podemos cometer, pero también es verdad que usamos al término de manera laxa, sin rigores cientificistas ni resabios académicos. Además, en España, se ha impuesto en las aproximaciones y recuentos últimos una suerte de decantación que suele depender más de la década en la que le ha tocado nacer al poeta que en el intervalo de los tres lustros. [. . .] No hay correspondencia directa entre las fechas de nacimiento y las de acceso a la publicación, y este es otro aspecto que cualquier caracterización debería tener en cuenta: son las obras —y no la edad o el grado

> de madurez de los autores— las que marcan las pautas. ("Hacia otra caracterización," 35, 36)
>
> [When we talk about a "generation," we know the inaccuracies we can make, but it also is true that we use the term with laxity, without scientific rigor or academic traces. Moreover, in Spain, it recently has become a common approach and a way to verify a kind of separational process that often depends more on the decade in which the poet happens to be born. (. . .) There is no direct correspondence between dates of birth and those of access to publication, and this is another aspect that any characterization should consider: the works—and not the age or wisdom of the authors—set the standard.]

The present study also is not an anthology. Reviewing the current lyric in the format of an anthology can be beneficial, as I noted at the outset in my chronological overview mentioning works informing my study. The anthological approach is especially fruitful when the work presents an instructive and objective preface or introduction, a brief statement on the poets whose works are featured, an illustrative "poetics" by the poet or an original written response by the poet to a questionnaire, a representative selection of poems, and, finally, a relevant bibliography. The anthological practice often can be useful for situating recent Spanish poetry in a linear, historic, and chronological pattern or for highlighting the evolution of emergent trends. These, however, are not the aims of my critical investigative monographic.

At times, authors combine a version of both the generational and anthological methodologies in portraying a specific gathering of poets and poetry. Luis Antonio de Villena's recent 2010 work serves as an example. But other critics do not follow this joint approach. Sánchez-Mesa, in his incisive 2014 article "Guardianes de la diversidad: Funciones de las antologías en la era de las multitudes" (*Ínsula*, 22–25), convincingly "deactivates" what he refers to as "la ecuación *antología = aparato generacional*" (22) [the equation *anthology = instrument for classifiying generations*], long dominating literary considerations reflecting the course of various eras. His own 2007 *Cambio de siglo*, unfortunately out of print, is an example of one such significant deactivation. In 2015, Visor published an innovative anthology encompassing a transatlantic examination of the newest poetry being published in the language of Spanish. This work is a collaborative effort by Remedios Sánchez García and Anthony L. Geist and is titled *El canon abierto: Última poesía en español 1970–1985*. No longer confined to geographic borders, the conventional literary canon, or the generational methodology, this work opens current poetry studies by including forty Latin American and Spanish poets from this era.

LITERARY EVENTS

Significant literary events and publications frame, shape, and ground my book. The 2014 January–February special issue of *Ínsula. Revista de letras y ciencias humanas*, Spain's foremost journal on poetry, is one of them. This superlative issue features first-rate investigations concerning Spanish contemporary poetry, as the title of this issue indicates. It is a cultural landmark in recent Spanish literary criticism, providing, on the one hand, a retrospective appraisal of the poetry written at the intersection of the years marking the end of the twentieth-century and the inaugural decades of the twenty-first century. Furthermore, the issue provides indisputable insights in the various critical articles it gathers for examining the course of the Spanish lyric of today. Admirably, this 2014 *Ínsula* issue presents in one place invaluable assessments by several of the leading Spanish literary critics. Essential to my book are the works of Prieto de Paula, "Poesía y contemporaneidad: Unas cuestiones de partida" (*Ínsula*, 2–5); Bagué, "La poesía española bajo el efecto 2000" (*Ínsula*, 5–8); Iravedra, "Función de poesía y función de la crítica: Del realismo a la realidad" (*Ínsula*, 8–12); Andújar, "El signo borrado: poéticas simbolistas para un nuevo siglo" (*Ínsula*, 12–15); Lanz, "Poéticas del fragmento y esquirlas dialógicas en la poesía española reciente (1992–2013)" (*Ínsula*, 15–18); and Sánchez-Mesa, "Guardianes de la diversidad" (*Ínsula*, 22–25), among others.

This special issue furnishes a copious assembly of poems, poetics, and commentaries by many exemplary poets currently publishing in Spain (30–48). This remarkable publication features all four of the poets whose work I investigate in my book. The 2014 *Ínsula* issue incorporates the most recent poetics of Luis Muñoz titled "El poema no escrito" (40–41) and "Poética I" by Abraham Gragera (44–45). It presents an illuminating analysis by Ada Salas of one of her most recent poems, "Fragmento III del poema 'Chanson du désir'" from *Limbo y otros poemas* (2013), in a study titled "El deseo es lo mudo" (40). Josep M. Rodríguez closely examines his poem "Fractura" from *Arquitectura yo* (2012) in a splendid study highlighting the intertextual dialogue elucidating this work (46–47). This indispensable issue also includes a bibliography of the works cited in the critical articles (28–29). This 2014 cultural, critical, and poetic compilation is fundamental to any scholarly investigation of the Spanish lyric of today and tomorrow, and notably, it has fueled my book.

With the aid of hindsight, Luis Muñoz's 1998 publication in *Clarín. Revista de nueva literatura* of his article-poetics titled "Un nuevo simbolismo"[15] could, perhaps, be viewed as a significant literary event launching a few of the fundamental views on the inventive expressive capacity of the lyric in Spain today. There, he establishes significant characteristics that also would soon stimulate the rejuvenation of language as relevant to his own poetry: "la vigilancia permanente sobre agotamientos expresivos del lenguaje, de la renovación constante de [. . .] ese lado de construcción lingüística que necesita de la buena novedad, de la novedad que abre el camino, de la novedad que ensancha el campo de la poesía" (21) [the permanent attentiveness to the depletion of language's expressivity, the constant renovation of (. . .) linguistic constructions in need of genuine innovation, inventiveness that blazes a trail, innovation that expands the field of poetry]. This view of attentive "vigilance" and vital "innovation" would become the hallmarks of the current lyric. It is Muñoz's 1998 poetics that establishes the groundwork for this poetry and my book: "los fenómenos expresivos y estéticos, toda la interacción de las palabras, de sonidos y de imágenes que conforman al poema" (21) [the meaningful and aesthetic phenomena, all interaction among words, sounds, and images that shape the poem]. In a 2016 published "dialogue" with fellow poet Ana Gorría, Muñoz self-reflectively observes: "La verdad es que no sé el peso que haya podido tener el artículo 'Un nuevo simbolismo', aunque algunos poetas de la promoción siguiente a la mía me han dicho que tuvo cierta importancia para ellos."[16] [The truth is that I don't know the importance that the article "A New Symbolism" might have had, although some poets subsequently have told me that it had a certain significance for them.]

Spain's premier, most distinguished, and admirably perceptive literary critic examining this era in poetry, José Andújar Almansa, underscores the undeniable presence of Luis Muñoz. He observes one decade after Muñoz's 1998 pioneering article, "El nombre que suena con mayor ascendente entre los poetas últimos es el de Luis Muñoz, quien desde *Manzanas amarillas* (1995) y, sobre todo, *Correspondencias* (2001) supo incidir de manera fértil en la revisión de algunos aspectos de las poéticas del simbolismo moderno" ("Paisaje de la poesía última," 33). [The name that rings the loudest among the recent poets is that of Luis Muñoz who, since *Manzanas amarillas* (1995) and, above all, *Correspondencias* (2001), understood how to influence productively the reconsideration of some aspects of the poetics of modern symbolism]. Without question, Muñoz's 1998 poetics holds a formidable place in Spanish letters because it offered new and exciting ways to engage in the poetic enterprise during the initial decades of the third millennium. Unmistakably innovative, this essay is a cornerstone poetics, and it was Muñoz's leading voice that began the process of enriching the evolving aesthetic ("Retrato robot," 27, 29). He further explains that Muñoz's own poetry, in following the premises that he outlined in 1998, also provided a new impetus for fostering the fresh exploration of "alternative routes" for new discovery ("El paisaje de la poesía última," 33) and the renovation of poetic discourse ("El signo borrado," 12). In her recent 2016 work, Araceli Iravedra underscores the "privileged point of reference" his poetry has and its inspiring allure, where both signal a decisive break with "the fossilization of the rhetoric of experientialism."[17] This 1998 article by Luis Muñoz undeniably assisted in shaping the trajectory of twenty-first-century poetry; the evidence of which is apparent in the works I examine in my book. This stimulus, in looking back, articulated with finesse and instructive guidance in 1998, is an instrumental poetics that could be considered as an early catalyst for the renovation of creative expressivity featured in many of the analyses in the present monograph. In 2014, José Andújar Almansa wisely explains why, "El poeta proponía allí una iniciativa posible de renovación, de superación de estériles debates entre la claridad y la oscuridad expresiva y, sobre todo, de vigilancia permanente sobre los agotamientos del lenguaje" ("El signo borrado," 12). [The poet proposed a possible plan of action for regeneration, for overcoming the sterile debates between expressive clarity and obscurity, and, above all, for permanent attentiveness to the depletion of language's expressivity.]

FINDINGS AND THE FUTURE

My book originates in the adventurous spirit with which each of the authors—Luis Muñoz, Abraham Gragera, Josep M. Rodríguez, and Ada Salas—enters a close examination of their own linguistic identity as a poet. Their collections of poetry and various poetics portray their individual strategies for establishing the essence of their craft and solidifying the foundations of their chosen vocation. Poetry becomes an exploration, a speleological expedition where the expressed desire to come to know and to appreciate "the instant," in the case of Luis Muñoz; "the word," in the poetry of Abraham Gragera; "the image," as conceived and displayed in the work of Josep M. Rodríguez; and the creative process evidenced in the "poetry and poetics" of Ada Salas. This quest results in new discoveries when the poem assumes the role of an epistemological mode of inquiry.

This is the first scholarly book to posit and trace this innovative thematic matter in the twenty-first-century works of Muñoz, Gragera, Rodríguez, and Salas. Is this a theme emerging in more Spanish poetry of this era? Answering this question requires further investigation, and I leave that to the exploratory work and investigative research endeavors of others. There are, however, other areas that I believe merit further study. When I first entered what was, in the beginning, an unknown territory to me, I encountered several poets whose works piqued my interest. I was drawn to poems by Luis Espejo, Martín López-Vega, Antonio Lucas, Erika Martínez, Elena Medel, and Ana Merino, alphabetically named. I found the range of poetic voices and the ontological concepts with which each of them grapples appealing and intellectually exciting. Their explorations of the nature of human identity and evolving self-knowledge is intriguing and worthy of study. In the afterword to my book, I shall point the way to a few of the newest poets whose works warrant attention.

Luis Muñoz, photograph by Cynthia Smart

1 * LUIS MUÑOZ: THE INSTANT

PERSONAL BIOGRAPHY BY MUÑOZ

Nací en Granada en 1966.[1] La biblioteca de mi abuelo paterno, que estuvo durante la guerra civil española encarcelado y condenado a muerte por tener libros "rojos", a la que tenía acceso cuando nos dejaba a mis hermanos y a mí las llaves de su casa la mitad del año que vivía en Canarias, me abrió los ojos a la poesía. Mis primeras lecturas: Juan Ramón Jiménez, Machado y Lorca, de quien mi abuelo tenía algunas primeras ediciones. Estudié en un colegio católico, los Maristas, que me dejó un recuerdo agridulce y como velado, unido al despertar de mi homosexualidad. En la Universidad de Granada, que vivía entonces un momento de efervescencia poética, estudié Filología. Siendo estudiante tuve mis primeras relaciones amorosas importantes. En 1989 me trasladé a Madrid para trabajar como secretario de Rafael Alberti, cuya forma de vivir la poesía me marcó profundamente. En 1991 publiqué *Septiembre*. Volví a Granada en 1992, donde dirigí la revista de poesía *Hélice* y el Aula de Literatura de la Universidad. En esos años publiqué *Manzanas amarillas*, *El apetito* y *Correspondencias*. En 2001 me trasladé de nuevo a Madrid donde trabajé como asesor literario de la Residencia de Estudiantes. Mi primera tarea fue trabajar con los archivos personales de Luis Cernuda que la Residencia acababa de adquirir. En 2006 publiqué *Querido silencio*. Desde 2013 soy profesor en la Universidad de Iowa, donde la comunidad de escritores es un estímulo constante. En 2015 he publicado *From behind What Landscape*, una selección de mi poesía que incluye nuevos poemas.

[I was born in Granada in 1966. The library of my paternal grandfather, who during the Spanish Civil War was incarcerated and condemned to death for having "red" books, was something I could access. He left my siblings and me his house keys for half of the year when he would live in the Canary Islands. His library opened my eyes to poetry. My first readings were Juan Ramón Jiménez, Machado, and Lorca, of whose works my grandfather had some first editions. I studied at a Catholic school, run by the Marist Brothers, and that left me with a bittersweet and veiled memory, connected to the awakening of my homosexuality. At the University of Granada, at a time of poetic effervescence, I studied philology. As a student, I had my first significant romantic relationships. In 1989, I moved to Madrid to work as a secretary for Rafael Alberti, whose way of living life and poetry had a profoundly long-lasting effect on me. In 1991, I published *Septiembre*. I returned to Granada in 1992 where I directed the poetry magazine *Hélice* and the university's Aula de Literatura. In those years, I published *Manzanas amarillas, El apetito,* and *Corrrespondencias*. In 2001, I once again moved to Madrid where I was the literary consultant for the Residencia de Estudiantes. My first project concerned the personal archives of Luis Cernuda, whose works the Residencia had just acquired. In 2006, I published *Querido silencio*. Since 2013, I have been a Spanish professor at the University of Iowa, where the community of writers is a constant stimulus. In 2015, I published *From behind What Landscape*, a selection of my poetry that includes new poems.]

ON THE EDGE OF THE PRESENT

"Limpiar pescado" [Cleaning fish]. With this surprising and intriguing image, Luis Muñoz confirms the prominence of the present instant in his poetry and poetics. "Limpiar pescado"—a common domestic situation, a daily occupation relying on the tides, an accurate and yet astonishing imaging of the brief and suspended moment in which what is fresh soon and suddenly can spoil. The analogy asserts an imperative. It also emphasizes an exacting, time-sensitive process. With imaginative insight and condensed expressivity, these two seemingly simple words summon and summarize the necessity of apprehending the present instant in the poetry of Luis Muñoz. The striking comparison is compelling and cannot be ignored because it signals, strangely enough, his views on the nature of time and on the creative act in time. The immediate task at hand for this poet is to seize the present instant as a propitious site for detailed inspection and incisive interpretation. The immediacy of the moment in the poetry of Luis Muñoz is palpable. It is his to examine and articulate, and he does so with refined finesse—choosing the precise word, offering pristine and unparalleled analogies, and presenting the poem as an epiphanic occasion for fresh illumination. For Muñoz, the instant is to be experienced fully and lived without delay. It is his task to present this moment before it diffuses into the future or is absorbed into the past. Creative activity occurs in the instant of the inception of the idea, the intense experience of the sensorial, the sudden illuminations arising from the everyday, the self-reflective moment of being in the world. The instant, like the poem, manifests a timely epistemic encounter inducing an inspiring and provocative response in the work of Luis Muñoz.

Muñoz explains his own discovery of this image as an epiphany. In his 2012 poetics, "Atracción de los opuestos"[2] [Attraction of Opposites], he discloses:

> La imagen de mi madre limpiando boquerones en la pila de cocina del pequeño apartamento de la playa, en Torre del Mar, con una pericia y una delicadeza que tenía grabadas en la memoria desde niño [. . .] Se me reveló aquel verano luminosamente parecida a las operaciones que se suceden en la escritura de un poema, a la manipulación de ese material tan fresco, pero tan perecedero de lo que está al punto de ser escrito.
>
> [The image of my mother cleaning anchovies in the kitchen sink in the small beach apartment, at Torre del Mar, with dexterity and finesse [was] etched in memory since childhood. (. . .) That summer, I experienced the sudden revelation that her activity was illuminative like the activities that occur when writing a poem, that manipulation of material so fresh and yet so perishable, like what is on the verge of being written.]

He further explains, in this same poetics, that for him, the image "limpiar pescado" embodies "la metáfora que más se acerca a cómo vivo la experiencia de escribir poesía. Es decir, me veo en ella, siento que me resume" ("Atracción de los opuestos," 82) [the metaphor that is closest to how I live the experience of writing poetry. In other words, I see myself in it, I feel it summarizes me]. Muñoz so fervently identifies with his analogy that he uses it as the title for the recompilation of the works that he published prior to 2005, *Limpiar pescado. Poesía reunida 1991–2005*[3] [*Cleaning Fish: Collected Poems, 1991–2005*].

The incomparable poetics "Transición" [Transition] introduces the regathering of his earlier work in *Limpiar pescado.*[4] In this introductory essay, Muñoz expresses his unique views concerning the interconnections of his concept of the instant, his poetry, and himself as a poet. He indicates, "La poesía creo está en el *todavía.* El poeta trabaja, como el pescadero que limpia el pescado, contra el tiempo. Tiene en sus manos un material que es la promesa de un alimento y de una descomposición" ("Transición," 7–8). ["I think the poetry is in the *yet.* The poet works, like the fishmonger who cleans the fish, against time. He has in his hands material that is the promise of both nourishment and of rot"] (*From behind What Landscape*, 123). This effective comparison prevails throughout his most recent work. It both fuels many of the thematic matters under scrutiny in his poetry and underscores the decisive technique he employs with unrivaled expertise. As a unifying feature of his work, this image firmly establishes Muñoz's remarkable gift for extracting from the ordinary of daily life the immediate opportunity for epistemic discovery.

Probing the present defines the enterprise in which Luis Muñoz engages in his work. It also characterizes the thematic matters under examination in the present chapter. For Muñoz, the present is an interval demonstrating the intrinsic vitality residing deeply within it. Accessing this innermost aspect of the present, the instant, is the task at hand. Muñoz finds that the instant offers an opportune occasion for portraying the genesis of the poem during the concentrated moment of the creative act. He also seeks to encounter the intricate structural components of the instant. Here, he discovers that the poem is his meticulous instrument for inspecting, in fine detail, the innermost essence of this most immediate event. Because the instant is transitory in nature, he comprehends the sense of urgency underlying his quest. Keen attentiveness is a required if he is to examine and appreciate the significance of being in time.

Fleeting aspects involving life in the everyday must be recognized. Commonplace objects and situations offer opportune moments for new discoveries. These findings point to the thematic matters under scrutiny in this chapter. At the same time, they reveal the existential ethic interwoven throughout Luis Muñoz's poetry and poetics: "la idea de vivir con intensidad el presente, un grado más elemental del *carpe diem*" ("Transición," 15) [the idea of living the present with intensity, a more basic form of carpe diem]. His unwavering commitment to this effort is one of the hallmarks of his work.

How does this poet go about elucidating this temporal interval in his works?[5] Several of his prose poetics and his responses during interviews explicate his distinctive methodology. In 2005, he provides an informative self-portrait, "El tiempo de la poesía para mí es el presente."[6] [For me the time of poetry is the present.] He also believes that the poet has a "responsibility," one to which he staunchly adheres throughout his trajectory: "atrapar del presente"[7] [to capture the present]. How? By remaining "vigilant" when "living" "en las encrucijadas del presente"[8] [at the crossroads of the present]. Two commentaries by Muñoz offer additional insights. In his 2006 "Poetica," he provides decisive views concerning key factors that figure into his methods of inquiry. These approaches are constants throughout his work:

> La poesía es una indagación en los resortes íntimos de la realidad y es una conversación. Es una indagación que sucede en la soledad más plena, en la soledad sin protecciones. Y los resultados de esa indagación uno pretende compartirlos.
>
> . . . .
>
> Por otra parte, la poesía es una conversación, o dos conversaciones simultáneas: con nuestra tradición [. . .] y por otro lado una conversación con nuestro tiempo, con los retos emocionales, con los espacios materiales y afectivos, con las imágenes, con las combinaciones sensoriales de hoy.
>
> Pero son conversaciones que confluyen, que se alimentan una de otra, que se provocan una a la otra. Porque tienen en común la búsqueda de algo esencial humano.[9]

> [Poetry is an inquiry into the most intimate aspects of reality, and it is a conversation. It is an inquiry that occurs in the most complete possible solitude, in the solitude without safeguards. And the results from that inquiry one aims to share.
> ....
> Furthermore, poetry is a conversation, or rather two simultaneous conversations: with our tradition (. . .) and conversely with our own era, with the emotional challenges, with the material and affective spaces, with the images, and with the sensory combinations of today.
>
> But they are conversations that coalesce, that nourish each other, that ignite one another. Because they have in common the search for what is essentially human.]

Muñoz further reveals facets of this "search" in 2007 when describing the writing process during the creative act:

> Para mí la palabra clave es ésa, la búsqueda. Seguir el rastro de lo más profundo a través de la piel de las cosas. No pienso en continuidad ni pienso en cambios. Porque creo que en poesía no se llega nunca a ningún lugar. Se parte una y otra vez, desde cero.[10]

> [For me the key word is search. To pursue what is deeply within through the outermost layer of things. I do not think about continuity or change. Because in poetry one never reaches any one place. Time and again, one starts from scratch.]

The objectives Luis Muñoz underscores in these self-reflective insights guide him to this day.

POETRY ADDICTS

The present instant is of the utmost importance to Muñoz. This is especially evident in his unique presentation of the poem and the writing process as evolving within this instant. This perspective positions him to enter this most precise, pure, and promising of time-based sites in order to partake of the essence of the moment by imaging it in the poem. Nowhere is this more apparent than in his stunning poem, "Dejar la poesía" [Leave Poetry]. This work was published in his estimable 2006 collection titled *Querido silencio*[11] [Dear Silence]. In "Dejar la poesía," Muñoz offers a dazzling analysis of the nature of poetry while he writes in the compressed present moment. As a superb metapoetics, "Dejar la poesía" articulates the imagistic perfection evident in his lyric. This representative work, moreover, reveals the convergence of the fundamental characteristics of his poetry: the innovative expressivity, the masterfully constructed analogy, the sensorial delights, the linguistic identity of the poet and the poem, and the meticulous examination of the present instant. In both style and concept, this poem is a polished and exquisite work displaying multifaceted moments of lucid discovery. By inspecting carefully the nature of poetry during its genesis, Muñoz skillfully conveys the intrinsic features of creative writing as a process of discovery. Incomparable in originality, "Dejar la poesía" is a breath-taking artistic achievement and an invaluable gem in Spain's recent lyric.

In this work, Muñoz depicts poetry in such a way that he permits his personified subject to express not only its mysterious intricacies but also its magnetic appeal. However, "Dejar la poesía" does even more than this. It also concisely demonstrates why Muñoz's poetry is unmistakably "inventive"[12] while also providing ample evidence supporting José-Carlos Mainer's important claim that Luis Muñoz is one of the most important young poets advancing the new lyric poetry written in Spain.[13] Intriguingly, by presenting poetry as an addiction, Luis Muñoz discloses the intrinsic identity of the poem's central voice.

He cleverly features an enlightening performance of two distinct dramatis personae while they engage in a lively and rhythmical conversation displaying the aims and effects of poetic discourse. Muñoz introduces and images "poetry," his lead "character," as a distinctive personality with a unique temperament and an extraordinary life of its own. As such, it knows exactly what it is and what it does. Possessing unparalleled self-knowledge, "poetry" exhibits a boundless potential, supremacy, and self-will. "Dejar la poesía" portrays a self-assured dramatic personality first identified in the title. This personage exhibits an impressive linguistic identity, an enticing conversational style, diverse behavioral patterns and motives, and an uncanny capacity to understand not only its primary functions but also its own captivating qualities. The poem allows the traits of its central *persona* to unfold in the compressed present instant and establishes, at the outset, its unique association with another fellow "character," an "impersonal you." This "tú" also makes its appearance as the poem begins. The "tú" character experiences poetry's effects and, at times, appears to be troubled by these. Yet it cannot resist the alluring central personality and its appealing self-expression. This dramatic staging is smart and original, but what is most exciting and inviting about this poem is the engaging exchange occurring between "poetry" and "you," two syntactically silent characters masterfully presented by means of ellipsis. Here, Muñoz skillfully utilizes and exploits expressivity by means of syntactic and rhetorical omission.

The poem's central "character," "poetry," appears only in the poem's title and, curiously, this immediate, direct, introductory, and phonetically realized naming does not occur elsewhere in the poem. Rather, as the poem develops, the presence of "poetry" makes itself known by means of its unmistakable absence. Ellipsis directly figures into "Dejar la poesía" at the outset: "Por restar mientras que tú sumas" [By subtracting while you add]. In the poem's initial line, the identity of the "empty subject" of the stated infinitive "restar" is derived from the closest preceding noun, in this case "la poesía," found in the title. It is "the presence" of such a "phonetically unrealized"[14] element, as the poem begins, that offers the first indication of the prevalent role syntactic omission will play in this dramatic presentation.[15]

In "Dejar la poesía," Muñoz also examines poetic discourse by revealing the addictive nature of his central character, "poetry," along with a series of persistent circumstances enveloping the other character, the "impersonal you," caught in a struggle to abandon an enticing habit.[16] Conscious self-expression assumes a significant role when Muñoz spotlights the self-referential linguistic identity of both personalities. The most refreshingly innovative aspect of this work resides in how Muñoz enriches the language of poetry. By attentively allowing condensed poetic expression to demonstrate its own enticing and unbound potential, "Dejar la poesía" manifests the incisive identity of this poet and his extraordinary exploitation of syntactic and poetic ellipses.

The measured cadence of "poetry" enriches its enticingly alluringly addictive appeal: it charms and attracts with its sonorously seductive nature. Heptasyllabic versification is the vital pulse of the poem, and captivating hendecasyllabic lines rhythmically underlie several of its fascinating and transformative images: "Por llenarte de pájaros la mesa" [By filling your table with birds], the unique combination of "por hablarte / cuando quieres dormir" [By speaking to you / when you want to sleep], "Por su orgullo de bestia descarriada" [By its silly pride], and the superb final line, "Por beberse la sombra de mañana" [By drinking up the shadow of tomorrow]. As Octavio Paz has explained,

> El poeta crea por analogía. Su modelo es el ritmo que mueve a todo idioma. El ritmo es su imán. Al reproducirlo —por medio de metros, rimas, aliteraciones, paranomasias y otros procedimientos— convoca las palabras. [. . .] La creación poética consiste, en buena parte, en esta voluntaria utilización del ritmo como agente de seducción.
>
> [The poet creates by analogy. His model is the rhythm that moves every language. The rhythm is his magnet. In reproducing it—by means of meter, rhyme, alliteration, paronomasia, and other procedures—he summons the words. (. . .) Poetic creation consists, to a marked degree, in this voluntary utilization of rhythm as an agent of seduction.][17]

"Dejar la poesía" displays epiphanic opportunities for appreciating the lure of engaging in the creative act on the part of the poet. And yet, this discovery also has the potential to affect another surprisingly different result. Muñoz self-reflectively recognizes both possibilities in his revealing 2012 poetics, when he comments on the process of writing this poem:

> En uno de mis poemas de mi libro *Querido silencio,* "Dejar la poesía," enumeré motivos posibles para el silencio definitivo, el silencio de no escribir. Mientras lo escribía me iba dando cuenta de que todos esos motivos eran reversibles, y que también podían servir para no dejar la poesía. Por otro lado, me atrajo la contradicción que supone tratar el tema de dejar la poesía precisamente escribiendo un poema. ("Atracción de los opuestos," 86)

> [In one of the poems in my book *Dear Silence,* "Leave Poetry," I listed possible motives for definitive silence, the silence of not writing. While I was writing it, I began to realize that all of these reasons were reversible and that they could also serve as reasons not to give up writing poetry. On the other hand, I was attracted by the contradiction involved in addressing the topic of abandoning poetry precisely by writing a poem.] (*From behind What Landscape,* 139)

This poet, however, does not remain silent nor do the dramatis personae in the spectacular performance they deliver. Muñoz is fully aware that as a poet he cannot "abandon" the poetic enterprise. In fact, in this same poetics, he explains why, "Escribir poesía es perder la oportunidad de callarse, es decir, de dejar intacta esa gran masa perfecta del silencio, que lo incluye todo, y es también ganarse la oportunidad de decir" ("Atracción de los opuestos," 85). [Writing poetry is losing the opportunity to keep your mouth shut—that is, to leave intact that huge, perfect mass of silence, which includes everything, and it is also earning the opportunity to speak.] (*From behind What Landscape,* 131). Put differently, is it possible for a poet to "leave poetry"? Spain's distinguished poet Francisco Brines, perhaps, has best answered this question. When awarded the prestigious international XIX Annual Reina Sofía Poetry Prize in 2010, Brines affirms, "Los que leen la poesía la necesitan como drogadictos."[18] [Those who read poetry need it like drug addicts]. This is true for the reader of poetry. Moreover, it is true, as well, for the poet as creator. Poetry addicts. This is the nature of poetry as evidenced in Muñoz's magnetic "Dejar la poesía."

A POETICS OF THE INSTANT

Muñoz's image "limpiar pescado" analogously characterizes the poet's activity of writing, in his words, "contra el tiempo" ("Transición," 7–8). This same image also is central to his exposition of the present. In his work, the present is the subject of his sustained inquiry. His poetry reveals the process of his intricate and exacting exploration and several unexpected and unique findings. Perhaps nowhere is this more apparent than in his seven-part poem fittingly bearing the title "El presente" [The Present]. That his investigation is in seven-parts points to the complexity of the time frame under investigation.

"El presente" appears in his 2001 *Correspondencias*[19] [*Correspondences*], a collection that garnered two prestigious awards in the Spanish lyric at the inception of the new century. These include the highly coveted Premio de Poesía de la Generación del 27 (2000), and the distinguished Premio El Ojo Crítico de Poesía (2001). *Correspondencias* itself is divided into five parts, of which the poem "El presente" constitutes part IV (185–193). The poem displays seven different and yet interrelated representations of the temporal interval that is the object of Muñoz's detailed study. This poem, however, is not a superficial survey of the present. Rather, this poem studies in detail its various parts, probes its innermost regions, and uncovers its indisputable essence—the instant. In his penetrating inquiry, Muñoz compresses that moment in order to inspect its constituent parts. His method is one of restricting his analysis to condensing the present into an immediate moment of discovery.

His findings disclose the dynamic activity of the instant as an active force propelling the present as it engages in its own becoming: "La cascada con fuerza, / cada una de sus gotas cada vez" [The powerful waterfall, / each of its droplets every time]. His is an attentive inquiry into a moment that always already exhibits the vigor of constant change: "la furia del arrastre, las aguas de marea" ("El presente 6," *Limpiar pescado,* 192) [the fierce pull, tidal waters]. These images expose a feature central to the essential nature of the instant, its dynamism in becoming what it is not yet *and,* simultaneously, its perpetual manifestations of exhibiting the residual effects of what it once was. For Muñoz, the instant possesses and divulges vitality, movement, transit. It is never still. How to image the ongoing temporal transformation of the instant is the matter under investigation for the poet of the exceptional epiphanic poem "El presente."

In this work, Muñoz does not attempt to harness the present. He accepts its energy, and he does not mourn its passing. His approach is one of keen analysis of the multifaceted and interconnected dimensions of the instant in time. Its complex nature cannot easily be grasped. Essentially, it is transitory and, thus, any effort to detain it for immediate inspection is but fleeting. None of this deters Muñoz. Instead, with artistic precision and pristine imagery, he directly engages in a profound exploration of the constituent elements of the present. The sheer density of his subject matter requires a framework for articulating his process of dividing, segmenting, and dissecting the essence of the present during it most concentrated and immediate inception: the instant. However, he knows that because the moment always is in motion, his findings will reveal it to be "la cifra de algo más" ("El presente 1," *Limpiar pescado,* 187) [the code for something more].

In his article on Luiz Muñoz's collection *Limpiar pescado*, the distinguished literary critic José Andújar Almansa raises two insightful points applicable to Muñoz's "El presente." Each should be considered as advancing additional aspects relevant to Muñoz's investigative strategies evidenced in this poem. When commenting on *Correspondencias*, Andújar observes that this work manifests "una poética del instante que es, precisamente, el tiempo de la analogía y de las correspondencias"[20] [a poetics of the instant that is, precisely, the time relevant to analogy and to associations]. "El presente" is a superlative illustration of Muñoz's art of writing poetry both about and in "the instant." Poem "3" in the assemblage of "El presente," briefly and succinctly conveys the nature of the transitory by means of an effective analogy: "donde el viento es un globo, / va el presente" (*Limpiar pescado*, 189) [where the wind is a balloon / the present goes]. Subtle, sensorial, and captivatingly fleeting, this imagery embodies the sensitivity and charm that Muñoz brings to his innovative poetry. In poem "4" (*Limpiar pescado*, 190), unexpected correlations among differing situations remarkably disclose fresh perspectives from which to consider the temporal moment, its limitations, its movement, its incessant activity of becoming. He writes,

También cortada así, como en filetes,
una porción de tiempo es antes y es después.

El carnicero esgrime su juego de chuchillos
como si diera paso.

Como si señalara un rumbo a la carrera.

[Likewise, cut that way, as into fillets,
a portion of time is before and is after.

The butcher wields his set of knives
as if he were clearing the way.

As if he hurriedly were signaling a direction.]

Domingo Sánchez-Mesa Martínez investigates "la percepción del instante" [the perception of the instant] in his excellent essay introducing his 2007 anthology.[21] This critic's various astute remarks also assist in underscoring features of the present interval applicable to Muñoz's poem. Sánchez-Mesa finds that some of the poets represented in his anthology, Muñoz included, exhibit a keen interest in the present as a site for studying time, in general, and the "instant," in particular. This "poética del 'instante'" [poetics of the "instant"], in his view, "es también del tiempo, pero más volcada, tal vez, en una labor de disección de estructura del tiempo presente, su vivencia, de sus capas y texturas" (*Cambio de siglo* [*Turn of the Century*], 47–48) [also is about time, but one that is, perhaps, more focused on the task of dissecting the structure of the present, its layers, its textures, its experience]. The critic's comments point to the process of detailed analysis that Muñoz uses in revealing the multiple facets of the instant. For Muñoz, these must be determined if the essence of the present is to be apprehended.

Another incisive observation by Sánchez-Mesa also serves to elucidate Muñoz's analysis in "El presente," as a poem and as a method of inquiry, "una disección penetrante y siempre brillante de las estructuras del instante" (*Cambio de siglo*, 48) [a penetrating and always illuminating dissection of the structures of the instant]. Muñoz introduces "El presente" with the synthetic affirmation made by the influential modern Spanish poet Juan Ramón Jiménez years earlier: "Hay un momento en el que el pasado es porvenir. Ése es mi instante" (*Limpiar pescado*, 185). [There is a moment in which the past is future. That is my instant]. The first poem of the seven-part series offers intriguing reasons as to why. An omniscient voice directly addresses the present and hypothetically surveys its compositional features:

> Como si dibujases
> tres calles de carrera con obstáculos
> y luego señalaras
> ese tono en los verbos que viene a ser el tiempo . . . ("1," *Limpiar pescado*, 187)
>
> [As if you were to draw
> three street lanes with obstacles
> and soon were to show
> that verbal hue becoming time . . .]

Muñoz begins his painstaking segmentation of the imaged "tres calles" when past, present, and future intersect revealing "recuerdos" [memories], "deseos" [desires], and "esperanzas" [hopes]. This imaginative crisscrossing taking place within the present instant resembles "ese tono de los verbos" [that verbal hue] when actions, states, or occurrences are inflected for tense and modified with correlative colorings. This is the intriguing "zone," where overlapping parts jointly convey that the present always already, as the closing line divulges, "es la cifra de algo más" [is the code for something more].

From the outset "El presente" establishes the attentive attitude that must be assumed in a concentrated examination detailing the essential nature of this site in time. Throughout this poem, as well as in each of its constituent parts, concentrated observation is most especially advantageous when it leads to undistracted and reflective awareness of the temporal. Poem "3" (*Limpiar pescado*, 189) refreshes the perspective of witnessing time as passage by offering, instead, a concise imaging and reimaging of the ephemeral present. The poem begins by describing the figurative site of the present: "También la intersección de dos conjuntos. / Dos elipsis perfectas y su zona en contacto." [Likewise, the intersection of two wholes. / Two perfect ellipses and their zone of contact.] The initial point of entry signals that it both will display and add to the facets of "The Present" that Muñoz depicts in the first two poems of his series. This new perspective, "likewise," probes the moment. Poem "3" expresses, however, that the present encompasses the absence of what it was and what it will be. Muñoz's second Alexandrine couplet in this poem reveals "el pasado repleto como un árbol con frutos, / el futuro disperso por luces inconstantes" [the past replete like a tree in fruit, / the future scattered by shifting lights]. The present emerges from within this figurative "intersection," a fleeting and transformative convergence when the instant reveals "donde el viento es un globo, / va el presente" [where the wind is a balloon / the present goes]. This singular epiphanic flash of sudden insight concisely renders that knowledge, too, is brief. Poem "3" exposes that the acute awareness of the instant occurs within the enterprise of its own becoming.

Andújar points out that in Luis Muñoz's poetry, "el instante, el presente analógico, es tanto una dimensión como una intuición, una intersección o un círculo que se contiene círculos" ("Correspondencias," 29) [the instant, the analogical present, is as much a dimension as it is an intuition, an intersection, or a circle containing circles]. In poem "5" (*Limpiar pescado*, 191) the poet approaches the inner dynamism of the present by configuring manifestations of the successive instances of its essence. The poetic voice considers the fixed and measurable aspects of time in its ordinary sense. These include the "day," "weeks," "months," "seasons," "years." Its progressive mobility, as each of these temporal phases advances, coalesce one into the other when days become weeks, weeks months, and months years as present time evolves during perpetual transformation. Imaginatively imaging the present as a spiral by analogously and inventively portraying first its corkscrew-like patterns in the universe, "los bucles de planetas" [ringlets of planets], and then its repetitious wheel-like belts or tracks that propel heavy machinery here on earth, Muñoz brilliantly conveys the essence of time as mutable, as instances exhibiting "círculos, eso sí, en movimiento" [circles, of course, in movement].

His probing analysis also provides an advantageous opportunity for engaging in further inquiry, "¿Es más que un intervalo? / ¿Es más que un movimiento?" ("7," *Limpiar pescado*, 193). [Is it more than an interval? / Is it more than a movement?] For this poet, as "El presente" demonstrates, this passing "interval" is a multidimensional space inviting various vigorous explorations into ascertaining its elemental features. His painstaking examination of the significant imaged segments structuring the present moment, in turn, illumine the essential nature of the instantaneous. Throughout his poetic production, these, in turn, will prompt a continuing "search" leading to discoveries about the moment.

It is worthwhile to call to mind the marvelous analogy that best "seizes" the fragility of the present moment in Muñoz's poetry: "limpiar pescado." It underlies "El presente" as a poem and as a concept. This image succinctly points to his method for inspecting the parts of the present that, once exposed, permit a new understanding of the precarious position of the instant in time. This intricate study of the temporal infuses the poem "El presente." As in the activity of "cleaning fish," time is of the essence. Muñoz comprehends that, as a poet, he must work carefully, his scrutiny of the thematic material in his hands must be sharp, his separation of the intricate parts under thorough examination must be exact, and his aims must be well-defined. This is Muñoz's approach as evident in his seven-part poem "El presente."

QUOTIDIAN CONVERSATIONS

By being in the moment, this poet recognizes that even in the most ephemeral and commonplace activities of daily human life reside exceptional opportunities for acquiring immediate and enlightening knowledge. By engaging in epiphanic conversations with the everyday, the poetry of his *Querido silencio* manifests and enriches the poetics of the instant. The self-reflective poet discloses in 2005, a new perspective concerning his creative activity when he explains,

> Yo ahora me hago muy poco caso en los poemas. Me interesa mucho más lo que está fuera. Es como en esa frase de *Adiós a Berlín* que dice: "I am the camera," y yo ahora soy alguien que se mete en situaciones vitales para poder escribir . . . poemas sobre cosas que ocurren. No, ahora no me veo como objeto de mis poemas.
>
> [Now my concerns are not about me in my poetry. What interests me much more is what is around me. It's like that phrase from *Goodbye Berlin* that says: "I am the camera," and now I am someone who becomes involved in real life situations in order to be able to write . . . poems about things that are happening. No, right now I don't see myself as the object of my poems.]

This viewpoint and attitude are the underpinnings of *Querido silencio* when quotidian dialogues with the ordinary yield astonishing results. By intermingling colloquial language with refined and nuanced imagery, Muñoz demonstrates that his poetry "es un campo de posibilidades" [a field of possibilities], as he also notes in this same interview.

Querido silencio robustly contributes to the clarity and artistry of style associated with Muñoz's lyric. The elegance, originality and imagistic precision evident in this inspiring work demonstrate a confluence of several of Muñoz's prose poetics and a refined and dedicated approach to his role in crafting the poem. The 2006 collection articulates several of the elements he identifies in his 1998 "Un nuevo simbolismo" [A New Symbolism] as essential ingredients of his own creative enterprise. He elucidates, for example, the role of imagery that suggests rather than directly declares. By advancing this fundamental role of nuanced expressivity, Muñoz characterizes his own work and plants the seeds for the suggestive capacity of the image that his work would come to exemplify in twenty-first-century Spain. In this key poetics, Muñoz also encourages the unique conjoining of an incisive exactness and a lucid ambiguity that, when considering the course of his work as a whole, displays "la novedad que ensancha el campo de la poesía"[22] [the innovation that expands the field of poetry].

These features coalesce in profoundly contemplative moments nurtured in solitude and later expressed in the poem, as Muñoz explains in his 2006 "Poetica" featured in Morales Barba's anthology (129). In another essay, published six years later, he analyzes the benefits of poetic creation disclosing, "La gana, al escribir poesía, es uno de los nombres que adopta la intuición, ese tipo de síntesis de la inteligencia que se precipita en los sentidos" ("Atracción de los opuestos," 82–83). [The want, in writing poetry, is one of the names that intuition adopts, that kind of intellectual synthesis that triggers the senses.] "Transición," the remarkable poetics introducing his *Limpiar pescado*, offers an additional and perceptive self-reflection on the part of Luis Muñoz:

> El poeta que escribe un poema es también un ser humano por hacer y el poema un producto, un organismo por hacer. Cuando voy a escribir un poema siento que el vértigo de lo que está por hacer es el primer material de trabajo y las inmersiones en la realidad una aventura que se justifica por sí misma pero busca sólo lo que necesita. La poesía, en esa operación, destaca las válvulas de los sentidos, nos convierte en esponjas. (*Limpiar pescado*, 17)

> [The poet writing the poem is also a human being in the making and the poem is a product, an organism still in the making. When I am going to write a poem, I feel that the dizziness that I experience when thinking about what yet needs to be done, is the raw material of my work and the immersions into reality an adventure justified in and of itself, but (the poet) seeks only what he needs. Poetry, in this process, emphasizes the senses as valves, it makes us sponges.]

When speaking with Javier Díaz Gil in 2007, Muñoz also underscores the role of the reader in his poetry: "Lo que procuro hacer es proponer al lector mirar la realidad de una manera determinada, a través de los sentidos."[23] [What I endeavor to do is to allow the reader to look at reality in a certain way, through the senses.] The confluence of these observations illustrates and illuminates the essence of *Querido silencio*.

This poet expertly discloses his immersions into and sensorial examinations of familiar surroundings in *Querido silencio*. Often the poetic voice emerging in these poems pauses to inspect and then to reflect on the most elemental details found in the everyday: the roots of a recently transplanted plant, a newly growing fingernail, toothbrushes, a solitary magpie separating itself from the flock, flies trapped on a window pane, three breakfast menus in a small café, and even the seats in the back of the bus, to cite a few examples.[24] Throughout *Querido silencio*, Muñoz, by accentuating the ordinary, reveals that acute awareness of incidents, events, and objects from daily life are a source of poetic inspiration. Recognizing and writing about what previously might not have been visible, or was forgotten, or, perhaps, was too mundane to be noticed, the quotidian becomes the unique subject matter of his 2006 collection. Muñoz masterfully demonstrates that the seemingly unimportant in the day-to-day offers endless opportunities for apprehending, appreciating, and acquiring new knowledge during the present instant of observation and reflection. His inquiry into and his conversations with the commonplace promote stimulating and striking epistemic discoveries. The poet of this 2006 work realizes that the quotidian is a source of delight, inspiration, and illumination and a fortuitous occasion in which to participate in the moment. Here, Muñoz put into practice the revelation that he ironically voices in his 2014 poetics "El poema no escrito" [The Unwritten Poem]. For him, as he expresses in this marvelous essay, his as yet "unwritten poem" will include "el asombro de los nuevos paisajes y de paisajes cotidianos repentinamente descubiertos"[25] ["the astonishment of new landscapes and everyday landscapes suddenly discovered"] (*From behind What Landscape*, 129). He achieves this six years earlier in *Querido silencio* and will continue to bring this aspect of his work to fruition in his most recent poetry, as will be demonstrated.

While engaging in these quotidian conversations, the poet presents what he explains in his 2005 interview in *Deriva. Revista digital literatura cine* as "una ruta [. . .] que nos refresque la mirada" ("Luis Muñoz") [a path . . . that refreshes our gaze]. Two poems from *Querido silencio* are illustrative examples. In "Raíces" (21), the "roots" of a plant are viewed in a transformative state. After having been uprooted, they are in a suspended condition, one of anticipating transplant. Plant roots, however, only will survive this process of transference if they are provided with the necessary conditions ensuring their survival. Uprooting leaves the plant in a precarious situation. This "maraña blancuzca y carnosa" ["whitish, fleshy tangle"] (*From behind What Landscape,* 83) only will continue to live if it remains mostly undisturbed. In this way, during the activity of transplanting, this living aggregate has the most optimal opportunity for encouraging new growth. In this outstanding poem, past actions reveal attempts at both considering and implementing such regeneration. All gardeners, including the personalized *yo-poético,* know the efforts involved:

> Cogimos tierra nueva,
> coloqué con cuidado las raíces
> y añadimos más tierra.
> Todo el espacio alrededor
> parecía crecer y acomodarse.
>
> [We took fresh dirt,
> I set the roots carefully
> and we added more soil.
> All the surrounding space
> seemed to expand and adjust.] (*From behind What Landscape,* 83)

The contemplative protagonist in this poem must wait to see if the transplant and the structure of roots meet with success. In the meantime, however, this self-reflective poetic voice draws from this ordinary situation an extraordinary lesson: "Las envidié en silencio / porque empezaban algo" (83). [I envied them in silence / because they were starting something new.] Muñoz masterfully transforms an everyday gardening activity into a condensed moment when his discourse of discovery images human existential concerns.

The finesse with which the poet introduces his analogy is astonishing. When the poetic speaker internalizes the experience of the moment of transplantation, Muñoz gently nudges the poem toward the thematic matter of the fragility of the present instant. The poem occurs in that moment. It is an unstable point in time, and it simultaneously signals the possibility, as well as the impossibility, of existence. Muñoz situates the life-support system of the roots of the plant precisely in the present instant during which it might achieve new life, and yet it also might fail to thrive. In the instantaneous, transplanting cannot be delayed. In the instantaneous, the plant roots can stimulate new growth. With stunning imagery of suggestion, Muñoz deftly hints at the contemplative speaker's haunting thoughts on human finitude.

"Continuidad" (47) [Continuity] provides another opportunity for self-reflection while being in the instant. In this poem, an unremarkable event of looking at a flock of magpies gathering in a tree develops in unexpected ways, the most surprising of which is the acquisition of new knowledge. The initial lines of the poem establish the overall scene unfolding in the present moment:

> Ya se están persiguiendo las urracas
> en el árbol de enfrente.
> No sé si es igual todo el tiempo,
> pero cada vez que las miro
> hay una que parece resistirse,
> la otra va detrás, y así.
>
> [Now the magpies are pursuing each other
> in the tree out in front.
> I don't know if it always is like this,
> but each time I see them
> there is one that seems to resist,
> another follows behind, like that.]

Muñoz presents the poetic protagonist as an eyewitness who, at first, takes in several visual aspects of activities taking place outside. This view from a distance demonstrates a particularized present moment in general terms. The vigilant voice of the poem, however, soon begins to pay closer attention to visible details he notices and, consequently, adjusts his gaze. His attention shifts from the flock to two specific magpies, and he begins to track their movements: "hay una," "parece resistirse," "la otra," "va detrás." The unexpected then occurs in the condensed present moment with the sudden emergence of the "right now" within which the viewer becomes much more attentive to one of the two magpies:

> Ahora se posa la más clara
> sobre la barandilla.
> Está solo un segundo.
>
> [Now the clearly visible one rests
> on the railing.
> Only for a second.]

Precision and verbal economy pinpoint imaged optical modifications that more clearly define the visual perceptions developing this scene.

Soon, however, this once very attentive onlooker becomes distracted by his own commonplace activities occurring inside. The singular bird perching outside, however, is much more vigilant than its human companion. Instantaneously, this individual magpie reacts not to the protagonist's actions, but rather to the appearance of a very alert eyewitness that now participates directly in the unfolding of an unexpected event: "La otra se acerca." [The other one approaches.] The isolation of the resting magpie is momentary. The condensed present is as transitory as the instant it embodies. The poet's superb, synthetic synesthesia masterfully transforms presence and absence when the unremarkable reveals the remarkable in the moment: "un trozo de papel en los dedos del viento" [a piece of paper in the fingers of the wind]. Although encounters with epistemic illumination may be brief, they are, nonetheless, profound in the poetry of *Querido silencio*. Keen awareness of the ordinary produces the extraordinary experience of epistemic discovery. Perceptive inquiry, even if brief, yields a significant finding: "la idea de vivir con intensidad el presente" ("Transición," 15) [the idea of living the present with intensity].

IMMERSIONS INTO REALITY

2015 marks the publication by Luis Muñoz of his bilingual edition, in Spanish and in English, of *From behind What Landscape: New and Selected Poems*. This pioneering work presents to a wider multicultural public an excellent selection of his poetry and portions of his poetics. In this work, Muñoz published for the first time a unique grouping of poems gathered under the overall title "Sierra de Guadarrama (fragmentos)" (106–113) [The Guadarrama Mountains (Fragments)]. What is of special interest to this chapter is that a number of these poems from "The Guadarrama Mountains" assemblage display fresh insights into Muñoz's inquiry into the present instant. Two works in particular, "Habla un vecino" (108) [A Neighbor Talks] (109) and "Bocadillo que vuelve de excursion" (110, 112) [The Sandwich That Comes Back from the Day Trip] (111–113), exemplify the importance of the condensed present moment as a unique site for unanticipated instances of sudden illumination. Here, however, various elemental constituents of a natural environment receive special attention during an imaginative outdoor trek when, in the words of Muñoz, "las inmersiones en la realidad" ("Transición," 17) [the immersions into reality] offer other ways to investigate the multifaceted present instant. Here too, Muñoz is acutely attentive to ordinary objects and events as stimulating sources for dialogues promoting discovery.

Original perspectives concerning the everyday and being in the moment converge in these unique portrayals that have, as their setting, the Guadarrama mountain range. The perceptive observer scrutinizes scenes, situations, and objects that could, at first, appear to be insignificant. However, during direct inspection, the poetic protagonist becomes captivated by and eagerly wishes to participate in learning from what previously he might not have noticed because he did not actively partake of being the moment. Now nothing escapes his consideration.

This poetic protagonist discerns the diminutive, "los mosquitos que hilan / sus elipses de encuentros" ("Efecto," 106) ["the mosquitos that twirl / their elliptical encounters"] ("Effect," 107), along with the vast, "el fondo hospitalario del paisaje" ("Habla un vecino," 108) ["the landscape's hospitable background"] ("A Neighbor Talks," 109). His focus is unswerving, his analysis is precise, and his discoveries are among the most inventive in the recent poetry from Spain.

The Guadarrama Mountains are a range that runs southwest-northeast, extending from the province of Ávila in the southwest through the Community of Madrid and then into the province of Segovia.[26] In Muñoz's poems, no trail or trails are indicated nor do any of the works establish a precise location. This lack of geographical specificity accentuates the immensity of the mountainous areas and, at the same time, presents a direct contrast to the exactness with which the personalized poetic voice attentively perceives specific aspects of nature during his different encounters.

Muñoz excels at presenting combined sensorial experiences stimulated by the vitality of different locales and multiple events during this imaged excursion through the Guadarrama Mountains. Here, the poetic protagonist-hiker is on an outing where city and domestic life have been left behind. Here, poetry is not only a "search" and an "inquiry," as he explained earlier in 2006 ("Poética," 128) but also an original adventure. Here too, Muñoz puts into practice one of the tasks of the poet that he articulates in his exceptional poetics from 2005, "propone al lector una mirada sobre el mundo y el lector completa las propuestas del poeta en una especie de corriente hecha de confianza y de sorpresa" ("Transición," 16–17) [offers the reader a view of the world, and the reader responds with a type of trust and surprise].

The poem "Habla un vecino" (*From behind What Landscape,* 108) ["A Neighbor Talks"] (109) serves as an excellent illustration. At first, there appears to be an immediate discrepancy given the poem's title and the plural verbal forms that follow. The gaze of the hiker reveals the interrelated features of a quiet scene in which this first-person speaker intently absorbs and is fully absorbed by the present moment. During this analogic immersion, the poetic voice comprehends, "Conmigo están tranquilos." [With me, they are at ease.] Who? What? Why? The mountain trekker pauses to behold the surroundings with fresh eyes:

> Se mecen con el viento,
> se platean, se doran, se zambullen
> en el estanque seco de la noche.
>
> [They rock themselves in the wind,
> they plate themselves in silver, in gold, they dive
> into the night's dry pond.]

It only is when the poem gradually begins to close that the reader discovers what the poetic voice already knows: the friendly neighbor is a tree, in fact, many different trees, "Hayas, fresnos, robles, sauces" [Beech, ash, oak, willow]. These active participants in their own daily lives exhibit a shared vitality in the forest they inhabit where "Hacen de su espesor / el fondo hospitalario del paisaje" [Of their density they make / the landscape's hospitable background]. The nouns naming these trees do not capture their essence nor do they indicate the unique role that each tree plays when perceived by this hiker. Each of these living trees, when considered singularly and when viewed as a cluster, constitute a constant source for new discoveries for this contemplative observer during this brief but elucidating moment, "Lo que hagan después, ya no lo sé." [What they do afterwards, I have no idea.] In his 2014 poetics "El poema no escrito" (41) Muñoz reveals:

> Mi poema no escrito tiene una vocación claramente contemplativa, pero no solo por la inevitable observación de cosas a la que suele someterse, que viene de una especie de lentitud íntima, sino porque cree que la poesía nace de ahí [. . .] y, además, porque aspira en ocasiones a poder representar en sus versos el acto mismo de la contemplación.
>
> [My unwritten poem has a clearly contemplative vocation, not only for the inevitable observation of things that it usually submits itself to, which comes from a kind of intimate slowness, but because it believes that poetry is born there . . . and also because sometimes it aspires to represent the very act of contemplation in its own lines.] (*From behind What Landscape*, 129)

This portion of his recent poetics precisely describes what Muñoz achieves in "Habla un vecino," a poem that, ironically, already has been written.

The intriguing "Bocadillo que vuelve de excursión" (*From behind What Landscape*, 110, 112) ["The Sandwich That Comes Back from the Day Trip"] (111, 113) is a superb example of an inventive poem displaying the "poetics of the instant" in an astonishingly compelling way. The poem tells the tale of an ordinary sandwich enduring a day trip to and from the Guadarrama Mountains. The unexpected personification of this everyday object is as surprising as it is revealing. In making the return trip, this object reveals the various components of its now unavoidable fate. The adventure was too long for its survival. As a food source, it now is an unwanted leftover. It was subjected to a test of durability, but it failed in this endeavor. Instead, at the end of the day trip, this commonplace object could only display the temporality of its existence. The inventive anthropomorphizing of the humble sandwich elevates it to a heroic status when Muñoz captures its courage during its process of becoming throughout the evolving present moment.

The poem is an extraordinary analysis of the present instant. On the one hand, "Bocadillo que vuelve de excursión" immediately provides unanticipated insight into the ephemeral: "Ha envejecido casi instantáneamente" (110) ["It has aged almost instantly"] (111). At the same time, by characterizing the existential and emotional states of the personified sandwich, the acutely observant poet divulges the unfortunate fate of this commonplace thing. Simultaneously, the object is considered subjectively when the poet describes and empathizes with its uncommon condition of suffering gradual deterioration throughout the day trip:

> Las arrugas del papel de aluminio
> son un mapa de carreteras
> de su dolor del día.
>
> [The wrinkles on the aluminum foil
> are a road map
> of the pain of its day.] (110, 111)

Imaged superimpositions of various compressed instances masterfully disclose the progressive decline of this "sandwich" and its various parts:

> La miga y la corteza no distinguen
> qué era qué.
>
> La loncha de jamón
> huele a cuarto cerrado . . .
>
> [The doughy part and the crust can't tell
> which was which.
>
> The slice of ham
> smells like a closed room . . .] (112, 113)

The unusual convergence of the edible with the natural at once conveys the more immediate recollections of the day trip in the mountains and the vulnerability of the poem's inventive protagonist during its transformation in the instantaneous:

> La mantequilla borda una pradera:
> vacas glaseadas, mirlos y caballos
> sobre las suaves lomas deseosas
> tocadas por el sol.

[The butter embroiders a prairie:
sugar-glazed cows, blackbirds and horses
on the gentle, desirous hills
touched by the sun.] (112, 113)

This is a poem of exceptional originality where Luis Muñoz demonstrates the agility of his analogic imagery, his refreshing colloquial expression, and his noteworthy conversational tone when examining occurrences in the everyday. His unique illuminations resulting from innovative and creative inquiry, together with his genuine understanding and appreciation for what transpires *ahora*, enliven a poem that could have been written as an elegy underscoring human finitude. Instead, the provocative, personified "bocadillo" is to be admired for its fortitude during the metaphoric experience of its journey. "Bocadillo que vuelve de excursión" exhibits what readers have come to value highly in the work of Muñoz: his artistry in crafting the language of the poem so that it conveys keen practical sense imaged in surprising, unconventional, and enlightening ways.[27] This poem is a stroke of genius. Only Luis Muñoz could convey the essence of human finitude in his unique rendering of the analogic "sandwich." His inventive reinterpretation of the carpe diem motif, from the subjective vantage point of this ordinary hiking companion, is extraordinary and enlightening. This poem is an exceptional manifestation of the compressed instant when *the* intensified present moment reveals new discoveries.

THE WELDER

Luis Muñoz characterizes the nature of poetry in 2007 in *Cambio de siglo* (405). In so doing, he provides both an illuminative summary and a perceptive prediction relevant to his poetry:

> Yo creo que la poesía intenta siempre lo mismo: dar con los núcleos de vida, los nudos de emoción, las situaciones, las historias, las imágenes, las ideas que resumen el estupor y la maravilla de estar vivo y proponer para ellos una estructura verbal, un orden de palabras.
>
> [I believe that poetry always tries to do this: to find the nuclei of life, the nodes of emotion, the situations, the stories, the images, the ideas that summarize the amazement and the wonder of being alive and to give these a verbal structure, a sequence of words.]

His explication remains relevant a little more than a decade later when considering the works and the themes examined in this chapter. One poem in Muñoz's trajectory stands out as a superb example of his self-reflective insights articulated above, "El soldador" (*Limpiar pescado,* 151) ["The Welder"] (*From behind What Landscape,* 67). The poem originally appeared in Muñoz's 2001 collection *Correspondencias.* In 2009, José Andújar Almansa examines this poem and establishes an astute correlation regarding this poet as a welder and the poem "El soldador" ("Correspondencias," 26). His perceptive views served as a stimulus for reviewing the thematic matters considered in the present chapter.

As a skillful imagist of the instant, Muñoz is a metaphoric welder. As a poet, he seeks union and harmony by fusing the like or unlike materials he has before him into significant figurative combinations of precisely perfected analogies. This poet joins the thematic matter of human existence to the intensity of apprehending the instant in the present interval. For him, this is a specialized moment embodying, fusing, and demonstrating the opportunity to seize "the amazement and the wonder of being alive" ("Luis Muñoz," 405). He is a poet of the present who imaginatively configures and reconfigures in his works the unique "intersección de dos conjuntos" ("El presente 3," *Limpiar pescado,* 189) [the intersection of two wholes]. In *Correspondencias, Querido silencio,* and the "Sierra de Guadarrama" poems, Luis Muñoz meticulously separates out the distinguishing constituents comprising the instant in order to solder them back together, to consolidate them, to affirm them as the most essential elements joined within, even if only briefly, the moment. He does so with superlative artistry and in such a subtle and intricate way that the poetics of the instant emerges as the essential bonding agent of his work. The present instant conjoins inquiry and findings as luminous events during which outstandingly new knowledge interpenetrates the activity of writing. For Muñoz, this is *the* moment for imaging discovery.

What does this poet solder? Muñoz's creative endeavors are his most immediate junctures for establishing his unique identity as a poet. His is a creative enterprise of interconnected and self-reflective poetics. His is an illuminative process where poems and poetics fuse in harmonious combinations expressing epistemic discoveries. His "inquiry," "conversation," and "search" ("Poética," 128) meld during writing. The temporal dimensions of the present emerge in his work as the metaphoric interval at once bound to the past and to the future. Conversations with the quotidian connect various explorations of the everyday as a unique juncture for coming to know the essence of the moment. The soldering consolidation of these approaches, as demonstrated in this chapter, both integrate and display the poetics of epiphany in the work of Luis Muñoz.

His recent poetics titled "El poema no escrito," conjoins the past, present, and future publications of his poetry. In this inventive 2014 work, Muñoz as a welder of poetry and poetics, outlines the combined elements that are the requisites for a poem that has not yet been written. He also, however, remains ever-mindful that this "unwritten" future work should unite essential elements. His 2014 poetics highlights "algunas variedades del lenguaje común" [some variations of ordinary language], "la capacidad expresiva del lenguaje" [the expressive capacity of language], "el asombro de nuevos paisajes y de paisajes cotidianos repentinamente descubiertos" [the astonishment of new landscapes and everyday landscapes suddenly discovered], and "una vocación claramente contemplativa" (41) [a clearly contemplative vocation]. These are the ingenious and the defining characteristics of the poems that Luis Muñoz already has written. At the same time, his clever title, "El poema no escrito," also indicates that that there still is much to anticipate in his future work.

POEM AND POEM ANALYSIS BY LUIS MUÑOZ

What follows is a poem by Luis Muñoz and his original analysis of this work. He wrote his study at the request of the author for inclusion in this chapter of the book. Personal in voice and epiphanic in nature this new poem together with his revealing analysis discloses unique insights into his poetics of the instant. This is an enticing sampling of his current work and the limitless creativity of his poetry.

"CAMBIO DE DIRECCIÓN"

Contando desde el andamio
de la malla morada,
la tercera ventana era la suya.
Huelo el resabio a lejía
y las olas del guiso de pescado
del hueco de las escaleras.
Siempre está frío.
Los azulejos silban
al pasarle los dedos.
Siempre subo de prisa,
la respiración acribillada por la gana.
Es tan perentorio
que coincide con mi fibra del mundo.
Lo tenemos a mano.
Quitamos accesorios.
Mantenemos en las supresiones
la tensión.

La fórmula de la felicidad,
cómo ancla en los cuerpos,
nos sobrecoge,
pero no la aireamos.
No damos pábulo al lenguaje
de lo mucho que nos falta.

[CHANGE IN DIRECTION]

Counting over from the scaffold
in the lattice of residences,
the third window was his.
I can smell the aftertaste of bleach
and the swells of fish stew
in the stairwell.
It is always cold.
The tiles whistle
when a finger rubs them.
I always go up in a hurry;
my breathing riddled by desire.
It is so insistent
that it coincides with my very being.
It is at hand.
We clear away incidentals.
We maintain in restraint
the tension.
The formula for happiness,
how it anchors the bodies,
overtakes us,
but we don't discuss it.
We don't fuel speech
about how much we want.]

ANÁLISIS

Escribí el primer borrador de "Cambio de dirección" en verano de 2017 en Granada. Cuando estoy allí, camino todo el tiempo que puedo. Hay un impulso que viene del aire de la ciudad, o mejor, de la sensorialidad de la mezcla de la luz y el aire, que adopta también la forma de presión en el pecho o de urgencia en los pies, que me lleva a salir y deambular. Parafraseando a Robert Smithson, en muchos de esos paseos, el andar condiciona la mirada, y esta condiciona el andar, hasta el punto de que solo los pies son capaces de mirar.

De cuando vivía en Granada en casa de mis padres, recuerdo la llamada de la calle, sobre todo en primavera, la danza de paseos que tenían que ver con un circuito, que era también de dentro hacia fuera, en la que se producía una recuperación del sentido del tiempo, la sensación de una temporalidad profunda y una especie de falta de motivo que era, a la vez, una forma de necesidad. No en todas las calles ni en todas las plazas sucedía lo mismo. En algunas, digamos en la Gran Vía, el tiempo me parecía que iba en línea recta, como la propia calle, mientras que en algunas pequeñas plazas del Albaicín, como la de San Miguel Bajo, giraba en redondo, o en cuadrado, con la misma plaza.

La tarde que escribí el primer borrador de "Cambio de dirección," estaba deambulando por el Albaicín Bajo y me topé con un edificio donde A. había vivido varios años. Aunque no compartíamos casa, dormíamos juntos todos los días, en su apartamento o en el mío. La clase de felicidad que sentía con él estaba hecha de pocos ingredientes, había una especie de elementariedad en ella, que resultaba ser su clave, y también un extrañamente constante sentimiento de sorpresa que se prolongó mucho tiempo. Al encontrarme con el edificio y observar la ventana, sentí el aviso de inquietud que en ocasiones anuncia la posibilidad de la escritura, algo así como una secuencia de saturación emocional, premura y ocasión. Además, el lugar me impulsó hacia el pasado, pero en tiempo presente. Empecé a componer el poema según continuaba el paseo, primero en la cabeza y luego con un lápiz en un pequeño cuaderno de bolsillo. Como otras veces, en este proceso, me acordé de la famosa imagen de Lorca, de su conferencia sobre Góngora, en la que dice que el poeta que va a escribir tiene la sensación vaga de que va a una cacería nocturna en un bosque lejanísimo. Y sentí la mezcla de sobreconciencia e inconsciencia que otras veces contiene y conduce la escritura de un poema.

Al volver a mi casa de Iowa City, semanas después, releí el borrador. En la primera versión había versos que trataban de ilustrar los componentes concretos de la felicidad con A. Estos los suprimí. Del último verso tenía tres o cuatro posibilidades. Elegí la más cercana a la "verdad" del poema y, por el mismo motivo, añadí la palabra "mucho."

[ANALYSIS]

[I wrote the first draft of "Change in Direction" in the summer of 2017 in Granada. When I am there, I walk as much as possible. Motivation comes from the city's air, or better yet, from the sensoriality of the blending of light and air, which also assumes the form of tightness in the chest or of insistence in the feet, prompting me to go out and wander around. Paraphrasing Robert Smithson, on many of these strolls, walking impacts sight, and this impacts walking, until only the feet can observe.

When I lived in Granada in my parents' home, I remember the call of the street, above all in the spring, the dance-like movement of following a route, from the inside out, that would produce a recapturing of the sense of time, the sensation of a profound temporality and a kind of lack of purpose that was, at the same time, a form of need. The same thing didn't happen in all the streets or in all the plazas. In some, let's say in the Gran Vía, it seemed to me that time would go in a straight line, like the street itself, while in some of the smaller plazas of Albaicín, like that of San Miguel Bajo, it used to turn in a circle, or in a square, like the plaza itself.

The afternoon that I wrote the first draft of "Change in Direction," I was wandering through the Albaicín Bajo and I came across a building where A. had lived for many years. Although we didn't share a home, we used to sleep together every day, in his apartment or in mine. The kind of happiness that I experienced with him had very few ingredients, there was a kind of simplicity to it, which was key, and an inexplicably constant emotion of surprise that used to continue for a long time. Upon finding the building and observing the window, I felt the warning of restlessness that sometimes announces the possibility of writing, something like a sequence of emotional saturation, a rush, and an opportunity. In addition, the place drove me toward the past, but in present time. I began to compose a poem as I continued my walk, first in my head and then with a pencil in a small pocket notebook. Like other times, in this process, I recalled the famous image of Lorca, in his lecture on Góngora, in which he says that the poet who is about to write has a vague sensation that he is going on a nighttime hunt in a faraway forest. And I felt that mix of subconsciousness and unconsciousness that in other cases contains and steers the writing of a poem.

Upon returning to my home in Iowa City, weeks afterward, I reread that draft. In the first version there were lines that were attempting to illustrate the concrete components of happiness with A. Those I eliminated. The last line had three or four possibilities. I chose the one that was closest to the "truth" of the poem and, for the same reason, I added the word "much."]

POEMS BY LUIS MUÑOZ

The complete text and translation of the poems examined in chapter 1 include the following:

"Dejar la poesía," *Querido silencio* (2006).
"El presente 1–7," *Correspondencias* (2001).
"Raíces," *Querido silencio* (2006).
"Continuidad," *Querido silencio* (2006).
"Habla un vecino," *From behind What Landscape: New and Selected Poems* (2015).
"Bocadillo que vuelve de excursión," *From behind What Landscape: New and Selected Poems* (2015).
"El soldador," *Correspondencias* (2001).

DEJAR LA POESÍA

Por restar mientras que tú sumas.
Por llenarte de pájaros la mesa.
Por llevarte a donde no sabes salir.
Por castigarte sin hablar.
Por decirte: estás solo.
Por preferir que cargues
con su dolor de siglos
cuando te sientes nuevo.
Por su imán descabellado.
Por la sed que produce
cuando finge ser agua.
Por su vida paralela.
Por hablarte
cuando quieres dormir.
Por su orgullo de bestia descarriada.
Porque mira a la muerte
con el rabo del ojo
cuando canta oh belleza.
Por no dar explicaciones.
Por suficiente.
Por insuficiente.
Por beberse la sombra de mañana.

[LEAVE POETRY]

[By subtracting while you add.
By filling your table with birds.
By taking you where you know no escape.
By punishing you without speaking.
By telling you: you are alone.
By preferring that you accept the burden
of its centuries of pain
when you experience something new.
By its unbridled magnetism.
By creating thirst
when pretending to be water.
By its parallel life.
By speaking to you

when you want to sleep.
By its silly pride.
Because it stares death
in the face
when it sings oh, beauty.
By not providing explanations.
By just enough.
By totally insufficient.
By drinking up the shadow of tomorrow.]

EL PRESENTE

1
Como si dibujases
tres calles de carrera con obstáculos
y luego señalaras
ese tono en los verbos que viene a ser el tiempo
en su gama color presente azul,
color pasado rojo, color blanco futuro
y dejaras correr tu dado negro
delante de la tromba de temores,
de recuerdos, deseos, de esperanzas.

Y como si después de la partida
creyeses que es la cifra de algo más.

2
Rayar una libreta no rayada.
Una extensión innumerable
por honda y por abrupta,
por monótona y cruel: acotar el presente,
el que no necesita acotaciones.
Rellenar su casilla, organizar los puntos,
distribuir los gastos.

3
También la intersección de dos conjuntos.
Dos elipsis perfectas y su zona en contacto.

El pasado repleto como un árbol con frutos,
el futuro disperso por luces inconstantes.

Donde los frutos muestran su corona incendiada,
en la zona de nadie, donde el viento es un globo,
va el presente.

4
También cortada así, como en filetes,
una porción de tiempo es antes y es después.

El carnicero esgrime su juego de cuchillos
como si diera paso.

Como si señalara un rumbo a la carrera.

5
Sólo pasa que el día se contiene.
Las semanas son círculos y los meses son círculos.
Las estaciones y los años
igual que la memoria y el deseo,
los bucles de planetas, los trenes de la oruga.

Círculos, eso sí, en movimiento.

6
La cascada con fuerza,
cada una de sus gotas cada vez,
el imán de moneda de la noche,
la furia del arrastre, las aguas de marea,
los flujos de saliva.

7
La mecha de un viaje si no se consume.
¿Es la llama que prende,
es la explosión final, si no hay final?

¿Es más que un intervalo?
¿Es más que un movimiento?

[THE PRESENT]

[1
As if you were to draw
three street lanes with obstacles
and soon were to show
that verbal hue becoming time
in its range of colors present blue
past red, white future

and you were to cast your black die
in front of the whirlwind of fears,
memories, desires, hopes.

And as if after the game
you were to think it is the code for something more.

2
Draw lines in an unlined notebook.
An incalculable addition
intense and brusque,
monotonous and severe: limit the present,
that which doesn't need limitations.
Fill in blanks, organize matters,
distribute expenses.

3
Likewise, the intersection of two wholes.
Two perfect ellipses and their zone of contact.

The past replete like a tree in fruit,
the future scattered by shifting lights.

Where fruits display their luminous crown,
in the zone of no one, where the wind is a balloon
the present goes.

4
Likewise, cut that way, as into fillets,
a portion of time is before and is after.

The butcher wields his set of knives
as if he were clearing the way.

As if he hurriedly were signaling a direction.

5
It just happens that the day is self-contained.
The weeks are circles and the months are circles.

The seasons and the years
the same as memory and desire,
ringlets of planets, crawler tracks.

Circles, of course, in movement.

6
The powerful waterfall,
each of its droplets every time,
the silver magnet of the evening,
the fierce pull, the tidal waters,
the flow of saliva.

7
The wick of a journey if not extinguished.
Is it the flame that begins,
is it the last explosion, if there is no end?

Is it more than an interval?
Is it more than movement?]

RAÍCES

En el trasplante se quedaron fuera.
Una maraña blancuzca y carnosa
Como con algo obsceno.

Pensé en transformaciones,
en galaxias perdidas, en intestinos.
Luego, al arañarme, solamente
en lo que me dirías.

Cogimos tierra nueva,
coloqué con cuidado las raíces
y añadimos más tierra.
Todo el espacio alrededor
parecía crecer y acomodarse.

Las envidié en silencio porque empezaban algo.

[ROOTS]

[They were left out during the transplant.
A whitish, fleshy tangle
like something a little obscene.

I thought of transformations,
of lost galaxies, of intestines.
Then, when they scratched me, only
of what you would say.

We took fresh dirt,
I set the roots carefully
and we added more soil.
All the surrounding space
seemed to expand and adjust.

I envied them in silence because they were starting something new.]
(*From behind What Landscape: New and Selected Poems*, trans. Curtis Bauer)

CONTINUIDAD

Ya se están persiguiendo las urracas
en el árbol de enfrente.
No sé si es igual todo el tiempo,
pero cada vez que las miro
hay una que parece resistirse,
a otra va detrás, y así.

Ahora se posa la más clara
sobre la barandilla.
Está sólo un segundo.
Y no porque me intuya
detrás de los cristales,
hojeando revistas y hablando por teléfono.
No es esa vibración.
Es que la otra se acerca,
un trozo de papel en los dedos del viento,
y le toca alejarse.

[CONTINUITY]

[Now the magpies are pursuing each other
in the tree out in front.
I don't know if it always is like this,
but each time I see them
there is one that seems to resist,
another follows behind, like that.

Now the clearly visible one rests
on the railing.
Only for a second.
And not because it senses me
behind the window panes,
thumbing through magazines and talking on the phone.
It is not the movement.
It is because the other one approaches,
a piece of paper in the fingers of the wind,
and it is time to depart.]

HABLA UN VECINO

Lo que hagan después, ya no lo sé.
Conmigo están tranquilos.
Se mecen con el viento,
se platean, se doran, se zambullen
en el estanque seco de la noche.
Lanzan brillos distintos
para el sol o la lluvia.
Hacen de su espesor
el fondo confortable del paisaje.
Llenan de la nostalgia de cosas no vividas
a los que se pasean.
Y ante sus claros nombres
ni siquiera se inmutan:
hayas, fresnos, robles, sauces.

[A NEIGHBOR TALKS]

[What they do afterwards, I have no idea.
With me, they are at ease.
They rock themselves in the wind,
they plate themselves in silver, in gold, they dive
into the night's dry pond.
They cast a different shine
for the sun or the rain.
Of their destiny they make
the landscape's hospitable background.
They fill those who walk by with nostalgia
for things they haven't lived.
And when someone says their clear names
they show no flicker of emotion:
beech, ash, oak, willow.] (*From behind What Landscape*, trans. Curtis Bauer)

BOCADILLO QUE VUELVE DE EXCURSIÓN

Ha envejecido casi instantáneamente.
Las arrugas del papel de aluminio
son un mapa de carreteras
de su dolor del día.
La miga y la corteza no distinguen
qué era qué.

La loncha de jamón
huele a cuarto cerrado
que empieza a ventilarse
abriendo una rendija de ventana
y moviliza rachas de memoria traslúcida.

El queso se le adhiere
—amor sin condiciones—
como tras una noche de inquietud y de frío.

La mantequilla borda una pradera:
vacas glaseadas, mirlos y caballos
sobre las suaves lomas deseosas
tocadas por el sol.

[THE SANDWICH THAT COMES BACK FROM THE DAY TRIP]

[It has aged almost instantly.
The wrinkles on the aluminum foil
are a road map
of the pain of its day.
The doughy part and the crust can't tell
which is which.

The slice of ham
smells like a closed room
someone's beginning to air out
by cracking a window—
it calls up gusts of translucent memory.

The cheese sticks to it—
unconditional love—
like after a night of anxiety and cold.

The butter embroiders a prairie:
sugar-glazed cows, blackbirds and horses
on the gentle, desirous hills
touched by the sun.] (*From behind What Landscape,* trans. Curtis Bauer)

EL SOLDADOR

Si no son los deseos,
habrán de ser las juntas con estaño
en la leve estructura de este día:
la voz hirviente que devuelve,
a través de las ondas de un teléfono,
el punto en que creías todo cerca,
los cojines encima del sofá,
que dan al horizonte como un caer mullido,
las páginas del libro que perforan recuerdos
o la sombra de un dedo que llega a señalarlas.

La idea de que faltan varias piezas
es mentira.
Tienes sólo que dar con sus extremos.
Y dar con la pestaña de los tuyos.

[THE WELDER]

[If they are not desires,
they must be tin joints
in this day's delicate structure:
the boiling voice that comes back
through the waves of the telephone,
the point where you thought everything was close,
the cushions of the sofa
that give the horizon a soft place to fall,
the pages of the book that pierce memories
or the shadow of a finger that could point to them.

The idea that several parts are missing
is mistaken.
You only need to find their edges.
And the seam that joins them to yours.]
(*From behind What Landscape*, trans. Curtis Bauer)

Abraham Gragera, Enrique Escorza/Cucamonga producciones

2 * ABRAHAM GRAGERA: THE WORD

PERSONAL BIOGRAPHY BY GRAGERA

Nací en Madrid, el 19 de noviembre de 1973, pero pasé la infancia y la adolescencia en un pueblo de Badajoz, Montijo, en Extremadura, de donde es mi familia.[1] A los 18 años me fui a estudiar a Salamanca, en cuya universidad me licencié en Bellas Artes y cursé estudios de Psicología y Filología Hispánica. Algo más tarde, en Córdoba, cursé estudios de Humanidades.

Escribí mi primer poema válido (desde mi punto de vista, claro) a los 21 años: "Estrella fugaz," incluido después en mi primer libro, *Adiós a la época de los grandes caracteres*. El libro se publicó 11 años después, a mis 32 años. Durante ese tiempo, profundicé en mis lecturas y estudios y viví en diversas ciudades de España y del extranjero.

A los 39, en 2012, publiqué mi segundo poemario, *El tiempo menos solo*, tras siete años de silencio. Y a los 43, *O Futuro*, mi último libro.

He trabajado como editor y como traductor. He formado parte del consejo de redacción de diversas revistas de poesía y he dirigido una, *Años diez*, junto a Juan Carlos Reche.

Soy, además, dramaturgo, director musical y co-director artístico, junto a Luz Arcas, de la compañía de danza contemporánea *La phármaco*.

[I was born in Madrid, November 19, 1973, but I spent my childhood and my youth in a town in Badajoz, Montijo, in the region of Extremadura, where my family is from. When I was eighteen years old I went to study in the city of Salamanca, at the University of Salamanca, where I received my degree in fine arts and pursued studies in psychology and Hispanic philology. Later, in Córdoba, I studied humanities.

I wrote my first acceptable poem (from my point of view, clearly) at twenty-one: "Estrella fugaz," later included in my first book, *Adiós a la época de los grandes caracteres*. The collection was published eleven years later, when I was thirty-two. During that period, I did extensive readings and furthered my education in various cities in Spain and abroad.

At thirty-nine, in 2012, I published my second collection of poems, *El tiempo menos solo,* after seven years of silence. And at forty-three, *O Futuro,* my latest book of poetry.

I have worked as an editor and as a translator. I have been on the editorial boards of various periodicals specializing in poetry, and I have directed one, *Años diez,* along with Juan Carlos Reche.

In addition, I am the dramatist, music director, and artistic co-director, together with Luz Arcas, for the contemporary dance company *La phármaco.*]

THE POETICS OF THE WORD

The poetry of Abraham Gragera exhibits a profound understanding of metaphor. Two noteworthy commentaries point to the underpinnings of this literary trope in his work. Edward Hirsch writes, "The transaction between the poet and the reader, those two instances of one reality, depends on figurative language—figures of speech, figures of thought. Poetry evokes a language that moves beyond the literal and, consequently, a mode of thinking that moves beyond the literal. [. . .] Poetry is made of metaphor. It is a collision, a collusion, a compression of two unlike things: A is B. [. . .] A metaphor transfers the connotations or elements of one thing (or idea) to another. It is a transfer of energies, a mode of interpenetration, a matter of identity and difference."[2] In his poetry, this transferring, this shifting of ideas, stimulates the poetics of the word as a generative force occurring during the activity of creating, what must be called in his case, the cognitive metaphor. An additional and vital aspect of this figurative expression further grounds his poetry of today: "Rather than simply substituting one word for another, or comparing two things, metaphor invokes a transaction between words and things, after which the words, things, and thoughts are not quite the same."[3] These are pivotal points of departure for exploring the artistic making of metaphor in *Adiós a la época de los grandes caracteres* [*Farewell to the Era of Grand Letters*], *El tiempo menos solo* [*The Less Lonely Time*], and Gragera's most recent work, *O Futuro* [*The Future*].[4] These collections exhibit his convincing ability to convey the intellectual force of metaphor when it stimulates the untold referential capacity of the word. Gragera accomplishes this by his striking metamorphosis of this literary trope when he shapes and reshapes the efficacy and impact of the word in his estimable poetry.

Unique and self-renewing expressiveness fuels Gragera's poetry, especially when his poetic voices attempt to comprehend diverse aspects of and encounters with reality. His lyric often manifests surprising and multifaceted semantic configurations when the word takes on newly charged dimensions. In his expert hands, once familiar language becomes strange whenever the word undergoes extraordinary transformations after which it "will never be quite the same." "Siete presentes" [Seven Presents][5] (*Adiós a la época*, 28–34) offers treasured examples of this process. The initial poem discloses:

> . . .
> Por eso ahora
> tras el relámpago
> cuando las nubes pugnan por echar raíces
> las palabras se reúnen para preguntarse
>
> dónde se encuentran
> los que desaparecen. . . . ("I," 28)
>
> [. . .
> That is why now
> after the lightning
> when the clouds struggle to put down roots
> the words gather to wonder
>
> where those that disappear
> might meet. . . .]

Igniting the spark of new knowledge is fundamental to the dynamism of the recreated word in Abraham Gragera's poetry. In *Adiós a la época de los grandes caracteres*, Gragera challenges familiar verbal expression within inventive contexts when metaphor assumes the illuminative capacity to defy the standard interpretive act. The magnificent series of poems, "Siete presentes," offers undeniable evidence. This poem, divided into seven parts, provides a compendium of the distinctive role of metaphor in Gragera's work. It also sets the stage for the adventurous spirit with which he will continue to challenge unimaginative verbal expression, one of his major stylistic pursuits, throughout his trajectory. It is in this way that Gragera's poetry invites the experience of the invigorated word in fresh and vibrant metaphoric combinations. The innovative and unexpected encounter with his inspired poetics of the word, is particularly evident in his "Siete presentes," therefore the poem merits special consideration. In each of the seven parts of the poem, he offers different perspectives concerning the perception of various facets of this ephemeral moment. His careful analysis yields superlative insights into both this temporal dimension and this poet's inventive diction, as poem "II" (29) displays:

. . .
Ya solo sé vivir entre dos letras
Dos cifras, dos palabras
Más allá o más acá
De duda de no saber si sé
Vivir

Porque vivir es casi

[. . .
I only know how to live in between two letters
Two ciphers, two words
Further or closer
From the uncertainty of not knowing if I know how
To live

Because living is almost]

Rhythmic variations of hendecasyllabic and heptasyllabic lines sonorously linked by the alliterative omnipresence of "s" bring this poem to its thematic essence: "living." This existential activity, nevertheless, is short lived "because" the present moment occurs in the metaphoric domain of the "almost." Throughout "Siete presentes," original discourse contributes to the metamorphosis of metaphor when the word, used precisely and with decisive effects, combines in astonishing ways. This will become the new expressivity that will come to characterize Gragera's singular poetry. Poem "VII" (34) offers another stunning example:

. . .
permítenos dormir

así

fetalmente abrazados

como dicen que duermen

las interrogaciones

[. . .
let us sleep

like this

fetally embraced

as they say

question marks do]

In word and in deed, Gragera's "Siete presentes" series of poems leads to epistemic discoveries when metaphor recreates ordinary discourse with extraordinary metamorphic effects. Throughout his creative trajectory, his eloquence is admirable, and his unique poetics of the word is epiphanic.

In 2007, José Andújar Almansa, in his article "Retrato robot de la poesía reciente" [The Composite Profile of Recent Poetry], explains the nature of language in the Spanish lyric. The critic provides an indispensable summary relevant to the works of Abraham Gragera published both before and after that date. Andújar indicates, "Esta mezcla de precisión expresiva e invención metafórica, el teclado de imágenes, de efectos y sugestiones que percuten sobre las posibilidades semánticas del poema, son rasgos que me parecen ya decisivos para caracterizar a la poesía reciente."[6] [This mixture of expressive precision and metaphoric invention, the keyboard of images, of effects and suggestions striking the semantic possibilities of the poem, are features that seem to me already crucial for characterizing the recent poetry.] His insights readily apply to the poetry of Abraham Gragera, one of the most resourceful voices resonating in contemporary Spain. Gragera reveres the word making it the cornerstone of his work whenever he exploits and expands its referential possibilities.

NEW WAYS OF SAYING

In the 2014 special issue of *Ínsula* mentioned in the introduction, Gragera articulates in his "Poética, I" [Poetics, I] what should be considered as the most fundamental stylistic component underlying his poetic production: "Amar las formas, despreciar las fórmulas."[7] [Love the forms, disregard the formulas]. In 2006, Manuel Borrás's observations concerning the task at hand for the poet, in general, are applicable to Abraham Gragera. He accurately elucidates, "El poeta busca entre lo obvio, busca obviedades no bautizadas por el verbo y también busca lo no tan obvio. El problema consiste en que son pocos los que logran alguna de las dos cosas."[8] [The poet searches among the obvious, searches for what is obvious but not yet baptized by the word while also searching for what is not so obvious. The problem is that very few of them achieve one of these two things]. For Borrás, both the poet and the reader of poetry share in a similar quest, "encontrar nuevas formas de decir" (*Adiós a la época*) [to encounter new ways of saying]. When considering Gragera's poetry, it is this activity of "encountering" that distinguishes his poetics of epiphany and manifests the fundamental purpose of his quest and its unique results.

Gragera's work demonstrates that he is readily cognizant of his own linguistic identity where "el poeta no es un hombre rico en palabras muertas, sino en voces vivos" [the poet is not a man rich in dead words, but in living ones], borrowing Octavio Paz's insightful phrasing from his famous study *El arco y la lira*.[9] Gragera's profound respect for the word and its vital capacity both to inspire and to infuse his works indicate the importance of his work today. Fifty years earlier, Octavio Paz elucidates the singular importance of the word, and his estimable insights are applicable to the works of Abraham Gragera:

> Cuando un poeta encuentra su palabra, la reconoce: ya estaba en él. Y él estaba en ella. La palabra del poeta se confunde con su ser mismo. Él es su palabra. En el momento de la creación, aflora a la conciencia la parte más secreta de nosotros mismos. La creación consiste en un sacar a la luz ciertas palabras inseparables de nuestro ser. Ésas y no otras. (*El arco y la lira*, 45)

> [When a poet finds his word, he recognizes it: it was already in him. And he was already in it. The poet's word is confused with his very being. He is his word. At the moment of creation, the most secret part of our selves comes to the surface of consciousness. Creation consists in bringing forth certain words that are inseparable from our being. Those words and not others.] (*The Bow and the Lyre*, 34)

This attitude toward artistic "creation" also is the foundation for Gragera's poetics of the word. His steadfast pursuit of a fresh and vibrant vocabulary manifests his desire to say now what before has not been said. This acute awareness of saying and writing anew is a one of the hallmarks of his work.

Impeccably written, extraordinarily imaginative, and profoundly innovative, Abraham Gragera's 2005 *Adiós a la época de los grandes caracteres* signals his twenty-first-century understanding of the unique role of the word. The twelve poems constituting this collection incarnate the rich and vast potential of language in the hands of a leading poet in Spain. What drives this collection is Gragera's exceptional portrayal of the revitalization of the word, and the titular poem, "Adiós a la época de los grandes caracteres" (16–17) indicates how. Throughout this book, Gragera solidly demonstrates that his poetry has bid adieu to the cliché, the formulaic, and the predictable linguistic expression. Instead, his work signals his own fostering of an inventive and fresh degree of a different use of the word, one that incarnates the epistemic intensity of his own pursuit of renovating poetic discourse. Provocative poems such as "Estrella fugaz" (11) [Shooting

Star], "El susurro del polvo" (22–23) [The Whisper of the Dust], and "Siete presentes" (28–34) [Seven Presents], manifest these aims. For Abraham Gragera, the word must convey a renewed referential potency engendering a wealth of opportunities, combinations, and effects. His richly metaphoric "telaraña" [spider web], in the poem naming the collection, is itself a fine example as it symbolically catches past verbal expression and worn out discourse completely unaware, revealing, "Así, la telaraña dice adiós a la época de los grandes caracteres, mecida por el aire, la presa, el cazador. . . ." [Thus the spider web says farewell to the era of grand letters, poised in the air, the prey, the predator. . . .][10] It is within this elliptical and suspended moment where this talented poet stimulates different expectations and exploits unexpected nuances when developing one of the most ingenious poems and collections in twenty-first-century Spain.[11] In the opinion of Manuel Borrás in his essay "Abraham Gragera: Adiós a la época de los grandes caracteres," this image highlights "el pasado se cancela" [the past is cancelled]. Why? A newly articulated verbal reality is at hand. Offering indisputable insight, this critic further explains that in this collection, Gragera demonstrates that "se necesita otro vocabulario, se necesita ordenar de nuevo el verbo que heredamos" [one needs another vocabulary, one needs to overhaul the word that we inherit]. Borrás maintains that Gragera's 2005 work is an expression of a "search" for "inventing" anew because for this poet the "codes" of the past have become "imprecise" and "diffuse."

In 2013, fellow poet Martín López-Vega elucidates that Gragera's 2005 work "llevaba a la práctica la evidencia de que buscar decir cosas nuevas . . . equivalía a buscar nuevas formas de decirlas"[12] [put into practice the proof that seeking new things to say . . . corresponded to seeking new ways for saying them]. Although not placed as the initial poem of the collection, "Adiós a la época de los grandes caracteres" epitomizes Gragera's scrutiny of timeworn expression. His is a commitment to vivify the word and he achieves this with iconoclastic expertise. The singularity of poetic expression resides in the word and, in his view, here and now the time is right to beget a distinctive discourse. In so doing, Gragera successfully displays that his poetry will embody a new diction as the poetic voice of the poem "Adiós a la época de los grandes caracteres" well knows: "depurar ciertas palabras de su exceso de infinito" [rid certain words of their infinite excess]. Throughout this collection, Gragera transforms the word during "un acto genesíaco"[13] [an act of genesis]. His singular approach to the creative act in this 2005 work signals that Gragera's own "farewell" to past "formulas" place him squarely at the forefront of recent Spanish poetry, where he welcomes and champions its future.

The poetics of the word resonates throughout *Adiós a la época de los grandes caracteres* where, with impressive agility, Gragera's inventive metaphors expose the known as unknown, the common as uncommon, and the similar as different.

His is an unconventional method for reinventing the identity of the word and for discerning its numerous expressive possibilities. Both processes greatly enrich epiphanic discovery in his work. The poems comprising this collection provide unique occasions to ponder the imaginative "transfer of energies" imaged in metaphor. They also afford opportunities to encounter the various poetic voices heard in his collections. A few distinctive examples display these points. In "Estrella fugaz" (11) [Shooting Star], the poet establishes, in this initial poem of his 2005 collection, that instantaneous perception results only in ephemeral knowledge:

Aún es pronto, demasiado pronto para el ojo
pero tarde, muy tarde ya para el pensamiento

[It's still early, too early for the eye
but late, too late for the thought]

Instructive conversations with everyday objects in "El susurro del polvo" (22–23) [The Whisper of the Dust] disclose the following:

. . .
sujeto por la percha
de una interrogación
vivir es predicado.

[. . .
Held by the hanger
of a question mark
living is predicated.]

"Siete presentes" (28–34) [Seven Presents] penetrates the compressed temporal moment by reinventing reality as poem "V" (32) from this series reveals:

Ah la realidad

                no se puede

permanecer en ella ni intentar

ir más lejos

[Oh, reality

you cannot

remain in it

nor try to go further]

Gragera's concept of and attitude toward the speakers in his poems illuminates these three works particularly, and his poetry in general. In 2003, when answering a question posed by Luis Antonio de Villena, Gragera explains the development of his poetic voices, "Básicamente presentando a mis personajes poéticos como voces que las confunden o que, más bien, son incapaces de diferenciarlas. Esto no implica que como autor y lector establezca esas diferencias. Ni lo contrario."[14] [Basically, I present my poetic characters as blended voices or, rather, they are unable to be told apart. This does not imply that author and reader establish those differences. Nor the contrary.]

OH, REALITY

In Andújar's 2008 article, "Paisaje de la poesía última" [The Landscape of Recent Poetry], the notable literary critic uses poem "V," from "Siete presentes," as an elucidating point of departure for his examination of what he terms "la conciencia de lo real"[15] [the awareness of the real] in Gragera's 2005 collection. In Andújar's view, reality assumes a new meaning in the innovative poetry of today in Spain. The poets scrutinize, as he explains,

> una realidad de distintas densidades y superficies, caleidoscópica y desconcertante, abierta a nuevas vías de significación, reclamando una sensibilidad y una atención distinta. Una realidad compleja (como nunca, como casi siempre) y contradictoria. [. . .] Lo dice en un poema de *Adiós a la época de los grandes caracteres* (2005) de Abraham Gragera, y lo resume de otro modo, con mayor atención crítica . . . Alberto Santamaría: "no es posible enfrentarse a la realidad desde una perspectiva, por eso no aparece viable reducir a un solo mecanismo poético la expresión de esa realidad". [. . .] ("Paisaje de la poesía última," 34)
>
> [a reality with distinct densities and facets, kaleidoscopic and astonishing, open to new routes to meaning, calling for a sensibility and a distinct focus. A complex reality (as ever, like almost always) and contradictory. (. . .) It is expressed in a poem from *Farewell to the Era of Grand Letters* (2005) by Abraham Gragera, and it is summarized in another way, with closer critical attention . . . (by) Alberto Santamaria:

> "it is not possible to confront reality from only one perspective, therefore it is not viable to reduce to a single poetic device the expression of that reality. (. . .)"]

These observations strategically place the poetry of Abraham Gragera and his 2005 book at the center of Andújar's superb presentation of "the landscape" of Spain's recent poetry and the works the critic examines therein.

Additionally, in this article, Andújar makes use of another outstanding example from *Adiós a la época de los grandes caracteres* when he further underscores many of the points he explicates above by indicating the following:

> Está la realidad, en imparable movimiento, en un continuo hacerse y deshacerse. Y están las conexiones, las imágenes, las metáforas, los símbolos, con que los nuevos poetas intentan hablarnos de la realidad y del mundo, asomarnos a la vida. [. . .] Me detengo por un momento en algunas de esas imágenes, esos ojos distintos con que la poesía actual quiere mirar y nos hace mirar la realidad: "Anocheciendo / como en el interior de las manzanas." ("Paisaje de la poesía última," 35)

> [Reality is in relentless movement, in a continuous making and unmaking. And the connections exist, the images, the metaphors, the symbols, with which the new poets try to speak to us about reality and the world, show us life. (. . .) I pause for a moment in a few of those images, those different eyes with which the poetry of today wants to see and to make us see reality: "Dusk / like in the inside of apples."]

The example originates in Gragera's poem "III" from "Siete presentes" (30). Andújar highlights that in this image Abraham Gragera captures "un movimiento pendular de dentro a fuera y de afuera dentro, activado por un voltaje lírico que condensa sensación y visión interior" ("Paisaje de la poesía última," 35) [a pendular movement inwards and outwards activated by a lyrical voltage compressing sensation and insight.]

No single poem from this collection better illustrates this point than "El susurro del polvo" (22–23) [The Whisper of the Dust]. The work is a sensorial delight, even though it offers somber insight into the precarious nature of human beings in time. This poem is paradigmatic of the epistemic and ontological endeavors evidenced throughout Gragera's trajectory. "El susurro del polvo," however, merits a noteworthy position because it demonstrates the finesse with which this poet writes about the dilemma of being mortal. By balancing a sincere appreciation for the endurance in time of common objects with imagery expressing poignant realizations of human finitude, this work manifests why Abraham Gragera is a premier poet. This work further articulates fresh perceptions of reality when Gragera gathers an exceptional assemblage of simultaneous encounters with diverse aspects of life. In doing so, he succeeds at demonstrating his astute "awareness of the real" during an illuminative conversation with the everyday. Exemplary, melodic, and incisive, "El susurro del polvo" exhibits, borrowing Andujar's just cited observations, "those different eyes with which the poetry of today wants to see and to make us see reality." The inventive energy of metaphor, together with the confluence of varied and unanticipated discoveries, render the familiar as unfamiliar and the unfamiliar as familiar in this striking work. Here, Gragera uncovers the *poiesis* of the word with enviable artistry in the making of this poem.

"El susurro del polvo" embodies what the legendary modern Spanish poet Federico García Lorca articulated in 1931 in "La imagen poética de Don Luis de Góngora"[16] [The Poetic Image of Don Luis de Góngora]. As García Lorca indicates below,

> un poeta tiene que ser profesor en los cinco sentidos corporales. Los cinco sentidos corporales, en este orden: vista, tacto, oído, olfato y gusto. Para poder ser dueño de las más bellas imágenes tiene que abrir puertas de comunicación en todos ellos y con mucha frecuencia ha de superponer sus sensaciones y aun disfrazar sus naturalezas.

> [a poet must be a professor of the five corporeal senses. The five corporeal senses, in this order: sight, touch, hearing, smell, and taste. To master the most beautiful images, (the poet) must open the doors of communication among all of them and often should superimpose these sensations and even cloak their nature.]

Gragera reveals multiple facets of reality in this poem by skillfully employing sensorial transference as a dynamic strategy for his revitalization of metaphor. García Lorca further underscores in his essay, "La metáfora une dos mundos antagónicos por medio de un salto ecuestre que da la imaginación" ("La imagen poética," 69). [Metaphor joins two opposing worlds by means of an equestrian leap of the imagination.] In this poem, Gragera neutralizes what might seem, at first, to be incompatible modes of existence in the everyday by combining synesthetic perceptions leading to imaginative cognitive discoveries.

Garcia Lorca's perceptive observations shed substantial light on Gragera's "El susurro del polvo" (22–23). In this poem, the first-person speaker participates in a dialogue with ordinary objects:

> Me sobreviviréis
> sin excepción, objetos:

lámparas, llaves, vasos
cuartillas, ceniceros

[You will outlive me
without exception, objects:
lamps, keys, glasses,
sheets, ashtrays]

Internal assonance and alliterative echoing enhance the cadenced heptasyllabic lines melodically presenting features of the everyday. At the same time, these commonplace things sonorously converse among themselves. Each reveal "su muda arqueología"[17] [their silent arcaheology], the well-kept artifacts stored and displayed during remembering in time:

Y sobreviviréis
también a la memoria
de todos los que un día
poblaran con vosotros
su lengua y sus vitrinas,
su muda arqueología.

[And you will outlive too
the memories of
all those who one day
might fill their language
and their display cases with you,
their silent archaeology.]

The reflective poetic voice achieves new knowledge concerning the significance of being when the commonplace of the everyday reminds this protagonist of the ephemeral nature of the human condition. The ensuing lines reveal the metaphoric mastery of this poet:

Sujeto por la percha
de una interrogación
vivir es predicado.
Y por eso os arrastro
más acá del silencio,
mientras cuelgo mi ropa
usada ya, sin dueño,
en un armario . . .

> [Held by the hanger
> of a question mark
> living is predicated.
> And that is why I drag you
> this side of silence
> while I hang up my clothes,
> already used, without an owner,
> in a closet . . .]

The artistic dexterity with which Gragera shapes verbal expression in this exemplary poem readily displays an important theme guiding recent Spanish poetry. Andújar best articulates this in 2014 explaining, "Aun así, verbalizar el secreto consiste en hacer el mundo habitable, devolver a las cosas una mirada de reconocimiento."[18] [All the same, verbalizing the secret consists of making the world more livable, giving things a look of recognition.] Earlier, in 2006, Túa Blesa offers insightful commentary on Gragera's *Adiós a la época de los grandes caracteres* by further explicating this "mirada":

> Y es que lo artístico debe vincularse a ese efecto epifánico de mostrar algo como si fuera la primera vez. Esta mirada tiene que ver con una intensa vivencia de las cosas, de los objetos —términos también reiterados—, porque "las cosas nos enseñan", porque "Me sobreviviréis / sin excepción, objetos" y porque en fin "Vivir . . . es . . . algo que sucede mientras las cosas callan." Mirada que se funde con las cosas. [. . .] Mirada hecha palabra cuyo poder también reside en esa "liberación," en ese forzarla a menudo hasta sus lindes o más allá. ("*Adiós a la época de los grandes caracteres*")

> [The artistic should connect to the epiphanic effect when demonstrating something as if for the first time. This look must see with an intense experience of things, of objects—also repeated terminology—because "things teach us," because "you will outlive me / without exception, objects," and because lastly "living . . . is . . . something that takes place while things remain quiet." The look that fuses with the things. (. . .) The look made word whose power also lies in its "release," by often forcing it to its limits or beyond.]

By seeing anew, Gragera transforms language into an instrument of striking illumination. The visual perception of quotidian things and situations converge in intense moments of discovery in this exceptional poem.[19]

Rafael Espejo, also a contemporary poet, captures the essence of the creative artistry of the poetry of Abraham Gragera when he delineates other important features of this poem and the collection that it represents:

> Su poesía, lenta y meditativa, devuelve al lenguaje aquella primitiva habilidad para fundar significados y establecer simbologías, de modo que cuando nombra parece crear contenidos de cada palabra, reinventar referentes que vivifican la inevitable clonación de nuestros hábitos sentimentales con una imaginación salvaje y doméstica, misteriosa y cercana, trascendental, insondable. Poemas que acompañan y fascinan. Poemas como gatos.[20]
>
> [His poetry, measured and meditative, restores to language that original will to discover meanings and establish symbolisms, so that when he names, he seems to create contents for each word, reinventing referents that vivify the unavoidable cloning of sentimental habits with an imagination wild and domestic, hidden and nearby, transcendental, unfathomable. Poems that accompany and fascinate. Poems like cats.]

This same author, in his 2007 article concerning Gragera's 2005 collection, perceptively explains, "Si tuviéramos que definir la poética de Abraham Gragera, bastaría una sola palabra: poesía." [If we were to have to define the poetics of Abraham Gragera, one single word would be sufficient: poetry.] His closing observation affirms the decisive role of this fundamental book when he situates it within the domain of recent Spanish poetry: "En definitiva *Adiós a la época de los grandes caracteres* es un pequeño libro mayor."[21] [In short, *Farewell to the Era of Grand Letters* is a small book with a major impact].

GENESIS

His 2012 collection, *El tiempo menos solo* [*The Less Lonely Time*], adds new dimensions to the poetry of Abraham Gragera by articulating the transformative possibilities of the referential capacity of the word during its genesis. This work, as indicated in Gragera's personal biography and in endnote 1 of this chapter, received the prestigious Premio El Ojo Crítico de Poesía in Spain in 2013. This is a significant poetry honor, and the objectives of this longstanding award are clear, "premiar a jóvenes talentos. Se han convertido en uno de los mejores apoyos para la promoción de artistas que comienzan sus carreras"[22] [to bestow an award on young talents. It has become one of the best ways to support promoting artists at the early stages of their careers]. The panel of judges recognized "la gran capacidad del autor para construir realidad desde la palabra" [the great ability of the author to construct reality from the word]. In their view, this collection claims success by "ensanchando los caminos de la poesía" [expanding the paths of poetry].[23] What energizes these poems is Gragera's firm belief in what Octavio Paz articulated years earlier: "La fuerza creadora de la palabra reside en el hombre que la pronuncia" (*El arco y la lira*, 37). [The creative force of the word resides in the man who utters it] (*The Bow and the Lyre*, 27). The 2012 work is an epiphanic act of voicing the nature of poetic creation by releasing the power of the word to express. Here, Gragera reconstitutes the word by energizing it with an electrifying metaphoric charge leading to new discovery. The poetry of *El tiempo menos solo* demonstrates an attitude intimately interconnected with one of the most distinguishing features of this poet and his poetry. His is a commitment to what Paz articulates in this way: "El poeta no quiere decir: *dice*" (*El arco y la lira*, 110). [The poet does not try to say: *he says*] (*The Bow and the Lyre*, 95). In the view of one of Gragera's contemporaries, the poet Antonio Mochón, the 2012 work is "un libro que nos dice"[24] [a book that speaks to us]. Gragera is a poet who "speaks," "says," "utters," and communicates with an inventively new expression, in ways that earlier had not been verbalized by others. The poetic discourse in this 2012 work is imaginative and nuanced, original and exciting, thoughtful and challenging because Abraham Gragera is a poet who "says."

The opening poem, "Los años mudos" (11–12) [The Silent Years], situates the role of the word in the collection, as the following first lines reveal:

> Pero también perdimos la palabra
>
> mucho antes, antes de que supiéramos siquiera
>
> que la palabra existía,
>
> mucho antes de nosotros y de los que existieron antes
>
> junto a nosotros, en los huecos que dejamos al cambiar de lugar, en cada instante
>
> que inauguramos. Así que no es motivo de preocupación, más bien una posibilidad inesperada
>
> de amar nuestra lengua porque una vez que amamos la palabra
>
> que dispersó las lenguas, sin ser estrictamente religiosos, ni vulnerables a las profecías.

[But we also lost the word

long before, even before we knew the

word itself existed,

long before us, and those who existed before us,

and amongst us, in the spaces that we left when we changed places, in each instant

that we started. So, this is no reason to worry, but rather an unexpected opportunity

to love our own language because one day we loved the word

that scattered all languages, without being strictly religious, nor vulnerable to prophecies.]

The poet abandons convention and invents the word, the new word, his word. Naming is genesis. Naming is inquiry. By naming afresh, the poet gives the word the new contents of the fertile terrain of the unexplored and the unexpected. For Gragera, naming is an opportunity to say, to divulge, to create, and to reinvent.

"La poesía" (16–17) [Poetry] is the cornerstone of the collection. In this outstanding poem, Gragera personifies "poetry" empowering it to speak as it never has spoken. Poetry comports itself as if it were a familiar lover, a constant companion assisting in imaging the imagination of the poet engaging in the creative act:

. . .

La imagino también imaginando
lo bello más que todo cuando es uno,
cada cosa más bella si fuese
única, porque ha sido imaginada

para serlo y, por tanto, imaginada
hasta el más mínimo detalle. . . .

[. . .

I also imagine her imagining beauty
rather than all that is singular,
everything more beautiful than if it were
unique because it's been imagined to be unique

and therefore imagined
to the very last detail . . .]

Writing both manifests and nourishes this intimate relationship:

es difícil imaginar que no
lo hemos estado siempre . . .

[it is difficult to imagine that
we haven't always been . . .]

The poetic voice also expresses a commitment to the activity of writing and finds comfort in this endeavor as a source for alleviating isolation. The reader witnesses the unfolding of the presentation of two dramatis personae, the *yo*-poet-character and the *tú*-poetry-character. Each voices unique perspectives concerning their own individual natures and achievements. When considered in this way, the poem innovatively reshapes the dramatic device of anagnorisis when the *yo*-poet-character comprehends a strikingly new revelation, "imagino también imaginando" [I imagine also imagining], while conversing with the central character, "la poesía," and while imaging her fundamental significance, "y tú has vivido el tiempo suficiente" [and you have lived enough time]. This illumination is central to the poetics of epiphany in Gragera's work.

The two readings offered here, however, neglect the presence of another formidable figure in the poem—the present moment. This is the temporal instant in which the articulated activities occur. The present moment also displays another significant aspect of poetic creation, as the two final quartets of "La poesía" also disclose. Because the past signals completion, it always already exhibits the absence of the vital presence of what now is unfolding in time. The word thrives in the present act of creation, and its vitality animates the poem whenever metaphoric language transforms the moment of composition into illumination. By vivifying the imagination, the poetic image flourishes here and now. When considered in this way, the creative act produces a powerful result: "Tú has vivido el tiempo suficiente." [You have lived enough time.] Here, poet and poem, word and metaphor, writing and reading converge in the suspended temporal interval imagined and imaged throughout "La poesía."

Nonetheless, this poem indisputably offers another viable and interrelated interpretation. The poem conveys, during the process of its genesis and development, the significant presence and recognition of the loved one. It also, however, conveys important aspects in the active construction of identity for the dramatis personae of the poet writing the poem. This is particularly evident when the first-person interlocutor addresses, in an original dramatic monologue, the presence of the *tú*. Metaphor transforms features of their intimately intertwined relationship, as the following perfected hendecasyllabic lines disclose:

> . . . Tú
> la imaginas como si fuese ella
> la que nos imagina juntos porque
>
> es difícil imaginar que no
> lo hemos estado siempre, hasta este día
> de la historia que acaba, como siempre,
> entre el polvo y los puntos suspensivos,
>
> o entre paréntesis como las grietas.
> Y por eso imagino que te amo
>
> [. . . You
> imagine her as if she were
> the one who imagines us together, since
>
> it is difficult to imagine that
> we haven't always been, until that day
> in history that ends, as usual,
> amongst the dust and the ellipsis,
>
> or inside brackets, like ruptures.
> That's why I imagine that I love you]

It is not that poetry appropriates the revered presence of the loved one, but rather that the loved one herself possesses the compelling capacity to inspire the poet and the word. Poetry, as an astute *personaje poético*, alters, even if only briefly, time as passage thereby permitting the immediate apprehending of the intensity of writing in the present moment. In this splendid work, the first person poetic voice engages in as well as records the process of luminescent new knowledge achieved during the creative enterprise. Gragera's inventive dialogue images the significant role of the noticeably silent and yet ever-present and inspirational "voice" of the loved one.[25] "Poetry" quietly portrays her extraordinary power to engender, to enlighten, and to energize the personal identity of her companion in time.

"La poesía" embodies the ars poetica of Abraham Gragera. In this work, he expresses a discourse of discovery in well-conceived hendecasyllabic quartets. Here too, metaphor reveals its transformative role during the inquiry into the essence of the poetics of the word, when this poet "says" he gives voice to the epistemic nature of poetry. Antonio Mochón's 2013 general observations concerning the poems constituting *El tiempo menos solo* are applicable to "La poesía." He maintains that Gragera's 2012 book is "meditación por momentos iluminada sobre el hombre y su tiempo, sobre el hombre y su tarea en el tiempo y en el lenguaje . . . que constituye un elogio de la poesía desde ella misma, sin recurrir a modas" ("El tiempo menos solo, Abraham Gragera") [illuminating meditation on humankind and its time, on humankind and its challenges in time and in language . . . constituting a tribute to poetry from the perspective of poetry itself, without resorting to trends]. In this amazing ars poetica, Abraham Gragera illuminates what, almost forty years earlier, the modern Argentine poet, Roberto Juarroz, affirmed as "el oficio de la palabra"[26] [the profession of the word].

THE MATTER OF METAPHOR

"Nuestros nombres" (21–22) [Our Names] is an excellent companion piece to "La poesía." Here, Gragera further stimulates the capacity of the word, as the opening of this poem discloses:

> Ahora
>
> imagina que fuésemos capaces de renunciar a cualquier ilusión,
> incluso la de ser inmunes a las ilusiones.
>
> Que callamos, y al callar descubrimos que el silencio también lo
> disfraza todo.
>
> Que todo lo que existe tiene un nombre para cada cosa que
> existe y existimos, porque las cosas saben cada nombre
>
> que cada una de ellas nos ha dado. Imagina

que al pronunciar un nombre, una sola palabra, recordásemos

lo que las olas insinúan, con sus innumerables lenguas . . .

[Now

suppose that we were able to forsake any hope,
even that of being immune to hoping.

That we remained silent and found out that silence also
masked everything.

That whatever exists has a name for each thing
that exists, and we exist, because things know the name

that each one of them has given us. Suppose that

when we utter a name, a single word, we were to recall

what the waves, in their countless dialects, suggest . . .]

By divulging the essential creative potential of the word, Gragera subsequently comes to understand the linguistic identity of the poet: "al decir nuestros nombres como las cosas los dicen, sabiendo / que callar es poco hospitalario con los que ya no tienen qué / decir" [when we say our names the way things say them, conscious / that remaining silent is not very kind with those who have nothing to say / anymore]. Revering the referential capacity of the word, Gragera renovates it by giving to it a new way to say, a different subject matter, a transformative energy through metaphor. Because the word conserves within it the unique ability to verbalize anew, for this poet it is imperative that it be allowed to do so.

"Nuestros nombres" realizes the self-expression of the word by endowing it with its own vivifying voice. In so doing, Gragera enriches the conceptualization of poetry articulated years earlier by Roberto Juarroz. The following observations from his fundamental work, *Poesía y realidad*[27] [Poetry and Reality] are relevant:

> La poesía [. . .] salta por encima de los nombres de las cosas, para nombrarlas de otra manera, sin el engaño y la arbitrariedad de la etiqueta. Desnombra [. . .] para ir más allá de la designación que fija, paraliza o petrifica [. . .] y alcanzar ese transnombre o metanombre que recupera el ser, por medio de la imagen inesperada,

de la metáfora [. . .] y despierta a través del lenguaje transfigurado una nueva mirada, una mirada que ve con palabras.

[Poetry (. . .) overcomes the names of things, to name them in another way, without deceit and arbitrary labels. It un-names (. . .) in order to go beyond the designation that standardizes, paralyzes, petrifies (. . .) to achieve the trans-name or the meta-name that reclaims being, by means of the unexpected image, of metaphor (. . .), and awakens through transformed language a fresh vision, a vision that sees with words.]

"Nuestros nombres" is another striking ars poetica. For Gragera, the creative process must involve his own conscious genesis of the word, not any word, *his* word, and this occurs during the condensed moment in which the poem becomes the site for singular revelation. This exceptional poem discloses writing as an opportunity, an act of freedom, an expression of the revitalization of language, as the following lines make clear: "Imagina que fuésemos capaces / de encontrarnos en lenguas que no han nacido aún. . . ." [Suppose that we were able to / meet each other in languages that have not been born yet. . . .] This poem discloses an indispensable and a defining discovery, "de donde las palabras nacen" [from where words are born]. This is what Gragera seeks. This is what he articulates with extraordinary efficacy and effect. In his poetry, he metaphorically transforms the word and offers it as a way in which to welcome the world in order to inhabit it afresh. His word, indeed, has something to say. He elucidates this poetics of epiphany throughout the course of *El tiempo menos solo*. He does so while engaging in efforts to define the nature of poetry and while disclosing that these efforts are the result of his self-awareness as a poet. In examining this 2012 collection, Mariano Peyrou, a poet contemporary to Gragera, sheds further light observing, "Abraham Gragera nombra con una voz nueva, y también pone nombre a lo que no lo tenía, pero sobre todo nombra lo que no existía, una mirada, una sensibilidad, una manera de estar en el mundo, es decir, de usar las palabras."[28] [Abraham Gragera names with a new voice, and he also places a name on what before did not have one, but above all, he names what was absent, a vision, a sensitivity, a way to be in the world—namely, to use words.]

El tiempo menos solo also further invigorates the epiphanic effectiveness of the word, or what Martín López-Vega accurately names as the "epiphanic capacity" of poetry in the works of Abraham Gragera.[29] Gragera is a master at expressing human situations with intuitive existential awareness. In this work, he does not provide a commentary on human finitude. On the contrary, there is no attempt to describe, to explain or to offer an account of human mortality. Nor does this poet mourn the precarious circumstance of the inevitable outcome of being. Rather, his is an act of naming its various and differing constituents. For him, naming is a process of knowledge, a means to discovery. The poetic voice of "Los años mudos" (11–12) [The Silent Years] asks the following:

> . . . ¿Qué pensarán las nubes, es el tiempo el que cambia
>
> o sólo lo hace nuestra forma de recordar? ¿Está nuestra ilusión del otro lado, por eso nos dispara por la espalda
>
> y nos sentimos la espalda del futuro, y lo sabemos? Nos ha costado tanto llegar hasta el presente
>
> que es demasiado tarde para ser mañana.
>
> [. . . What will the clouds be thinking: is it
> time that changes
>
> or is it just the way we remember? Are our hopes
> on the other side, and that is why they shoot us in the back
>
> and why we feel the back of the future, and we know it? It has
> been so hard to make it to the present
>
> that it is too late to be tomorrow.]

This personalized plural protagonist is fully cognizant of the human condition shared with others, as these striking metaphors remind the reader. Confronting mortality is no easy task. Nevertheless, in "Obedecí" (34) [I Obeyed], another poetic protagonist learns from the past, inhabits the present, and embraces a certain optimism when distancing extant contemplation from future recollection. Temporal metaphoric transference animates time in this poem. In its closing moments, Gragera skillfully brings the future forward when personified "objects" manifest their own extraordinary and perceptive ability to be longstanding witnesses to a transitory human existence:

> los días van borrando el país donde el amor nos hizo. Pero el amor no sacia.
> Leo de noche a los grandes poetas que escribieron desde el después de cualquier cosa
> para dormirme pensando que al abrir los ojos las cosas nos recordarán.

[the days erase the country where love made us. But
love doesn't satisfy.
At night, I read the great poets who wrote in the
aftermath of anything,
and I go to sleep thinking that when we open our eyes the objects
will remember us.]

In "A la altura, a medida" (38) [This Size, This Height] the narrative tone is deceiving. This is not a straightforward explication of time as passage. This is not the telling of a tale. Rather, here metaphor assumes a most significant role in transferring visualized portrayals into insightful opportunities for pondering anew the results of being in time. With refined expertise, Gragera presents a cognitive metamorphic rendering as these internally cadenced lines reveal:

. . . A veces los descubro entre la multitud, en
ceremonias campesinas, y a veces los convierto en ciudadanos
de una ciudad ideal, la pincelada de una naturaleza

muerta, o unas simples figuras en un paisaje simple, cuyo
único deseo es quedarse un poco más ahí, de pie, frente a los
campos vacíos, como si el hombre fuese sólo

la forma humana del tiempo, y no la forma temporal del
hombre el tiempo que los ha soñado así, a la altura de la
siembra, a medida de la siega.

[. . . Sometimes I find them amongst the crowd, in a pastoral scene,
other times I turn them into the dwellers of an ideal city,
into the moving brushstrokes of a still life,

or into simple figures in a simple landscape whose sole ambition
is to stay there for a little longer, standing before the
empty fields, as if man were simply

the human embodiment of time instead of time being the
transient form of man that it dreamt of this way,
just the same size as the crop, the perfect height for harvest.]

Ana Corroto accurately points out in 2013 that *El tiempo menos solo* presents poetry as a "bridge" leading the reader to the poet's desire to recover "el contacto con algo perdido" [contact with what has been lost]. She positions the thematic matter of this work within the fluidity of time—past, present, and future—providing insights into Gragera's overall commitment to communicate, in her words, "la condición de expresarse, de existir y ser"[30] [the condition of self-expressing, of existing and being]. She further clarifies, "Las palabras de Abraham, nos sitúan ante nuestra propia amnesia. Dan luz para lidiar con la oscuridad que acompaña lo que no somos y pie para tratar de dirigirnos hacia lo que queremos ser, dejando atrás o no, todo aquello que echamos de menos." [The words of Abraham place us up against our own amnesia. They shed light on our struggle with the obscurity that accompanies what we are not, and they give us reasons that attempt to direct us toward what we wish to become, leaving behind or not, everything for which we long].

Abraham Gragera allows the word to manifest its transformative power to speak. His poetry restores to the word this ability, something it had lost during years of its predictable and unimaginative use. His is not merely a renovation of linguistic expression. His is an entirely new way to conceive and to articulate poetic discourse. His too is a fresh understanding of what it means to be a poet. Octavio Paz writes that a poet is "alguien que trasciende los límites de su lenguaje" (*El arco y la lira*, 23) [one who transcends the limits of his language] (*The Bow and the Lyre*, 13). Abraham Gragera fulfills this role. In 1961, the Argentinian poet Aldo Pellegrini offers an additional dimension to the position of a poet. His view enriches this term when considering Abraham Gragera and his work. He explains,

> El poeta busca en la palabra no un modo de expresarse sino un modo de participar en la realidad misma. Recurre a la palabra, pero busca en ella su valor originario, la magia del momento de la creación del verbo, momento en que no era un signo, sino parte de la realidad misma. El poeta mediante el verbo no expresa la realidad sino participa de ella misma.[31]
>
> [The poet seeks in the word not a way to express himself but a way in which to participate in reality. He resorts to the word but seeks in it only its own original value, the magic of the moment of its creation, the moment in which it was not a sign but rather a part of reality itself. The poet by means of the word does not express reality, rather he participates in it.]

EXISTENTIAL ETHICS

Throughout his work Abraham Gragera demonstrates his resolute faith in poetry. This continues to be apparent in his newest work, *O Futuro*, appearing in 2017.[32] The title is in Portuguese. It is a curious naming, where, as readers of his poetry have come to expect, the transformative power of the word continues to make itself known. The title is elucidating. The most obvious way to translate to Spanish his title is "El futuro" [*The Future*]. Gragera, however, due to his detailed inspection of diction, subscribes to a subtle play on words by giving the *O* of his title additional content. In Spanish, the "o" is rendered as the definite article "el" [the]. It also calls to mind the lingering grammatical presence of the word "o" [or], functioning as the disjunctive conjunction. In Spanish, it signals difference, and it also serves to exclude one of the two expressed options. It thus presents an alternative and implies a choice. From the outset of his newest collection, Gragera's ingenious title immediately positions his poetry in different temporal planes, "the present or the future," as well as "the past or the future." These are the time-based circumstances thematically structuring the collection. Simultaneously, these different temporal dimensions both signal and inspire the underlying existential ethic empowering this poetry.

Additional discoveries lie ahead. The title *O Futuro* originates in the poem numbered IV (*O Futuro*, 56) that pertains to the fifth section of the collection. Whether in fact or fiction, the poetic protagonist in this poem ponders a simple object, a decorative tile purchased in a marketplace during "nuestro paso por Altura"[33] [our stop in Altura]. This town on Portugal's southeastern Algarve coast is famous for its artisanal tiles. The poem's speaker indicates the following:

> . . . elegimos éste, por su punta
> de proa de barquilla
> con una banda blanca en la que pone *O Futuro*,
> para conmemorar nuestro paso por Altura. ("IV," 56)
>
> [. . . we chose this one, because the tip
> of the prow of the small boat
> had a white flag with the words *O Futuro*,
> as a way of commemorating our stop in Altura.]

This metaphoric memento, encounter, and sentimental find launches Gragera's portrayal of several of the motifs evident in his newest work. This tile is no ordinary keepsake. It commemorates a past trip. It also simultaneously signals a metamorphic journey of discovery in the present. The collection's title symbolically functions as a type of compass, and the poetic voices in this collection must navigate among personal experiences portrayed in the present, as well as in the past. Because they are grappling with different reflective and self-reflective existential situations, they seek direction. The fundamental question underlying the collection is central to the personal circumstances, present and past, portrayed in *O Futuro*. What is the importance of being in the world today?

Some readers might be led to believe, when taking the title of this collection at face value, that "The Future" is the focus of this poetry. The title might even be incorrectly assumed to be an apostrophe, where the poet invokes what might seem to be a new and better future for humankind. In this work, there is an existential ethic, however, that Gragera elaborates in the present. His focus centers on the individual, on personal existence, on how to live life now by connecting with the past, with the loved one, with the experience of loss. Private life—in the sense of the individual and her or his right to respect, to dignity, to well-being, to personal existence, to expression of sincere and intimate love, to family, to community—must be safeguarded. To preserve this, the individual must assume a responsibility for self and for others. Only then can the individual shape the present for the future.

The point of departure for this work is the present moment continually engaging in its own dynamic process of being and becoming. Gragera looks inward and intimate self-reflection assumes a major role in his 2017 work. Self-study is a mode of being and it takes place when thoughtfully considering past events and situations in such poems as "Lavandera" (15) [Laundress] and "Enigmas de la naturaleza" (43–44) [The Enigmas of Nature].[34] It occurs also during poignant moments portraying the loved one and the bond of love between two individuals. One brilliant poem exemplifies special "scenes" from *O Futuro* when the self-reflective personalized poetic voice imagines the impermanence of the presence of the loved one. Metaphoric transformation reveals the following:

> No me acostumbro a despertar contigo
> oyéndonos latir el corazón descalzo,
> en la noche de siempre, por la casa desierta. ("IV," 57)
>
> [I am not used to waking up with you
> hearing our heartbeat barefoot,
> in this perpetual night, through the deserted house.]

In another, the poem's protagonist divulges a deeply moving and profound expression of love for the loved one, despite the relentless passage of time:

> No vi en tu cuerpo propaganda alguna
> del eterno retorno de la eterna juventud
>
> lo amé sabiendo que envejecería
> lo amé sabiendo que te perdería
> lo amé más allá de la euforia y la elegía . . . ("III," 55)

[I do not see in your body any misleading information
about the eternal return of eternal youth

I loved it knowing it would grow old
I loved it knowing that I would lose you
I loved you beyond euphoria and elegy . . .]

What can the individual in the present moment preserve "now" given the uncertainty of personal being in time? "Enigmas de la naturaleza" (43–44) offers a response. In the collection, the poet looks both forward and backward. This exemplary poem demonstrates the personalized poetic voice reflecting on past existential circumstances during a period when the present seemed to encompass a perpetual and infinite future. This is the view of a young child pondering the days that lie ahead with anticipation and without fear. This poem recollects childhood, and thus the personalized voice expresses a view of the present moving toward a future that already has been experienced and recorded in familiar memories. The self-portrait of the young child reveals instructive events concerning how to be in the world and how other living entities have learned about being and being in the world. Science, history, biology, archaeology, all provide useful guideposts for the child trying to understand the "enigmas" of being. The poem exemplifies a self-reflexive autobiographical dimension also found in other poems from this 2017 collection.

The curious child examining the origin of being soon will come to know that the nature of existence is finite. Even personal being, which was thought to be engaging in becoming what you wish to become later, itself evolves toward what it will become both now and also later than now in each temporal moment: nonbeing. Gragera captures the finitude of being human in two succinct heptasyllabic lines constituting a single poem:

Sí. Somos. Existimos.
Aunque sea improbable. ("XI," 70)

[Yes. We are. We exist.
Although it may be unlikely.]

By expanding the poetics of the word in this collection, he allows his expression to assume a content enriched by the underlying existential ethic. Given human finitude, his word shapes and explicates how to live life now and influence "the future." In uppercase, the word initial "F" gives this temporal dimension a wider importance and impact. It further underscores an implicit attitude toward a forthcoming state, situation, event that always already is immediately at hand. In this work, "The Future" cannot be ignored. It is in this sense that Gragera presents "una poesía que sea útil para la vida" [a poetry that is useful for life], as fellow poet Martin López-Vega recently observed in his excellent article, "el futuro como presente perpetuo"[35] ["The Future" as the perpetual present]. He further emphasizes the essential features of *O Futuro* and the creative work of Abraham Gragera in Spain today:

> Su poesía enseña a vivir en el punto medio entre todas las contradicciones, con una inteligencia humilde y generosa, honda, ilusionada y desengañada a partes iguales, con una curiosidad inagotable y a la vez reflexiva. Su contrato con el lenguaje es igual. Y todo esto hace de su poesía un manual de instrucciones perfecto para este tiempo raro, enseñándonos a vivir todo de todas maneras, sin cinismo ni exhibicionismo, honestamente, como quien sabe lo que tiene y no pide más que renovarlos día a día con ilusión y trabajo. Con vida.
>
> [His poetry teaches us to live at the mid-point between all the contradictions, with a humble and generous intelligence, deep, hopeful, and undeceived in equal parts, with an unlimited and yet still reflective curiosity. His bond with language remains the same. And all of this makes his poetry a handbook of instructions that is perfect for this strange period, showing us ways of living, without cynicism or extravagance, honestly, like one who knows exactly what he has and does not ask for more than renewal day by day with dreams and work. With life.]

In *O Futuro,* Gragera personifies this temporal mode transforming it into a witness to all occurring now in time. He endows this figure with the ability to listen to and to heed the various testimonials voiced by his various poetic protagonists in this work. Whether observing the poet's attempts to recover childhood memories, to imagine life in the absence of the loved one, to contemplate the finitude of personal being, or to consider the individual as part of a collective, these might all, at first, seem to suggest a passive bystander. In this collection, however, Abraham Gragera summons this eyewitness and requests that it assume an active role in orienting the present toward instructive moments applicable to now *and* for the time that is yet to come. The decorative keepsake tile alluded to in the title metaphorically embodies the existential ethic guiding the course of this recent collection of poems by Abraham Gragera.

On October 19, 2017, *O Futuro* was awarded the prize for *The Best Book of Poetry for 2017* by the Madrid Booksellers Guild. It was the first time that the genre of poetry was included as a category in these awards. The observations of the judging panel provide significant insights concerning this work and this poet's creative trajectory. The panel indicates, "Gragera desgrana su visión del mundo con una poesía que ilumina sin estridencias ni falsas retóricas como un recopilatorio de su propia alma en construcción constante, de sus vivencias que lo conforman como ser humano preocupado por el presente y esperanzado con el futuro [. . .], ya reconocible como un poeta de deslumbrante futuro."[36] [Gragera addresses his vision of the world with a poetry that illuminates but without being blatant or grandiloquent; his vision is a compendium of his own soul under constant construction, of the experiences shaping him as a human being concerned with the present and hopeful for the future (. . .), already recognizable as a poet with a stunning future.]

In twenty-first-century Spain, the distinguished work of Abraham Gragera manifests his singular ability to liberate the word so that it can express its creative power. The fresh referential dimensions of the word, together with Gragera's innovative metaphors, energize the linguistic revitalization that has come to be associated with this poet and his work. Past and present, the poetry of Abraham Gragera displays a discourse of discovery uniquely his own. This same panel of judges affirms that he "already has been recognized as a poet with a stunning future." The works studied in the present chapter further confirm this fact.

POEM AND POEM ANALYSIS BY ABRAHAM GRAGERA

What follows is a poem by Abraham Gragera and his original analysis of this work. He wrote his study at the request of the author for inclusion in this chapter of the book. Here, he reveals his own stellar insights into the epiphanic nature of his poetry. At the same time, this poem promises the novel and invigorating contributions that Abraham Gragera will express in his forthcoming creative endeavors.[37]

"LA VOZ DE NUNCA"

Teme al silencio, pero cada tarde le pide ser su amigo, y se levanta, mientras los otros duermen,
y camina por la penumbra fresca del pasillo hasta llegar al patio, donde espera.

Pero el silencio no aparece nunca, porque hasta nunca tiene también voz, y ojos que miran a través del ámbar que lo ha enjoyado todo con él dentro: el caudal de las grietas que ahora siente latir sobre las líneas de su mano, bajo la nueva capa de pintura; la sombra del jilguero que aletea en la jaula vacía; los crujidos del mimbre destrenzado en la butaca; los planetas de moscas y de avispas flotando alrededor de los limones . . .

Y así hasta el infinito, que se abría, igual que los limones, en el zumo amargo que su abuela le ofrecía cada tarde, para que no temiese más la voz de nunca: luz de beber que alumbraba los cuerpos por dentro. (*O Futuro*, 25)

[THE VOICE OF NEVER]

[He is afraid of silence, but each afternoon he pleads to be his friend and stands up, while the rest sleep, and walks the fresh length of the shaded corridor to the patio, where he waits.

But the silence never comes forth, because even never has a voice too, and eyes that look through the amber that has embellished everything with him inside: the course of the cracks in the walls he can feel pulsing in the lines of his palm, under the new coating of paint; the shadow of the goldfinch beating its wings in the empty cage; the crackle of the chair's frayed straw; the planets of flies and wasps floating around the lemons . . .

And likewise to the infinity, that opened up to him, like the lemons, in the bitter juice that his grandmother handed to him every afternoon, so that he might not fear the voice of never anymore: drinking light that brightened bodies from the inside.]

ANÁLISIS

"La voz de nunca" es un poema de revelación del mundo, un poema que recrea una epifanía.

Transcurre durante una siesta, una tarde de verano, en el sur de España. Para quien no esté familiarizado con estas coordenadas espacio-temporales, hay que decir que a esas horas, con más de cuarenta y cinco grados centígrados a la sombra, el silencio se adensa, se vuelve materia. La impresión es la de estar en el interior de un cuerpo, solo que este cuerpo no es oscuro, sino violentamente luminoso, y uno, como probablemente les ocurra a los fetos en el útero materno, está sometido a todo tipo de estímulos e impresiones auditivas. Es la densidad del silencio la que hace que el sonido se traslade a más distancia y con mayor volumen, como sucede debajo del mar. Cigarras, crujidos de maderas, pájaros ambulantes, alguna voz humana penetran en las estancias oscuras de la casa y el personaje poético se levanta, como obedeciendo una llamada. Lo que se encuentra, al salir al patio de la casa es, al mismo tiempo, absolutamente concreto y escurridizamente abstracto. El personaje poético mantiene el juicio en suspensión. La duermevela y el violento choque de la luz vespertina le provocan una especie de kenosis, un vacío sagrado, una despersonalización. Es un estado genuinamente receptivo, una extrañeza, previa a la revelación. La revelación, en este caso, no es racional, no es moral, sino circular, musical, física. El protagonista poético se siente dentro de la materia, se siente parte de ella y capaz, por tanto, de extenderse desde sus mismos orígenes hasta sus límites. De ahí las imágenes que aluden a la conciencia de saberse observado desde fuera (los ojos que le miran a través del ámbar que lo ha enjoyado todo con él dentro). La epifanía se produce cuando esta lejanía, esta experiencia de despersonalización, encuentra su analogía con la vida personal, biográfica (el personaje de la abuela y el propio cuerpo del protagonista). Esta analogía, o correspondencia, la posibilita el lenguaje que, en lugar de enunciar y de clarificar, trata de encarnar, de convertir en un objeto las distintas dimensiones temporales y perceptivas de la experiencia en cuestión.

[ANALYSIS]

["The Voice of Never" is a poem that concerns the revelation of the world, a poem that recreates an epiphany.

It takes place during siesta on a summer afternoon in the south of Spain. For those not familiar with it, at that time of the year in that part of the world and that time of day, when temperatures rise more than 45 degrees Celsius, silence becomes thick, it almost materializes. One gets the impression of being inside a body, only the inside of that body is not dark, but violently bright, and you are exposed to all sorts of stimuli and aural impressions, in a probably similar fashion to what happens to a fetus inside the womb. It is this solidity of the silence that makes sounds travel longer distances and at a louder volume, like under the sea. Cicadas, the crackle of wood, passing birds, some human voices penetrate the shaded rooms in the house and the character in the poem rises as if compelled by a call. What he finds when he goes out to the patio is something that is, simultaneously, both undeniably concrete and elusively abstract. The poetic persona suspends judgment. The experience of a light sleep and the wild shock of the afternoon light incite in him a kind of kenosis, a sacred emptiness, a depersonalization. It is a genuinely receptive state, the perplexing strangeness preceding revelation. The revelation is not, in this case, rational, or moral, but circular, musical, physical. The poetic character feels inside of matter, he feels part of it and, thus, capable of stretching all the way from his very beginning to his limits. Therefore, the images allude to the realization that he is being observed from the outside (the eyes that watch him through the amber that has bejeweled everything with him inside). The epiphany happens when this strangeness, this depersonalization, finds its analogy in his personal life, his biography (the grandmother character and his own body as the poetic protagonist). This analogy, or correspondence, is made possible by language that rather than enunciating and clarifying instead attempts to incarnate, to turn into an object, the distinct temporal and perceptive dimensions of the experience in question.]

POEMS BY ABRAHAM GRAGERA

The complete text and translation of the poems examined in chapter 2 include the following:

"Siete presentes I, II, III, IV, V, VI, VII," *Adiós a la época de los grandes caracteres* (2005).
"Estrella fugaz," *Adiós a la época de los grandes caracteres* (2005).
"El susurro del polvo," *Adiós a la época de los grandes caracteres* (2005).
"Los años mudos," *El tiempo menos solo* (2012).
"La poesía," *El tiempo menos solo* (2012).
"Nuestros nombres," *El tiempo menos solo* (2012).
"Obedecí," *El tiempo menos solo* (2012).
"A la altura, a medida," *El tiempo menos solo* (2012).
"Enigmas de la naturaleza," *O Futuro* (2017).

SIETE PRESENTES

I
Ya las conoces
en cierto modo son como la gente
están deseando encontrarse:
las nubes, las palabras.

Por eso ahora
tras el relámpago
cuando las nubes pugnan por echar raíces
las palabras se reúnen para preguntarse

dónde se encuentran
los que desaparecen.

Y los silencios mudan de lugar.
Y la vida es
casi más rara aún
menos nuestra

de lo que suponíamos.

Ya nos conoces.

II
Mi amor por ti compite con tu amor por todo

Pero si no te amo no puedo estar en todo

Ya sólo sé vivir entre dos letras
Dos cifras, dos palabras
Más allá o más acá
De la duda de no saber si sé
Vivir

Porque vivir es casi

III
Anocheciendo

Como en el interior de las manzanas
En su piel

Como un olor
Un objeto perdido

Una sombra
Carne desorientada

En ciudades y campos
Locamente semánticos donde vivir
No es privilegio ni signo de nobleza
Sino algo que sucede
Mientras las cosas callan

Anocheciendo

Hasta que cante el mirlo

Noche oscura del alba

IV
Cuando no despertemos

Cuando no despertemos y se mezclen
tus rasgos y los míos

Cuando la hierba tararee una canción
sobre nosotros

Y el topo ya no cante
el mito del murciélago

Cuando de la palabra identidad sólo se entienda
la última sílaba

¿Quién se preguntará
qué quería yo decirte

Como ahora me pregunto
si lo sabré entonces?

V
Ah la realidad
                no se puede

permanecer en ella ni intentar

ir más lejos

VI
Estas ropas encima de la silla . . .

Esta lluvia sin cuerpo que la precise . . .

VII
Amor que empobreces

al que recibe tanto

como al que no

aléjanos del reino
de las intenciones

permítenos dormir

así

fetalmente abrazados

como dicen que duermen

las interrogaciones

[SEVEN PRESENTS]

[I
You know them by now
they are somehow like people
looking forward to meeting each other
the clouds, the words.

Therefore now
after the lightning
when the clouds struggle to put down roots
the words gather to wonder

where those that disappear
might meet.

And silences change places

and life is
even stranger yet
less ours

than we thought.

You know us by now.

II
My love for you challenges your love for everything

But if I don't love you I cannot be in everything

I only know how to live in between two letters
Two ciphers, two words
Further or closer
From the uncertainty of not knowing if I know how
To live

Because living is almost

III
Dusk

Like in the inside of apples
Inside their skin

Like a scent
A lost property

A shadow
Disoriented flesh

In towns and fields
Madly semantic where living
Is not a privilege nor a sign of dignity
But something that happens
While things keep quiet

Dusk

Until the blackbird sings

Dark night of dawn

IV
When we might not be awake

When we might not be awake and your features
and mine blend

When the grass might murmur a song
about us

and the mole might not sing
the myth about the bat

When what might be understood about the word uniqueness
is its last syllable

Who will wonder
what I meant to tell you

like I now wonder
if I will then know?

V
Oh, reality
            you cannot

remain in it nor try

to go further

VI
These clothes on the chair . . .

This rain that no body requires . . .

VII
Oh love you that impoverish

the one who receives as much

as the one who doesn't

keep us away
from the kingdom of intentions

let us sleep

like this

fetally embraced

as they say

question marks do]

ESTRELLA FUGAZ

Aún es pronto, demasiado pronto para el ojo
pero tarde, muy tarde ya para el pensamiento
si veloz ilumina
esta árida extensión de la noche,
este manso terreno donde el girasol
se despereza, se astilla, se equivoca.

[SHOOTING STAR]

[It's still early, too early for the eye
but late, too late for the thought
when it suddenly shines over
this dry expanse of night
this tranquil field in which the sunflower
stretches, shrieks, mistakes]

EL SUSURRO DEL POLVO

Me sobreviviréis
sin excepción, objetos:
lámparas, llaves, vasos,
cuartillas, ceniceros,
líneas rectas y curvas
que ajenas dibujáis
mi camino y mi cuerpo.
Y sobreviviréis
también a la memoria
de todos los que un día
poblaran con vosotros
su lengua y sus vitrinas,
su muda arqueología.
Lo que venga después
no habita en las palabras
y puesto que la tierra
reclama cuanto es suyo
—forma, no sentido—
es inútil trataros
como a un testamento.
El bien y el mal
no pasarán de aquí,
ni el frío, ni el infierno.
Sujeto por la percha
de una interrogación
vivir es predicado.
Y por eso os arrastro
más acá del silencio,
mientras cuelgo mi ropa
usada ya, sin dueño,
en un armario, al fondo,
donde sólo se escucha,
como nieve que cae,
lenta, sin viento,
el susurro del polvo.

[THE WHISPER OF THE DUST]

[You will outlive me
without exception, objects:
lamps, keys, glasses,
sheets, ashtrays,
straight lines and bends
that barely outline
my path and my body.
And you will outlive too
the memories of
all those who one day
might fill their language
and their display cases with you,
their silent archaeology.
Whatever comes next
does not dwell in the words
and since the land
reclaims all that belongs to it—
form, not meaning—
it is useless to treat you
as a testament.
Good and evil
will not go further than here,
nor cold, nor hell.
Held by the hanger of
a question mark
living is predicated.
And that is why I drag you
this side of silence
while I hang up my clothes,
already used, without an owner,
in a closet, at the back,
where all that can be heard,
like snow that falls
slowly, with no wind,
is the whisper of the dust.]

LOS AÑOS MUDOS

Pero también perdimos la palabra

mucho antes, antes de que supiéramos siquiera

que la palabra existía,

mucho antes de nosotros y de los que existieron antes

junto a nosotros, en los huecos que dejamos al cambiar de
lugar, en cada instante

que inauguramos. Así que no es motivo de preocupación, más
bien una posibilidad inesperada

de amar nuestra lengua porque una vez amamos la palabra

que dispersó las lenguas, sin ser estrictamente religiosos, ni
vulnerables a las profecías.

Me pregunto por qué pasó de largo la poesía

frente a nuestros intentos de adquirir dominio público, y nos
dejó de este modo, imaginando

con tanta imprecisión tragedias generalmente aceptadas, por los
que sufren y por los que persiguen

transformar sus asuntos en ejemplos. Por qué es difícil de escribir,
por qué no basta

el simple amor porque las cosas sean

incapaces de aceptar el yugo, lo literal de nuestras voluntariosas

aproximaciones: los barcos mugen, crepusculares, las gaviotas
levantan

su torre de Babel en la corriente térmica; el sol se agita como un
saltamontes entre el bajo voltaje de las chicharras

y en los muros del solar abandonando las telarañas recuerdan

a la espuma marina. ¿Qué pensarán las nubes, es el tiempo el que cambia

o sólo lo hace nuestra forma de recordar? ¿Está nuestra ilusión del otro lado, por eso nos dispara por la espalda

y nos sentimos la espalda de futuro, y lo sabemos? Nos ha costado tanto llegar hasta el presente

que es demasiado tarde para ser mañana.

Por eso es cada vez la última.

Y agobiados hasta lo interminable, con vergüenza de ser como las falsas etimologías,

con aire silencioso, de futuros conocidos, tratamos de encarnar en lo posible

este amor imposible

por todo lo que es, perece y muda.

Porque en nuestro futuro no hay memoria

y somos el futuro de todo lo que está a nuestras espaldas.

[THE SILENT YEARS]

[But we also lost the word

long before that, even before we knew the

word itself existed,

long before us, and those who existed before us,

and amongst us, in the spaces that we left when we changed

places, in each instant
that we started. So this is no reason
to worry, but rather an unexpected opportunity
to love our own language because one day we loved the word
that scattered all languages, without being strictly religious, nor
vulnerable to prophecies.
I wonder why poetry was unimpressed
with our efforts to reach the public domain, and left
us this way, guessing vaguely
generally accepted tragedies, for those
who suffer and for those who wish
to turn their own issues into examples. Why is it difficult
to write, why just love is not enough,
since things are unable to accept
the yoke, our often too literal, well-intentioned
approaches: the ships, crepuscular, moo, the
seagulls build their Babel tower
in the thermal currents; the sun shakes like
a grasshopper in the cicadas' low-voltage buzz
and on walls of the abandoned sites the spider webs
recall sea surf. What will the clouds be thinking: is it

time that changes

or is it just the way we remember? Are our hopes

on the other side, and that is why they shoot us in the back

and why we feel the back of the future, and we know it? It has

been so hard to make it to the present

that it is too late to be tomorrow.

That is why each time is the last time.

And overwhelmed to exhaustion, ashamed of being

like false etymologies,

in a quiet manner, like that of future acquaintances, we try to embody in the possible

this impossible love

for all that exists, perishes and changes.

Because there is no memory in our future

and we are the future of all that is behind us.]

LA POESÍA

Yo la imagino aún siendo capaz
de imaginarlo todo sin hacer
sentir a quien la escucha irresponsable
de sus propios delirios y razones.

La imagino también imaginando
lo bello más que todo cuando es uno,
cada cosa más bella que si fuese
única, porque has sido imaginada

para serlo y, por tanto, imaginada
hasta el más mínimo detalle. Tú
la imaginas como fuese ella
la que nos imagina juntos porque

es difícil imaginar que no
lo hemos estado siempre, hasta este día
de la historia que acaba, como siempre,
entre el polvo y los puntos suspensivos,

o entre paréntesis, como las grietas.
Y por eso imagino que te amo,
que la luz se desnuda en tus orillas
y va a dormir donde la noche duerme;

y que si el tiempo alguna vez sonríe,
si esta nostalgia de los propios rasgos,
que enciende el aire del amanecer,
hace al tiempo sentirse menos solo,

será porque recuerda cada vida,
y el tiempo de la flor entró en la rama,
y sube hasta tus pies la tierra entera,
y tú has vivido el tiempo suficiente.

[POETRY]

[I still imagine her being able
to imagine everything without
making the listener feel irresponsible
of his own reasons and delusions.

I also imagine her imagining beauty
rather than all that is singular,
everything more beautiful than if it were
unique because it's been imagined

to be unique and therefore imagined
to the very last detail. You
imagine her as if she were
the one who imagines us together since

it is difficult to imagine that
we haven't always been, until that day
in history that ends, as usual,
amongst the dust and the ellipsis,

or inside brackets, like ruptures.
That's why I imagine that I love you,
that light undresses on your shores
and goes to sleep where night rests;

and that if ever time smiles,
if this longing of our own features
that lightens the air at dawn
makes time feel less lonely,

it must be because it remembers each life,
and the time of the flower seeped into the branch,
and the whole earth reaches up to your feet,
and you have lived enough time.]

NUESTROS NOMBRES

Ahora

imagina que fuésemos capaces de renunciar a cualquier ilusión,
incluso a la de ser inmunes a las ilusiones.

Que callamos, y al callar descubrimos que el silencio también lo
disfraza todo.

Que todo lo que existe tiene un nombre para cada cosa que
existe y existimos, porque las cosas saben cada nombre

que cada una de ellas nos ha dado. Imagina

que al pronunciar un nombre, una sola palabra, recordásemos

lo que las olas insinúan, con sus innumerables lenguas, a los
peces reunidos en la luz de los últimos reflejos, como oscuras
sinapsis extraviadas

esta tarde de marzo: que nosotros también fuimos dichos, que
nada de lo dicho pertenece a quienes administraron las palabras,
que verdad

es lo que no se puede poseer y, por tanto, somos verdad ahora,
al decir nuestros nombres como las cosas los dicen, sabiendo

que callar es poco hospitalario con los que ya no tienen qué
decir.

Imagina que fuésemos capaces

de encontrarnos en lenguas que no han nacido aún, que nuestra
larga canción de despedida naciese en realidad de un miedo
más profundo

el de la permanencia, de donde las palabras nacen.

Que todo nacimiento es un perdón.

Mirar como se miran las cosas entre sí.

O este amor animal del que volvemos, sabiendo que no hemos
perdido el mundo pero sospechando

que nunca merecimos su belleza.

[OUR NAMES]

[Now

suppose that we were able to forsake any hope,
even that of being immune to hoping.

That we remained silent and found out that silence also
masked everything.

That whatever exists has a name for each thing
that exists and we exist, because things know the name

that each one of them has given us. Suppose that

when we utter a name, a single word, we were to recall

what the waves, in their countless dialects, suggest to the
fish that gathered in the light of the last reflections,
like disoriented synapsis

on this March evening: that we were also uttered, that
nothing that was said belongs to those who organize the words,
that truth

is what cannot be possessed, and therefore we are true now
when we say our names the way things say them, conscious

that remaining silent is not very kind with those who have nothing to
say anymore.

Suppose that we were able to

meet each other in languages that have not been born yet, and
that our long farewell song might in fact be born out of a
deeper fear,

that of stillness, from where words are born.

That each birth is an acquittal.

Imagine that we look at each other the way things look at each other.

Or this animal love we are returning from, certain that
we have not lost the world but suspecting

that we never deserved its beauty]

OBEDECÍ

Como justos que arrojan al fin sobre la tierra baldía su
primera piedra,
como niños que no pueden dormir porque saben que no se
librarán de nada,
los días van borrando el país donde el amor nos hizo. Pero el
amor no sacia.
Leo de noche a los grandes poetas que escribieron desde el
después de cualquier cosa
para dormirme pensando que al abrir los ojos las cosas nos
recordarán.

[I OBEYED]

[Like righteous men who over wasted land finally cast
the first stone,
like children who can't sleep because they know there's
nothing to hide from,
the days erase the country where love made us. But love
doesn't satisfy.
At night, I read the great poets who wrote in the aftermath
of anything,
and I go to sleep thinking that when we open our eyes the objects
will remember us]

A LA ALTURA, A MEDIDA

En museos, en libros de arte, trato de adivinar siempre en
qué cuadros les gustaría vivir a las personas que admiro, los
seres que amo, aquellos que recuerdo por soñar

todavía. A veces los descubro entre la multitud, en
ceremonias campesinas, y a veces los convierto en ciudadanos
de una ciudad ideal, la pincelada viva de una naturaleza

muerta, o unas simples figuras en un paisaje simple, cuyo
único deseo es quedarse un poco más ahí, de pie, frente a los
campos vacíos, como si el hombre fuese sólo

la forma humana del tiempo, y no la forma temporal del
hombre el tiempo que los ha soñado así, a la altura de la
siembra, a medida de la siega.

[THIS SIZE, THIS HEIGHT]

[In museums, in art books, I always try to guess
which paintings the people I look up to, or those ones whom I love
or the ones I realize having not yet dreamt of, would choose to live in.

Sometimes I find them amongst the crowd in a pastoral scene,
other times I turn them into the dwellers of an ideal city,
into the moving brushstrokes of a still life,

or into simple figures in a simple landscape whose sole ambition
is to stay there for a little longer, standing before the
empty fields, as if man were simply

the human embodiment of time instead of time being the
transient form of man that it dreamt of this way,
just the same size as the crop, the perfect height for harvest.]

ENIGMAS DE LA NATURALEZA

Era mi libro favorito.
Era un regalo de mi padre
lleno de gráficos y epígrafes,
fotografías en color
de máscaras, de buceadores
en el antártico, entre nubes
de krill; de esquirlas de cristal,
de ocelos y cefalotórax
vistos con microscopio cien
veces más grandes, e indecibles,
como lo que sentía con:
Y los árboles se volvieron
piedra, escrito junto al fósil
en el que me costaba un poco
dar con el árbol. O al llegar
a lo de la partenogénesis.
O al tratar de entender qué fue
lo que llevó a las procariotas
a fagocitar otras células,
y a convertirse en eucariotas,
inaugurando la noción
misma de vida, separando
lo vivo y lo inerte en el mar
primordial.

¿Fue de mutuo acuerdo,
la carencia de núcleo y de
membrana respectivamente?
¿O el hambre sin más y la lucha
por la supremacía? ¿Fue
un acto rutinario, ciego,
o una singularidad? ¿Cómo
se llega a ser nosotros?

Qué hacemos aún allí,
mi padre y yo, sin responder;
yo con mi libro favorito,
él con mi vida por delante;
los dos mirando al infinito

más próximo, no con nostalgia,
sino con nuestra única certeza:
que no nacemos, no morimos,
sólo nos separamos.

[THE ENIGMAS OF NATURE]

[It was my favorite book.
It was a present from my father
full of diagrams and epigraphs,
color photographs of
masks, of divers
amongst clouds of krill in
the Antarctic, of crystal splinters,
of ocelli and cephalothorax
a hundred times bigger under the
microscope, and things beyond words,
like what I felt with:
*And the trees turned into
rock*, written beside a fossil
in which I struggled slightly to
make out the tree. Or when you got
to that section about parthenogenesis.
Or when I tried to understand what
was it that impelled the prokaryotes
to phagocytize other cells
and become eukaryotes,
initiating the very notion
of life, separating
the living from the inert in the
primordial sea.

Was it a mutual agreement,
to surrender their nucleus and
membrane, respectively?
Or was it simply hunger and the fight
for supremacy?
Was it a blind, random act
or a singularity? How
did we become us?

What are we still doing there,
my father and I, without an answer,
me with my favorite book,
him with my life in front of him,
both looking at a close infinity
not with longing
but with our only certainty:
that we are not born, we do not die,
we simply part] (Translations Juan de Dios León Gómez)

Josep M. Rodríguez, ©xavirue

3 ✱ JOSEP M. RODRÍGUEZ: THE IMAGE

PERSONAL BIOGRAPHY BY RODRÍGUEZ

Nací el mismo día que nació Stendhal, aunque en 1976.[1] Fue en una pequeña localidad de la Cataluña interior llamada Súria. De niño compaginé el colegio con los estudios musicales. De ahí la importancia que tiene para mí la música del poema. De hecho, empecé escribiendo letras de canciones para una banda de rock que formé en mi adolescencia. Estudié Filología en la Universidad de Lleida, ciudad donde ahora resido y donde publiqué mi primer libro de poemas: *Las deudas del viajero*. Fue en 1998. Desde entonces he publicado otros cinco libros de poemas. La antología *Ecosistema* (2015) recoge parte de esa obra. También he publicado un ensayo, dos antologías críticas y algunas traducciones. Actualmente trabajo como docente, aunque la mayor parte de mi actividad laboral se centra en escribir o en realizar conferencias y talleres de lectura. La Universidad Autónoma de Madrid celebró un encuentro sobre mi poesía en 2016. Ese mismo año, la revista *Fragmenta* dedicó un número monográfico a mi obra.

[I was born on the same day that Stendhal was born, although in 1976. It was in the small inland town of Súria in Cataluña. As a child, I combined my work in school with the study of music. As a result, the music of the poem has significance for me. In fact, in my youth, I began writing the lyrics for songs for a rock band that I formed. I studied philology at the University of Lleida, the city where I now live and where I published my first collection of poems, *Las deudas del viajero*. That was in 1998. Since then, I have published an additional five books of poetry. The anthology *Ecosistema* (2015) gathers selected poems from those five collections. I also have published an essay, two critical anthologies, and several translations. Currently I am a teacher, although most of my working life focuses on writing or giving lectures and readings and conducting workshops. The Universidad Autónoma de Madrid held a conference on my poetry in 2016. That same year the journal *Fragmenta* dedicated a special monographic issue to my work.]

A METEOR

Wallace Stevens writes, "A poem is a meteor" ("Adagia I").[2] Although brief, a meteor emits an immediate light that suddenly calls attention to the brilliance of its innermost essence. This is the approach to the poem in the work of Josep M. Rodríguez. His poems are impressive, luminous verbal constructions where he employs a rich vocabulary, painstaking attention to diction, and the startling capacity of his most essential literary device: the image. In 2008, he discloses, "La imagen se me antoja una herramienta imprescindible. Hasta el punto de considerarla el corazón de mis poemas."[3] [The image strikes me as an indispensable tool. To the point where I consider it to be the heart of my poems.] A renowned aspect of the writings of Josep M. Rodríguez is the artistry with which he shapes his remarkable imagery. As a poet, he possesses an extraordinary and sophisticated sense of the image, and he crafts it with impeccable technical expertise. This dazzling origin and matter of his poetry is evident in *Frío* [*Cold*], *La caja negra* [*The Black Box*], *Raíz* [*Root*], *Arquitectura yo* [*Architecture I*], and his most recent *Sangre seca*[4] [*Dried Blood*].

With spectacular speed, his imagery discharges a flash of immediate understanding, and it is in this way that Rodríguez both summons and exploits the definition offered by the modern poet Ezra Pound in his famous essay "A Few Don'ts (sic) by an Imagiste." In 1913, he explains the image as "an intellectual and emotional complex in an instant in time."[5] Throughout the course of his work, Rodríguez demonstrates that the poem is an assemblage of such images where each stimulates fresh and unexpected understanding. This is the process of his creative activity. His works are stellar clusters of luminescent cognitive and emotional moments of epistemic discovery. Within each poem, the collection of which it forms a part, and during the illustrative trajectory of Josep M. Rodríguez, his unique imaging sparks many astounding instances igniting his poetics of epiphany.[6] In his 2003 poetics appearing in *La lógica de Orfeo*, Rodríguez establishes his views on poetry as a method of inquiry and knowledge, views he continues to maintain today:

> La poesía, como ya dejara escrito Altolaguirre, "es mi principal fuente de conocimiento. Me enseña el mundo y en ella aprendo a conocerme a mí mismo." Pero la poesía es conocimiento en la medida en que también es misterio, comunicación o refugio: un lugar donde descansar y donde cobijarse, como un área de servicio. Ahora bien, si lo dicho hasta aquí sirve igual para el lector que para el poeta, la tarea de este último exige algo más: un punto de partida, una especie de palanca de Arquímedes que le permita empezar a moverse, empezar a construir su propia voz.[7]

> [Poetry, as Altolaguirre has written, "is my main source of knowledge. It instructs me about the world and in it I learn to know myself." But poetry is knowledge

since it is also mystery, communication, or refuge, a place to rest and to take shelter, such as a service area. That said, what has been referred to up until now serves the reader and the poet, the task of the latter demands something more: a point of departure, a type of Archimedean lever that allows the poet to begin to move, to begin to construct his own voice.]

For Rodríguez, poetry is the intersection of the imagination with reality, and he is unique in his ability to convey its effectiveness in divulging the capacity of this convergence. A vivid and unforgettable instance of this ingenious merging underlies the remarkable poem "Erosión I" (*Raíz*, 30) [Erosion I], which is part of a two-part poem. Rodríguez writes the following:

El sol es un faquir
que se ha tumbado
                    lento
sobre pinos de aguja.

Miro las montañas.

Hay algo de la piedra
que se pierde en el viento.
Erosión.

[The sun is a fakir
that has laid down
                    slowly
on the needles of the pine trees.

I look at the mountains.

There is something in the stone
that is lost in the wind.
Erosion.][8]

The poem "Morgue" presents this indisputable quality characteristic of his lyric in its opening lines:

Porque todos los cuerpos
encierran una historia,

quisiste ser forense. (*Arquitectura yo*, 55)

[Because all bodies
hide a story,

you wanted to be a forensic surgeon.]
(*Radar*, trans. Monika Izabela Jaworska, 69)

Such is the nature of imaging epistemic discovery in his work. What does this poet come to know? Rodríguez excels at pondering what is essential to human existence, and here, two central themes distinguish and unify his poetry. With superb stylistic exactness, the poem images lifelong lessons presenting how to be in the world. Throughout his poetic trajectory, he also elucidates another equally important mode of being, that of engaging in the indispensable human enterprise of avid self-study for activating the construction of personal identity.[9]

THE POEM

The poetry of Josep M. Rodríguez also manifests a profound and relentless search for the "Poem." He explains this quest early in his trajectory in his 2003 poetics titled "El grito":[10]

> Todo poeta persigue una idea de Poema, absoluta, previa, no menos volátil que el resto de abstracciones. Y cada poema escrito es una tentativa que le acerca y, a la vez, le aleja de su objetivo: una tentativa fallida, un grito inalcanzado. [. . .] En mi caso, conozco algunos rasgos del Poema que busco: equilibrio, precisión, sugerencia, respeto por la tradición.
>
> [Every poet pursues an idea of the Poem, absolute, exact, no less volatile than the rest of the abstractions. And each written poem is an effort getting closer to and, at the same time, getting further away from the goal: a failed attempt, a scream never achieved. (. . .) In my case, I know some of the features of the Poem that I seek: balance, precision, suggestion, respect for tradition.]

Rodríguez is ever mindful of his pursuit of "the Poem," and in a 2009 interview titled "Dejo huecos para que el lector se cuele por ellos" [I leave gaps so that the reader can fill them] with Paché Merayo, he sheds considerable light on this quest. He indicates, "No solo busco una limpieza formal, también ha de ser comunicativa. Tiene esto que ver con la voluntad y la necesidad de aportar algo, de dar cauces de emoción y mente a la vez, pues eso es lo que quiero aportar."[11] [I not only pursue a formal elegance, it also must communicate. This has to do with the will and the need to contribute something, to provide channels for emotion and thought together; that is what I want to contribute.] The polished expressivity of the image coalesces in the noteworthy achievements of Rodrí guez in his creation of "the Poem."

The skill with which he presents the image coincides with the underlying premise of his poetry. He explains in 2001, "Cada autor debe bucear en la tradición, trazar su propia ruta de acceso a la poesía."[12] [Each author should dive into tradition, chart his own access route to poetry.] He further articulates in 2008, "Cada poeta establece su propio árbol genealógico, ya sea en función de sus gustos, de sus prejuicios, de sus intenciones o del azar. [. . .] Creo en una tradición lo más plural y abierta posible" ("Memorias de un lector" [Memories of a Reader], 199). [Each poet establishes his own family tree, it may be a function of his tastes, biases, intentions, or chance. (. . .) I believe in the most plural and the most open possible tradition].

In his case, he learns from Ezra Pound the value of the refined image conveying only verbal precision. Aspects of his search for "the Poem" and the exacting image are evident when considering Pound's 1913 essay and cautionary instructions to poets. Rodríguez's work demonstrates that he is mindful of this advice:

> Use no superfluous word, no adjective, which does not reveal something. [. . .] Use no ornament or good ornament. [. . .] Don't imagine that a thing will 'go' in verse just because it's too dull to go in prose. [. . .] Don't be "viewy"—leave that to the writers of pretty little philosophic essays. Don't be descriptive; remember that the painter can describe a landscape much better than you can, and that he has to know a deal more about it. [. . .] When Shakespeare talks of the "Dawn in russet mantel clad" he presents something which the painter does not present. There [is] in this line of his nothing that one can call description; he presents.[13] ("A Few Don'ts by an Imagist")

Rodríguez does not hesitate to acknowledge that he has been inspired by the poetic form of the Japanese haiku. He recognizes this in his poetics; in interviews; in critical anthologies he has edited and translated, *Alfileres. El haiku en la poesía española última*[14] [Pins. The Haiku in the Most Recent Spanish Poetry]; in his essay *Hana o la flor del cerezo*[15] [*Hana* or the Cherry Blossom]; in his literary criticism "Un mismo cielo: Aproximación a extremo oriente"[16] [The Same Sky: An Approach to the Far East]; and in his translation work *Kobayashi Issa: Poemas de madurez*[17] [Kobayashi Issa: Later Poems]. His 2008 poetics explains why:

> Gracias a los poetas japoneses del *haiku* he aprendido a matizar el concepto de brevedad . . . el *haiku* es un ejercicio de desnudez. Un poema en el que no hay ninguna palabra superflua ni ningún adjetivo que sobre . . . el *haiku* nos enseña que es posible prescindir de algunos elementos del discurso tradicional. ("Memorias de un lector," 201)

> [Thanks to the Japanese poets of the haiku I have learned to nuance the concept of brevity . . . the haiku is an exercise in laying bare. A poem in which there is no superfluous word no adjective in excess . . . the haiku teaches us that it is possible to dispense with some of the features associated with a more traditional discourse.]

A recent essay provides other significant observations concerning the exquisite haiku poem and its influence on other poets:

> Escribir un *haiku* equivale a bailar encima de un ladrillo. A disparar una Polaroid. A encerrar un instante en una jaula de solo tres barrotes: de cinco, siete y cinco sílabas respectivamente. Sin duda su brevedad y aparente sencillez han contribuido al éxito de esta estrofa japonesa en Occidente. De Ezra Pound a Federico García Lorca. De Guilherme de Almeida a Edoardo Sanguineti. Pasado por Luis Cernuda, Allen Ginsberg, Jorge Luis Borges, Salvador Espriu, Octavio Paz o Juan Ramón Jiménez.[18] ("Un mismo cielo: aproximación a Extremo Oriente," 186–187)

> [To write a haiku is equivalent to dancing on top of a brick. To take a Polaroid. To enclose an instant in a cage with only three iron bars: of five, seven, and five syllables, respectively. Without a doubt, its brevity and apparent simplicity have contributed to the success of this Japanese poetic form in the West. From Ezra Pound to Federico García Lorca. From Guilherme de Almeida to Edoardo Sanguineti. Passing through to Luis Cernuda, Allen Ginsberg, Jorge Luis Borges, Salvador Espriu, Octavio Paz, or Juan Ramón Jiménez.]

He further indicates in a 2013 interview, "No me interesa el exterior de la literatura japonesa: su cáscara. Me interesa su economía verbal. Su capacidad de sugerencia. La mirada que se detiene en el detalle. Y ese *kokoro*, ese corazón que también es pensamiento. Pero sin renunciar al yo, porque uno nunca puede escapar de su sombra."[19] [I am not interested in the exterior of Japanese literature, its outer shell. I am interested in its verbal economy. Its capacity for suggestion. The gaze resting on the detail. And that *kokoro*, that heart-mind. But without rejecting the I because one never can escape from its shadow.] In an earlier interview conducted in 2009, when defining the concept of *kokoro*, Rodríguez reveals the aim of what he hopes to contribute to the Spanish lyric. He explains that *kokoro* "significa corazón y mente a la vez, pues eso es lo que quiero aportar. Aquello que decía Unamuno de sentir el pensamiento y pensar el sentimiento" (Rodríguez, "Dejo huecos") [means heart and mind together, that is what I want to contribute. That which Unamuno said was feeling with thought and thinking with emotion]. Rodríguez puts into practice this concept by revealing its pulsating presence in his work when he conveys only what is essential. A singular quality characteristic of his poetry is the echo of this ancient and brief form of poetry when he expresses only what is necessary in the exquisite concision of his imagery.

A POETICS OF THE IMAGE

In 2008, Rodríguez published *Raíz,* where he meticulously examines what he refers to in a 2009 interview as "the roots of all things" (Rodríguez, "Dejo huecos"). In this collection, the exacting image enriches his refined discourse of discovery. He examines the interconnection of attentive observation and perceptive contemplation as methods for achieving fresh knowledge. Two illustrative poems display how. "Indecisión" (*Raíz,* 51–52) [Indecision] and "Mantra" (*Raíz,* 11–12) [Mantra] disclose distinct facets of daily life as instructive opportunities for comprehending how to be in the world. This is a vital theme in his poetry and an essential mode of being for his poetic protagonists. José Andújar Almansa's excellent 2009 article on this collection presents several accurate insights. He elucidates, for example, what he refers to as "una poética de la imagen"[20] [a poetics of the image], and this revelatory naming is applicable to the poetry of *Raíz,* as well as numerous other works in Rodríguez's trajectory. This distinguishing characteristic also is significant because it underlies the epistemic dimensions of Rodríguez's poetry to date. It is fundamental to expressing the concept of *kokoro* in Rodríguez's poetry as well as the existential mode of discovering how to be in the world. The poem "Indecisión" (51) is a superlative example:

> Dura pocos segundos.
> Tras la lluvia,
> el pájaro está atento
> y le arranca a la tierra una lombriz
>
> y vuela hasta que ya no puede verse.
>
> [Lasting a few seconds.
> After the rain,
> the bird is attentive
> snatching an earthworm from the soil
>
> and flying away no longer to be seen]

Scrutiny of a common quotidian event divulges informative findings. Hesitation must be brief. Attentiveness to significant details, at times overlooked during direct observation, is required. Seizing an opportunity to inspect diligently essential events and circumstances can be rewarding. Being fully cognizant of these undertakings has beneficial results to the ever-mindful observer. Learning from the oftentimes overlooked particulars of daily existence, this poem's voice offers instructive insight and worthwhile advice:

La vida se reinventa a cada instante:

Aprende su lección
y sé valiente.

[Life reinvents itself every second.

Learn its lesson
and be brave]

Verbal economy, exact diction, and a melodic combination of heptasyllabic and hendecasyllabic lines and immaculate imagery coalesce to disclose a well-integrated positive attitude on the part of the speaker of this poem. This elucidates the work's central thematic matter, acute attentiveness to the activity of being in the world. The succinct and final hendecasyllabic line, separated briefly by white space on the printed page, calls attention to the cadenced imperatives. These mandates, at the same time, also underscore Rodríguez's clever deconstruction of the poem's title. Finally, engaging directly and decisively with the real is not a hidden mode of being. It is critical to knowledge of the world and the self.

These directives, in the familiar *tú* form, point to the intrinsic importance of steadfastly maintaining unwavering mindfulness of the everyday. This is the requisite attitude for being in the world that Rodríguez also develops in other poems of *Raíz*. For example, "Erosión I–II" (*Raíz*, 30–31) [Erosion I–II] and "La charca" (*Raíz*, 55–56) [The Pond] readily come to mind. The closing instructions in "Indecisión" also underscore another noteworthy feature of his poetry. The first-person poetic voice summons the presence of the reader by articulating directives in the *tú* command form. Attentive to the proximity of the reader, the poem's personalized voice proposes guidelines both for delving into the essential nature of everyday reality and for positioning writing and reading as interrelated access points for gaining new knowledge. In a recent 2014 poetics, Rodríguez explains the invaluable role of the reader: "Respetar al lector, saber qué él también forma parte del acto poético. [. . .] Al escribir, hacer sitio al lector. Dejando que intervenga, que haga suyo el texto."[21] [Respect the reader, know that he also forms a part of the poetic act. (. . .) When writing, make room for the reader. Letting him intervene, so that he might make the text his own.] By "making the poetic text his or her own" the reader of "Indecisión" learns an instrumental approach to daily existence that will, if adopted, become an important mode both of being and of reading.

"Mantra" (*Raíz,* 11–12) further embodies his "poetics of the image" while also communicating a significant existential ethic. This poem offers a lesson concerning daily life, how to live it more fully and, most especially, how to engage in being in the world in such a way that allows the ordinary to reveal and affirm an extraordinary truth. It is in this way that "Mantra" poetically embodies the existential belief underlying much of Rodríguez's lyric. Being in the world is a cognitive enterprise having many beneficial results. The first-person speaker of "Mantra" asserts, "Fijar la realidad / me ayuda a comprender lo que sucede" (11). [Taking note of reality / helps me understand what is happening.] By following sage advice, the personalized *yo* voices the recollected instructions learned earlier in life:

> "No hay que bajar los ojos —me decía mi padre—,
> quien sólo mira el suelo
> se acaba lastimando con las ramas."
>
> ["Mustn't look down—my father would tell me—
> whoever only looks at the ground
> ends up getting hurt by the branches."]

In many ways, this poem masterfully realizes the guiding principle of the 2008 collection as a whole:

> No hay que bajar los ojos:
> Estar atento a lo que me rodea
> como una forma de conocimiento.
>
> [Mustn't look down:
> Be attentive to what surrounds me
> as a form of knowledge.]

At the same time, this brilliant poem succinctly expresses the crucial "mantra" for both the writer and the reader. Above all, however, "Mantra" explicates facets of human identity that are, in this poet's view, vital for acquiring an understanding about being in the world.

The powerful awareness of a concrete and common detail from daily life, clothing drying on a clothesline in the heat of a summer afternoon provides the personalized speaker of "Mantra" with a unique opportunity to engage in compressed concentration and epistemic contemplation. In this magnificent poem, Rodríguez eloquently demonstrates his innovative use of the condensed image, its verbal exactness, and its suggestive capacity. At the outset, the poem presents a specific moment in the everyday:

> La ropa pierde lustre
> si se tiende
> cuando más arde el día.
> Es verano.
>
> [The wash loses its luster
> if hung
> during the hottest part of the day.
> It is summer.]

A subtle pristine image uncovers time as elemental essence as well as personifies daily temporality, as the poetic voice discovers:

> y el tiempo
> se ha hecho imagen:
> Mira cómo gotea.
>
> [and time
> becomes an image:
> Watch how it drips.]

The poet intensifies the presentation of an ordinary laundry line, alluded to earlier, by giving it an extraordinary figurative dimension and new identity, "El tendedero es un reloj de agua." [The clothesline is a water clock.] In one brief, compact, immediate instant, this eloquent imagery instantly illuminates time as passage and the poetics of epiphany:

> Mira cómo gotea:
> Deja un rastro en el suelo
> que poco a poco secará la noche.
>
> [Watch how it drips:
> Leaving a trace on the ground
> that little by little the night will dry.]

By imaging afresh, the age-old instrument for measuring the passing of time, the poet skillfully expands the transitory moment so that it also, and simultaneously, embraces the past, the historical instrument of the ancient *clepsydra,* and the future, when the afternoon soon wanes into evening. This poem is a dazzling manifestation of Pound's concept or technique of imagist superposition because it layers and compresses one idea into another. Not only does Rodríguez reimage historical and daily temporal occurrences, but he exploits the sensorial capacity of the image by creating an overlapping ensemble of auditory, visual, and tactile sensations. These are further expressed by and culminate in the concentrated moment transforming the instantaneous perception into exceptionally new and condensed knowledge: "El tendedero es un reloj de agua." [The clothesline is a water clock.] As a master craftsman of words, Rodríguez centers and releases the potential of the image by engendering brief and provocative insights into the everyday.[22]

The linguistic concision of this image itself embodies another one of Pound's principles. The momentary and melodic "El tendedero es un reloj de agua" in Rodríguez's poem, succinctly captured by a hendecasyllabic "musical phrase," subtly echoes the natural rhythmic droplets dripping from clothing drying on a clothesline. At the same time, this synesthetic activity also sonorously repeats the regulated and momentary movement of water in the age-old device for measuring time. Sound is essential to Rodríguez's imaged presentation of the external world in this poem and to his superlative ability to ground his imagery in rhythmic patterns. For example, the vocalic rhyme of the predominant *e* sound in and across both words and poetic lines creates an acoustic fluidity from beginning to end in "Mantra." The resonant vocalic *a* rhyming pattern, first introduced in the poem's title, is rhythmically distributed in various instances in the poem. It is audibly apparent in significant poetic words such as *ropa, arde, día, verano, refrescara, mira, gotea, pisadas, bajar, acaba, ramas, agua,* and so on. This recurring sound returns the reader both to the poem's symbolic title and to repetition as an aid for sustaining concentration during the process of recollecting the lifelong guiding watchwords meditatively echoing throughout the poem, "No hay que bajar los ojos." [Mustn't look down.] Heptasyllabic lines harmoniously merge into hendecasyllables evident in the poem's opening moment. The alliterative *s* sound highlighted in, for example, "pero qué significan los recuerdos. / Son un eco invisible de las pisadas" [but what do memories mean. / They are the invisible echo of footsteps], calls attention to the role of remembrance in the passage of time and in recalling and then repeating the existential mantra guiding daily human existence as well as the poem.

During a 2009 interview, Rodríguez replies to the following statement concerning his poems: "Dicen de sus versos que muestran una actitud contemplativa del mundo." [They say that your lines of poetry demonstrate a contemplative attitude toward the world.] His response illuminates his exemplary "Mantra," "Si entendemos por contemplativo que parte de la observación directa, de la contemplación de la vida, acepto la afirmación. La rechazo si habla de pasividad, porque yo estoy implicado en esa realidad que veo transformarse. Pienso como Huidobro que el poeta debe decir aquello que no puede decirse sin él" (Rodríguez, "Dejo huecos"). [If we understand contemplative as part of direct observation, meaning the contemplation of life, then I accept the statement. I reject it if it speaks to passivity because I am implicated in that reality that I see transforming itself. I think the same way that Huidobro does, the poet must say what cannot be said without him.] It is, in this sense, that "Mantra" is a "contemplative" work where Rodríguez emphasizes the cause and the effect of being in the world.

In "Mantra," Rodríguez foregrounds the existential ethic and the epistemological process of his poetry. Whether the personalized protagonist looks outwardly, as the first example below illustrates, or introspectively, as the second example discloses, intense attentiveness stimulates the invaluable insight found in epiphanic awakenings. In "Las nubes. *Versión segunda*" (*Raíz*, 50) [The Clouds: *Second Version*] the personalized voice explains

que en la mirada empiezan nuestros límites
y nuestra forma de entender el mundo.

Pienso en Borges:
                    No es abrir los ojos,

es ser abierto.

[our limitations begin with the gaze
and our way of understanding the world.

I think about Borges:
                    It is not about opening your eyes,

it is about being open.]

In "Autorretrato" (*Raíz*, 54) [Self-Portrait], the self-reflexive poetic speaker explains,

Un sol
    deshilachado y pálido
igual que la envoltura de un gusano de seda.

Me pregunto qué hay en su interior
y la pregunta
                también me incluye a mí.

[A sun
        frayed and faint
just like the sheathe of a silkworm.

I ask myself what is inside of it
and the question
                also includes me.]

The reader of "Mantra," like the reader of "Indecisión," must assume an active and participatory role. Compressed concentration in the everyday moment also must take shape during the "contemplative," in Rodríguez's sense of the word, act of reading when the reader is allowed, in fact, invited, by the poet to "intervene" and thereby "make the text his or her own" ("Cuaderno de viaje," 89). It is while realizing that enhanced perception directs the senses to a new understanding of reality that the reader also comes to comprehend that an enriched participatory act of reading will reveal a new opportunity to come to know more about the outside world and the inner self. Not only is Pound's definition of the image applicable to Rodríguez's poetry but also his additional clarifying comments to this definition must be considered when carefully examining the poetics of epiphany in Rodríguez's work. Pound writes, "It is the presentation of such a 'complex' instantaneously which gives that sense of sudden liberation; that sense of freedom from time limits and space limits; that sense of sudden growth, which we experience in the presence of the greatest works of art" ("A Few Don'ts by an Imagist"). When reading poems such as those discussed here, the same keen concentration that the first-person poetic voice calls for when scrutinizing situations and events in the everyday also should be assumed by the self-reflective and "contemplative" reader. In Rodríguez's work, directly experiencing the process of reading the poem becomes a critical method for acquiring indispensable knowledge.

BE ATTENTIVE

In his work, such clear self-awareness of being in the world requires undivided vigilance. Rodríguez expresses with concision and concentrated inspection the elemental constituents in his surroundings. This poet and his various poetic protagonists comprehend the need to see anew and thus afford the opportunity to look "with new eyes" ("Memorias de un lector," 203). In his words, "Todo poema tiene más de cuadro que de fotografía. Más de interpretación que de representación. Las cosas que nos rodean esconden pistas de lo que oculta o guarda una realidad más amplia. La mirada nos muestra sólo un fragmento" ("Memorias de un lector," 203). [Every poem has more to do with a painting than a photograph. More interpretation than representation. The things that surround us cover hidden clues or store a larger reality. The gaze shows us only a fragment.] Rodríguez uses the image in such a way that it too requests being "seen" afresh and with the mind's eye when engaging in inquiry. These brief but spectacular imagistic sightings disclose an important feature of his poetry. His works require full immersion into finding, penetrating, and unveiling the fundamental nature of various essentials populating reality.[23] It is in this way that he positions himself to seize opportunities for imaging revealing epistemic discoveries.

The poem "Hormigas" (*Frío*, 28–29) [Ants], presents a perfect example. Here direct observation is indispensable:

> En un bosque de encinas,
> bajo una sombra antigua como el miedo
> unas pocas hormigas se encaraman
> a la mano que las acoge.
>
> [In a holm-oak forest,
> under a shadow old as fear
> a few ants perch
> on the hand that greets them.]

By closely examining these tiny and industrious insects "transportando / migas de pan, semillas, ramas secas / y todo lo que encuentran a su paso" [carrying / bread crumbs, seeds, dried twigs / everything they find in their path], their undertakings disclose a daily and seasonal work schedule grounded in survival, "Es fácil encontrarlas, / previsoras, / aguardando un invierno que se acerca." [It's easy to find them, / forward-looking, / awaiting the coming of winter.] And yet, when imagining the impending threats facing these diligent insects—"los días de lluvia," [rainy days], "el vuelo de un gorrión" [the flying sparrow], "cerrar la mano" [closing the hand]—it is human knowledge that exposes their inevitable vulnerability: "Es la ley del más fuerte." [It's the law of the strongest.]

In two poems from his 2004 collection, "Mediodía" (*La caja negra*, 38) [Noon] and "Reflejo" (*La caja negra*, 29) [Reflection], Rodríguez further enhances the epistemic dimensions of the image. These exquisite works explicate unique opportunities for discovery occurring during the everyday experiences of being in the world. In both poems, he elegantly condenses the image by revealing the abstract in concrete terms. Incorporating features of the haiku also enhance the indisputable original expressivity evident in both poems. His own 2004 study and anthology on the Japanese poetic form establish its essential qualities by explaining the following:

> Intuición, espontaneidad y frescura, interrelación, mutabilidad de lo que nos rodea, contradicción, y la visión de la realidad como un "continuum" devenir que convierte cualquier instante en todos los instantes. Suma, ésta, de factores que convergen, como los radios de una rueda de bicicleta, en la esencial y elemental de la brevedad del *haiku*. Pero, como insinúa el *Tao te king*, lo importante en una rueda no son los radios —la materia—, sino su vacío: el velado misterio que aflora en cada una de las diecisiete sílabas de esta estrofa. El *haiku* rechaza la evidencia. Por ello, lo que se dice es tan importante como lo que no se dice. [. . .] En la capacidad de sugerencia radica la belleza del *haiku*.[24]
>
> [Intuition, spontaneity and freshness, interrelation, mutability in what surrounds us, contradiction, and a vision of reality as an unfolding "continuum" transforming any instant into all instants. A combination of factors converging, like the spokes of a bicycle wheel, in the essential and fundamental concision of the haiku. But, as *Tao te king* suggests, what matters most in a wheel aren't the spokes—the material—but rather the empty space, the veiled mystery emerging in each one of the seventeen syllables of the stanza. The haiku rejects the evident. Thus what is said is as important as what is not said. (. . .) The beauty of the haiku lies in the capacity of suggestion.]

When asked about his writing haikus in a 2013 interview, the poet responds,

> Yo prácticamente no he escrito *haikus*. O, todo lo contrario, hay algo de haiku en todos mis poemas. Pero supongo que te refieres a un poema basado en las diecisiete sílabas tradicionales, te citaré uno de los poquísimos y de los últimos que he publicado. Pertenece a *La caja negra* (2004) y es un *haiku* en el que precisamente quise alejarme en cierta medida del haiku, empezando por el hecho de que lleva título,
>
> "MEDIODÍA"
>
> Tiendo la ropa.
> Es una cuerda más
> el horizonte. (Rodríguez, "Entrevista," 27)

[I practically don't write haikus. Or, on the contrary, there is something of the haiku in all my poems. But I suppose if you are referring to a poem based on the seventeen traditional syllables, I shall cite one of the very few and the latest that I have published. It pertains to *La caja negra* (2004) and it is a haiku in which I precisely wanted to distance myself to a certain extent from the haiku, beginning with the fact that it has a title,

"NOON"

I hang the wash.
Another clothesline
the horizon.]

In this marvelous haiku, the poet also incorporates the perspective of a personalized voice and in so doing provides another inventive aspect to this traditional poetic form. This speaker discloses an immediate and perceptive self-awareness of being in the world. Within even the most elemental details of daily life reside astounding discoveries. These he images with refined impressions when the visual and the tactile combine in a singular experience. Here too, Rodríguez intensifies a concrete moment in ordinary human existence by giving it the extraordinary capacity to reconfigure its surroundings. In a single stunning instant, the image transforms perception into knowledge.

His imaginative imagery in "Reflejo" [Reflection] presents an unsurpassed attention to detail that is mirrored in the poem's brevity. Rodríguez's linguistic acumen is extraordinary, and the delicate suggestion of immediate impressions both contribute to and expose his mastery of the haiku. The poem is a sensorial delight. Nine words uniquely convey the synesthetic event of witnessing the splendor of the sunrise:

El azafrán,
tirado por el suelo
de la mañana.

[Saffron
strewn across the terrain
morning.]

Being in the world requires uninterrupted mindful observation where the epiphanic image instantaneously charges a luminescent moment. The dispersal of a golden-hue joins earth and sky during a sunrise that stimulates, as well as radiantly reflects, the participatory role of the senses. For Rodríguez, being in the world requires an ardent appreciation for the vitality of the moment.

A prominent poem in Rodríguez's early trajectory is "Ramas" (*Frío*, 40–41) [Branches]. This work manifests the intersection of the two principal themes that he would continue to refine and develop throughout the course of his poetry and poetics. The expert crafting of a series of images intriguingly reveals this thematic coalescence. What seems, at first, to be an account of the visual experience of an X-ray photograph of the lung in a medical examination office, soon becomes an exceptionally original analysis of the innermost essence of this organ when the illumined film reveals the details of body tissues and bones. This first glimpse evolves into a transformative moment. When seeing "with new eyes," the poetic protagonist encounters a striking discovery:

A contraluz,
tu pulmón al desnudo.

Y en su interior
(aunque no puedas verlas)
ramas como de almendro o de avellano

y una especie de florecillas blancas
brotando en sus extremos:

Una radiografía.

[Against a backlight,
your lung laid bare.

And in the inside
(even if you cannot see them)
branches like an almond or a hazelnut tree

and a type of small white flowers
sprouting from their ends:

An X-ray.] (*Radar*, trans. Ben Clark, 27)

Self-examination yields perceptive results. The poem's protagonist, as an alert human being, becomes more cognizant of the life-giving capacity of the now personalized and innermost branching respiratory passages. The ever-attentive poet adeptly transfers the visualization of this human experience into inventive imagery. These activities brilliantly converge in Rodríguez's poetic triumph:

Ramas en tus pulmones
y en la mesa

y en el papel de un libro.

Todo es parte de todo,
un mismo árbol.

[Branches in your lungs
and on the table

and on the page from a book.

Everything is part of everything,
the same tree.]

In 2016, Andújar identifies a fundamental conceptual linchpin in the works of Josep M. Rodríguez, "No es que la poesía vea cosas distintas, pretende verlas de un modo diferente."[25] [It's not that poetry sees different things, but that it endeavors to see them differently.] This is the vision that "Ramas" presents. This singular work also unveils a superlative example of Rodríguez having found "the Poem" that he seeks. Andújar's exceptional 2007 "Retrato robot de la poesía reciente"[26] [Composite Portrait of Recent Poetry], offers insight into Rodríguez's imagistic expertise. He comments that "Ramas" demonstrates "the new semantic possibilities" that he finds in Spain's current poetry. In the case of this poem, however, the critic cements the cognitive capacity of Rodríguez's imagery by underscoring that this work expresses "una experiencia rigurosamente mental" (37) [a rigorously mental experience]. This synthetic elucidation adroitly characterizes "Ramas." Finally, it is noteworthy that "Ramas" has been published in various anthologies displaying the development of Spain's twenty-first-century lyric. It is easily understandable as to why.

BEING IN THE WORLD

In this poetry, how to be in the world is under continuous construction. This enterprise involves realizing and articulating various human encounters with aspects of the actuality of being. In living life, this poet voices possibilities for coming to know the nature of reality while it unfolds before his eyes. Writing sustains this observant mode of being because it serves as an epistemic mode of inquiry. Writing, thus, emerges as another way in which Rodríguez studies and comes to comprehend aspects of reality. His poems often formulate existential modes offering illuminative insight into various methods of discovery. He comes to know the self as integral to what constitutes the real: "Yo estoy implicado en esa realidad que veo transformarse" (Rodríguez, "Dejo huecos"). [I am implicated in that reality that I see in continuous transformation.] Finely tuned attentiveness is essential as is a mindful responsiveness to change. Central to this poet's approach, however, is a participatory immersion into what Andújar considers "la consciencia de lo real"[27] [the awareness of the real]. Rodríguez's works divulge, as he images, "que en la mirada empiezan nuestros límites / y nuestra forma de entender el mundo" ("Las nubes. *Versión segunda*," *Raíz*, 50) [that our limitations begin with the gaze / and our way of understanding the world]. Acute inspection is requisite. In the aptly titled poem "Autorretrato" [Self-Portrait], the poet further explicates, "Me transforma / la realidad" (*Raíz* 54). [Reality / transforms me.] In his commentary on "Autorretrato," Andújar makes clear that Rodríguez implicates the poetic self in his scrutiny of his own "awareness of the real." The critic rightly maintains that "cualquier indagación sobre la realidad incluye al propio yo-poético"[28] [any inquiry into reality includes the poetic I].

In Rodríguez's work, these existential approaches also serve to underscore what fellow poet and literary critic Alberto Santamaría accurately characterizes in this way:

> El objetivo de buena parte de la poesía joven supone no el romántico *hacer visible lo invisible*, sino, de otro modo, *hacer más visible lo visible* . . . desde una clara pluralidad estética. [. . .] Se trata de poetas conscientes de que no es posible enfrentarse a la realidad desde una sola perspectiva, por eso no aparece como viable reducir a un solo mecanismo poético la expresión de esa realidad.[29]
>
> [The objective of a good part of the poetry of the young poets involves not the romantic notion of *making visible the invisible* but, put differently, *making more visible the visible* . . . with a clear aesthetic of plurality. (. . .) It concerns poets who are aware that it is not possible to confront reality from only one perspective; therefore it is not viable to reduce to a single poetic device the expression of that reality.]

Raíz provides several examples explicating Santamaría's incisive views. Rodríguez, however, furnishes additional insight by establishing various modes of being as illustrative approaches to obtaining new knowledge. The sterling poem "Erosión I, II" (*Raíz*, 30–31) establishes pertinent evidence. At first, the poem's protagonist carefully considers a few elements comprising aspects of an external environment:

Camino por el bosque.

Hace frío
y el arroyo está helado.

En su interior,
se ha quedado atrapada una pequeña hoja.

La mirada está atenta:
Esa imagen resume
qué pasa en la memoria. (“Erosión I,” 30)

[I walk through the forest.

It is cold
and the stream is frozen.

Inside it,
an oak leaf, caught.

My gaze is aware:
this image shows
what happens with memory.] (*Radar*, trans. Clark, 55)

This encounter engenders a pensive self-examination that, in turn, initiates a reconsideration of the activity of being in the world. The resulting discovery is unequivocal. Personal being is finite:

Camino por el bosque.

Estoy alerta.
La mirada me explica cuanto soy.

Por eso me he negado a la elegía.

¿Acaso la memoria
es algo más que el eco de lo que ya hemos sido?

Sólo tengo interés por el instante.
El resto es erosión
o me erosiona. (“Erosión II,” 31)

[I walk through the forest.

I am alert,
My gaze explains to me what I am.

That is why I have disallowed elegies.

Is memory anything else
other than an echo of what we were?

I am only interested in this instant.
The rest is erosion
or my own erosion.] (*Radar*, trans. Clark, 57)

The poem "La charca" (*Raíz*, 55–56) [The Pond] portrays the results of epistemic findings once having penetrated the visible to see beyond it. The poem's speaker thereby gains further understanding concerning how to be in the world. Perceptive and acute awareness of elements in nature are essential. Being mindful of unique opportunities to engage in constructing ways to enhance actively participating in the world also is fundamental. In this poem, Rodríguez divulges the nature of his poetics of epiphany—brief, lucent, and exact imagery disclosing striking insights for coming to know and to appreciate ways in which to discover and enhance personal being. In "La charca," the first-person protagonist divulges requirements for absorbing the surroundings, be they natural or personal. Fascination and engagement, however, are insufficient. Direct observation can lead to a breakthrough, however, that also seems to be insufficient. In this exceptional work, Rodríguez places the poem and the personalized self as poet into the activity of writing. These too, contribute to the setting under scrutiny. Here, however, the poem is not a site for exploration, rather it is the site for penetrating surface level understanding in order to achieve a richer and a deeper comprehension of existence. The present condenses into the more immediate now in time, especially when the poetic voice provides instructive imperatives concerning how to approach the activity of being in this masterful poem:

Profundiza.
Fíjate en los patos:
parece que nadar les sea fácil

y es algo muy distinto bajo el agua.

Ondulación:
Vivir la vida en círculos crecientes
y nazcan y se extiendan desde mí.

La emoción necesita un proceso.
No olvides los anillos de los árboles.

[Fathom.
Pay attention to the ducks:
it seems that swimming is easy for them,

and it is very different under the water.

Undulation:
Live life in increasing circles
originating and expanding from me.

Emotion needs a process.
Don't forget the rings of the trees.]

Andújar draws on Santamaría's article in his own 2008 essay highlighting salient features found today, "Lo real, hablando de los nuevos poetas, es una mirada otra sobre la realidad. Sus menudos y múltiples acontecimientos, sus objetos, su transcurso son como luces de posición que nos hacen en conciencia, significando" ("Paisaje de la poesía última," 35). [The real, in the case of the new poets, is another way to look at reality. Its insignificant and its multiple events, its objects, its course, they are meaningful spotlights making us more aware.] In a later article appearing in 2014, this same critic explains, "La poesía de hoy [. . .] más que otra realidad, persigue una mirada 'otra' sobre la realidad, abandonando la tumba de los lugares comunes y los automatismos cotidianos."[30] [Today's poetry (. . .) rather than pursuing another reality, seeks instead "another" way of looking at reality, abandoning the gravesite of the commonplace and the automatic considerations of the everyday.] The poem "La charca" is but one revelatory manifestation of this outlook. Other examples in Rodríguez's work, to mention a few, include "Las esquinas" (*Frío*, 39) [The Corners] and "El corazón del bosque." (*Raíz*, 10) [The Heart of the Forest]. For his various poetic protagonists, it is not the case that knowledge is provisional. Rather at times, it is difficult to arrive at a clear and singular understanding of the complexity of the real. In the poetry of Josep M. Rodríguez, reality is not impenetrable. It is, instead, a vast and rich territory that invites, rather than deters, different operative existential modes for exploring it. This requires willingness, initiative, and ardent alertness, even during daily and routine matters. No activity escapes notice. Andújar provides an enlightening and unparalleled commentary that is applicable to "La charca" when he observes the following:

> Hacer más visible lo visible consiste entre otras cosas en ensanchar el concepto mismo de realidad: la realidad de lo que entendemos y la realidad de lo que no entendemos. [. . .] Lo no perceptible forma parte también de lo perceptible, de una realidad que la poesía quiere iluminar, indagar, acechar, ensanchar. [. . .] Por eso no debe resultarnos extraña una "Poética" como la de Josep María Rodríguez en *La caja negra* (2004), apostando por la iluminación momentánea antes que por el conocimiento reflexivo: "Buscar la aguja del instante eterno. // La memoria, / después, / impone un orden." La perplejidad, el asombro, la extrañeza, lo imprevisto, lo insólito, lo desconocido, conforman ese apartado menos visible de lo visible, esa realidad otra de lo real. ("Paisaje de la poesía última," 34–35)

> [To make more visible the visible consists of, among other things, expanding the very concept of reality: the reality that we understand and the reality that we do not understand. (. . .) What is not perceived also forms a part of the perceived, of a reality that poetry wants to illuminate, question, stalk, expand. (. . .) Therefore it should not seem strange that a "Poetics" like the one by Josep María Rodríguez in *La caja negra* (2004) wagers in favor of momentary illumination before reflective knowledge: "Look for the needle in the eternal instant. // The memory, / afterward, / imposes order." Perplexity, wonder, strangeness, the unexpected, the unusual, the unknown conform to that part that is less visible of the visible, that other reality of the real.]

Throughout the course of his poetry, Rodríguez himself offers new and illuminative insight into the human activity of participating in the real. He does so by directly observing features of it that otherwise could have gone unnoticed or, perhaps, could have been regarded by others as too insignificant to invite further study. As a poet, his own heightened awareness of reality demonstrates an attitude paramount to being in and among the multiple features, situations, objects, and events that he scrutinizes in and around him. Such acute skills of observation reflect the most significant aspects of being in the world in his poetry: "Ser abierto" ("Las nubes. *Versión segunda*" [The Clouds: *Second Version*], *Raíz,* 50). [Be open.] This "mantra" energizes Rodríguez's poetry principally when he assumes poetic voices that become metaphoric extensions of one who fully engages in being, as well as someone who desires to render his ontological findings in an unparalleled discourse of discovery.[31]

REFLECTIVE SELF-AWARENESS

For Rodríguez, the essential mode of being in the world is a lifelong process intimately connected to the construction of personal identity. In this effort, keen awareness is also fundamental. Engaging in the existential mode of self-reflective introspection and contemplation also is imperative. In *Arquitectura yo* [*Architecture I*], Josep M. Rodríguez proposes several different opportunities for revealing how the poem, in his expert hands, is a unique exploratory instrument for his assiduous analysis of the self. Imaging this ontological endeavor is the aim of this remarkable 2012 collection. In this singular work, Rodríguez embarks on examining "reflective self-consciousness" as essential to creating human identity.[32]

During his poetic trajectory, Rodríguez presents an examination of this human characteristic in various "seed" poems. It is in *Arquitectura yo*, however, where his ontological self-investigation germinates and flourishes. Earlier in his trajectory, he images in "Distancia" (*Frío*, 31) [Distance], for example, an intriguing self-definition. As if filming a subjective close-up, the poet inspects and discovers the self by indicating the following:

> La distancia mayor entre dos puntos
> es también la más corta:
> la coincidencia exacta,
> yo.
>
> [The greatest distance between two points
> is also the shortest:
> the exact convergence,
> me.]

Self-awareness is both the point of departure and the point of return in this poem, "Miro mis pies, / desnudos como el tiempo que persiguen." [I look at my bare feet / chasing time.]. By living in each precarious present moment, the poetic speaker learns the essence of human finitude. The inevitability of personal nonbeing repeatedly displaces being thereby closing the "distance" between these two competing existential modes.

In "Intersección" (*Frío*, 38) [Intersection], condensed linguistic expression mirrors the compressed temporal moment of human existence. The poem presents an attempt to objectify personal identity when scrutinizing an imaged self-reflection in a mirror. This effort proves to be fruitless, "como el ciego, delante de un espejo" [like a blind man, in front of a mirror], revealing instead, "Así, / saberme yo también desconocido." [Thus, / I know I also am unknown.] In both examples, the construction of personal identity features the self as representative of the human condition. Poems from his 2004 collection further examine the thematic matter of being in time, as a few exemplary manifestations disclose. He writes in "Inicio" [The Beginning], "La nieve del tejado se deshace / poco a poco, / igual que la belleza de la mujer que amo" (*La caja negra*, 9). [The snow on the roof slowly / melts / just like the beauty of the woman I love]. This inaugural poem sets the tone for those that follow.[33] For example, "Ecuación" [Equation] reveals "la carne sólo es cauce para el tiempo" (*La caja negra*, 39) [the flesh is only a channel for time], while in "No impreciso, incompleto" [Not Imprecise, Incomplete], the personalized voice discovers, "Siempre hay pérdida: / incluso ahora / una parte de mí no me pertenece" (*La caja negra*, 47). [There is always loss, / including now / a part of me doesn't belong to me.] This collection also advances Rodríguez's scrutiny of the finitude of being in the temporal moment. Here, he gives it an added dimension: self-examination as a poet. This perspective emerges in the fittingly titled "Inicio" [The Beginning], when the poetic *yo* considers the cyclical nature of the transient moment while, simultaneously, engaging in the corresponding activity of writing:

Todo es cuestión de ciclos.
Lo que ahora se va,
                    después ha de volver
para irse de nuevo.

Todo es cuestión de ciclos:
yo sólo escribo círculos sobre el papel de nieve. (*La caja negra*, 9)

[Everything comes down to cycles.
What now leaves,
                    is sure to return
to then leave again.

Everything comes down to cycles:
I only draw circles on the paper of the snow.] (*Radar*, trans. Clark, 17)

In *Raíz*, Rodríguez continues to develop the existential mode of self-awareness of human finitude, as these selections further elucidate. In "Despertar" (*Raíz*, 14) [Awakening], he writes, "También ahora sé que estoy de paso." [Now I also know that I am passing through.] In the poem "Contradicción" (*Raíz*, 16) [Contradiction], he discloses,

La infancia de mi padre.
En eso pienso

mientras voy de visita al hospital.
. . .
¿Cómo puedo decirle
que lo mejor no está en lo que ya fuimos?

[My father's childhood.
I am thinking about that
during my visit to the hospital.
. . .
How to tell him
that the best is not in what we were?]

Self-scrutiny is multifaceted and complex, compelling a vigilant extraction of the most essential features of human identity. The figurative title of the opening poem "Amanecer" (*Raíz*, 9) [Daybreak] divulges, "Ahora todo ha cambiado. / He aprendido a importarme a mí." [Now everything has changed. / I have learned to care about me.] "Erosión II" offers insight as to why, "Estoy alerta. / La mirada me explico cuanto soy" (*Raíz*, 31). [I am alert. / My gaze explains to me what I am.] These revealing introspective self-analyses culminate in *Arquitectura yo*. The entire collection of poems constitutes a profound and pensive immersion into self-identity.

In 2013, fellow poet Antonio Lucas elucidates in his essay on poetry, in general, and on his own work, "Lo visible en el poema es parte de lo indecible. Esa realidad aumentada en la que uno se adentra como en peregrinación por un extraño destino. Y en ese viaje la realidad se genera a sí misma. De ahí la construcción de lo visible tenga algo de reemplazo; de espeleología íntima por las profundidades del ser que escribe, de quien lee."[34] [In the poem, the visible is part of the unutterable. That enhanced reality into which one ventures on a pilgrimage with a peculiar destination. And on that journey, reality creates itself. From there, the structure of what is visible offers a replacement; an intimate speleology into the depths of the human being that writes, and who reads.] In part, Lucas's observations can be applied to Rodríguez's collection. What is expressly beneficial about Lucas's commentary, as viewed in retrospect given that Rodríguez already had published his collection in 2012, is that he renders the exploration of the depths of the self as a metaphoric expedition into the evolving complexities of the inner self and human identity. This is not spelunking or caving, rather this speleological trip has a defined mission: charting, mapping, exploring, and finding the varying constituents forming *Arquitectura yo*. It is this activity that describes the penetrating process of Rodríguez's expedition into "reflective self-consciousness" in this stunning work. Poems, as acts of introspection, present and explicate "Yo, o mi idea de yo" (36) [Me, or My Idea of Me], the thematic matter of his study.

Attentive self-investigation is the cornerstone of *Arquitectura yo*. It is evident in Rodríguez's probing of the existential aspects and precarious nature of personal being in time, a nascent subject in a poem such as his earlier "Ecuación" (*La caja negra*, 39–40) [Equation]. In this work, the poetic speaker, at first, contemplates an external bleak landscape displaying animate and inanimate objects where even "la piedra testimonia lo fugaz" [the stone bears witness to the fleeting]. When internalizing the figurative funereal environment, however, the subjective existential preoccupation of the personalized poetic voice emerges:

> Extraña paradoja,
>
> la piedra testimonia lo fugaz,
> la carne sólo es cauce para el tiempo.
>
> (Cada hueso que tengo es una lápida
> por los muertos que escondo en mi interior.)
>
> ¿Por qué contar el tiempo que nos queda?
>
> [Strange paradox,
>
> the stone bears witness to the fleeting,
> the flesh only is a channel for time.
>
> (My every bone is a headstone
> for the dead ones that I hide inside of me.)
>
> Why count the time we have left?]

This poem concludes with imagistic precision explicating the transient nature of human existence, "Quién mira un tren pasar comprende el resto." [Whoever watches a train pass understands the rest.] The first-person protagonist of *Arquitectura yo*, however, is now more fully aware of the paradox of finite-being, and this existential mode no longer remains hidden "within." Rather, finite being is exposed as the poem "Madera" (37) [Wood] expresses with economic exactness, "Es por el ataúd que comprendo quién soy. // A cada instante existo un poco menos." [It is because of the coffin that I understand who I am. // Every passing minute, I exist a little less.][35] The outstanding "Yo, o mi idea de yo" (36)

[Me, or My Idea of Me], one of the definitive poems of this book, exquisitely discloses the essential ontological perspective penetrating personal being:

Y sin embargo a ratos me construyo.
Y sin embargo a ratos me derribo.
O incluso las dos cosas:

como un niño que nace
en un barco que se hunde.

[And yet at times I build myself up.
And yet at times I knock myself down.
Or even both:

like a child born
on a sinking boat.] (*Radar*, trans. Jaworska, 53)

CONSTRUCTING PERSONAL IDENTITY

The poem "Crudo" (9) [Crude], initiating the collection, is one of the cornerstones of *Arquitectura yo*. This is a superb work imaged with meticulous concentration on distilling from self-exploration the essence of being human. Acute "reflective-self-consciousness" provides the existential framework for Rodriguez's metaphoric construction of personal identity. Despite the images that the title might evoke, "Crudo" is a refined explication of human temporality. Here, autogenesis defines the transformative process of being becoming nonbeing intersecting in the moment.[36] This is the brutally stark ontological fact of personal existence in all its facets:

Nos construyen las pérdidas:
instante
        tras instante
                tras instante.

[We are constructed by our losses:
moment
        after moment
                after moment.] (*Radar*, trans. Clark, 49)

Unlike "la inocencia del fósil" [the fossil's innocence], forever unaware that it is fixed in time, the first-person poetic voice of "Crudo" is keenly attentive to the experience of continual transition as constituting being human. Each intense moment, each fragile "instant," reenacts and metaphorically embodies the singular temporal site for the persistent instability of being in time.[37]

Immersion into the self provides unique opportunities for scrutinizing the fluctuating circumstance of personal being when, in this collection, Rodríguez's attempts to come to know and to define self-identity. "Enseñanza" (22) [Instruction] articulates and clarifies this perspective. The splendid opening image, "Cruzo una habitación y soy otra persona" [I cross the room, and I am another person], establishes an unusual as well as provocative focus of attention for the *yo* protagonist in this poem—the self in the state of ongoing transformation. The imaginative imagery underscoring the immediacy of this self-revelation portrays the self as becoming that which it is not yet. In this estimable collection, "reflective self-consciousness" is an existential activity, a mode of being, and a means for achieving self-instruction on the nature of human identity.[38]

The self-construction of personal identity is an evolving process for a human being constantly engaging in various attempts at comprehending "Yo, o mi idea de yo" (36). This fundamental poem centers the thematic matter of *Arquitectura yo*:

> Tengo tendencia a generalizar:
> por eso escribo "bosque"
> aunque sé que no hay dos árboles iguales,
>
> por eso escribo "yo".
>
> [I have a tendency to generalize:
> that is why I write "forest"
> in spite of knowing there are no two trees alike,
>
> that is why I write "me."] (*Radar*, trans. Jaworska, 53)

The "idea" of personal being adapts and changes, and this poem reflects this ongoing process of self-construction as self-discovery. Andújar indicates, "El yo es una generalización que uniforma o compacta muchas otras identidades, igual que la lejanía hace indivisible la masa verdosa del bosque" (30). [The I is a generalization that levels out or compacts many other identities, just like from a distance the forest's dense greenery seems indivisible.] Subjective awareness of being, as well as of being in the world, is dynamic and so is the activity of engaging in reconstructing personal identity. This too is the thematic matter of this impressive 2012 book where Josep M. Rodríguez images "mi forma de buscarme en cada verso" ("Creer" [Believe], 12) [my way of searching for myself in each line].

In *Arquitectura yo,* being is not static like a snapshot. Any attempt at capturing the moment in a photographic image is merely an illusion because that instant, as "Enseñanza" (22) [Instruction] manifests, exposes personal being as always already having become something else:

Somos tan solo una fotografía:
sonrientes
y jóvenes.

No saben que escondemos
tras el marco
los márgenes gastados y las esquinas rotas.

[We are just a photograph:
smiling
and young.

They don't know that we conceal
behind the frame
the worn-out edges and the torn corners.]

The pertinent poem titled "Prospección" (43–44) [Prospecting] images introspection in a surprising way when the personalized voice surveys not outer reality but rather the innermost recesses of the self. Self-scrutiny is another thematic building block of *Arquitectura yo*:

¿Seré capaz de acostumbrarme a todo?

Los fracasos se enlazan,
crean hábitos,

y a menudo me escondo en mi interior
como si fuese una muñeca rusa,

cada vez más adentro.

[Will I be able to get used to everything?

The failures interconnect,
creating habits,

and frequently I hide within myself
as if I were a nesting doll,

more and more inside.]

What is learned from this self-prospecting? In *Arquitectura yo*, "Tejados" (21) [Rooftops] represents one response. The experience of the outer world leads to discovery of the inner self when elusive sensory impressions intermingle and elucidate a new understanding of (non)being:

En los tejados,
                    nieve,
y en los dedos la misma sensación,
el lento
deshacerse
de todo lo que toco.

[On the rooftops
                    snow,
and on my fingertips the same sensation,
the slow
melting away
of all that I touch.]

The poem "Interior" (35) [Interior] reveals yet another fundamental existential fact, "Otra vez me equivoco: / la vida no está fuera, sino dentro." [Once more I am mistaken: / life is not outside, but inside.]

Arquitectura yo also unveils other aspects of self-reflexive awareness of being that is integral to Rodríguez's construction of the nature of human identity. The ingenious poem "Morgue" (55–56) presents the metaphoric site for exhibiting the fragility of personal being. The unusual and yet exact title is a superb summation of human temporality. Placed as the final poem of *Arquitectura yo*, the work expertly signals the figurative merging of the modes of being and the nature of human self-identity that thematically unite the book. In one sense, Rodríguez localizes the poem in a morgue, the site where dead human bodies are temporarily kept pending identification. Within this imaged setting, the inspection of the deceased person occurs during the postmortem examination. The predominant first-person voice heard in the collection, often has engaged in analyzing the nature of self-reflexive human identity. In this poem, however, the observation is directed to the activities of *tú*, another dramatis personae, performing an equally attentive inspection of another human being during an autopsy.

Comprehending the medical analysis of a corpse is not of interest to the alert poetic voice. Rather, the object of focus is what the forensic examiner has learned and continues to learn from the process of inspecting the subject in question in this figurative morgue. The requisite examination by sight, necessary during the imaginative imaging of the autopsy taking place in "Morgue," also is required of the poem's perceptive onlooker. During the precisely imaged convergence of intense scrutiny and incisive inquiry, the spectator summons the medical specialist's own self-awareness and lessons learned after performing an autopsy:

> ¿Alguna vez pensaste que tu cuerpo
> es solo la envoltura
> del gusano de seda de la muerte?
>
> Su crisálida deja tras de sí
> tumbado en la camilla,
>
> un cadáver
> abierto.
>
> [Have you ever thought that your body
> could be nothing but the cocoon
> of the silkworm of death?
>
> Its chrysalis is left behind,
> laid out on the stretcher,
>
> an open
> corpse.] (*Radar*, trans. Jaworska, 69)

The human body is but a casing, a physical remnant of what is "left behind" for identification and forensic study. Imaging the essence of human identity is the task at hand for the poet of *Arquitectura yo*. Here, in this figurative "Morgue," Rodríguez strikingly discloses the undeniable human condition of inevitable mortality.

Literary critic José Andújar Almansa's explication of this poem offers perspectives that must be taken into consideration:

> Al final de toda disección aguarda siempre un cadáver abierto. Como en los versos de 'Morgue' que concluyen este libro. [. . .] Convertir la mesa de escritura en intempestiva mesa de forense es un gesto que tiene antecedentes en otros exploradores del abismo como Lautréamont o Gottfried Benn. Indagar con insistencia,

> sin escrúpulos, en lo subjetivo implica, como poco, dar por muerto a alguno de los yo que subyacen en el yo. Ineludible ejercicio este de echar tierra encima para recomenzar (una vez y otra) desde alguna parte. ("*Arquitectura yo*," 33)
>
> [The open corpse awaits the finished dissection. Like the lines from "Morgue" that conclude this book. (. . .) Converting the writing desk into an untimely mortuary examining table is a gesture that has antecedents in other explorers of the abyss like Lautréamont or Gottfried Benn. Unrelenting and unscrupulous investigation into the subjective implies, at the very least, to give up for dead any of the I's underlying the I. This is an inescapable exercise in covering up, in order to start over (time and again) from somewhere.]

This stunning poem presents "reflective self-consciousness" as an essential undertaking in the construction of human self-identity. This is the profound subject matter imaged throughout *Arquitectura yo*. This important state of being also fuels the existential imperative underlying the collection. Only intense self-inspection will result in the indispensable knowledge of forming, of shaping, of building personal human identity. Rodríguez excels at presenting the human self and placing it on display so that it can be inspected in detail and verbally realized in astonishing new ways. This is apparent in "Morgue" and the collection it remarkably represents. By examining being human with distilled imagery, this poet extracts the essential constituents of "reflective self-consciousness."

This collection is a penetrating exploration of the depths, the inner-most regions, the imaged dissections of the nature of being human. Throughout the work, Rodríguez and his assumed poetic protagonists, openly grapple with intense awareness of the inevitable finitude of human being. This is a shared condition and the sensational poem "B+" (40) establishes Rodríguez's findings. The metonymic title references the third most commonly occurring blood type. Donors of B+ blood are valued members of their community when they help sustain the blood supply. The poem's imagery presents the self-reflective activity of receiving a transfusion of additional lifeblood.[39] Even if only momentary, this acute self-awareness reveals a possible way in which to strengthen the existential enterprise in order to postpone, even if only briefly, the relentless activity of personal being unavoidably progressing toward nonbeing. But what does the reader learn? One obvious response is that this poetry calls for a keenly attentive self-reflective reader who is to engage in the act of reading as an introspective opportunity to contemplate the precarious nature of his or her own ephemeral being in time. This is one possible instructive existential example. What is the reader's "transfusion"? The poem "B+" divulges a response when the self-reflective poetic *yo* addresses the reader directly as the possible *tú* in the poem. This latter personage is imagined as one of many other "blood brothers" when/while being the recipient(s) of the imaged lifeblood personified as the poem. When pondering, however, the possibility of these "hermanos de sangre," the self-reflective poetic *yo* wonders, "¿Y qué sentiré yo / al saber que mi sangre circula por sus venas?" [And what will I feel / knowing that my blood is running through their veins?] Poetry, here inventively imaged as a common "blood type," might enable the continuance of being, both the poet's and the reader's, even if only temporarily. Indeed, both mortals might attain a form of immortality. However, the poet of *Arquitectura yo* does not seek nor present facile answers. Rather, the response that the poem offers is not only somewhat ambiguous but also provocative:

> Abro y cierro la mano
> mientras pienso si eso no es también la poesía:
>
> tomar sin merecer,
>
> ser en el cuerpo de otro.
>
> [I open and close my hand
> while thinking if this is not poetry as well:
>
> taking without deserving,
> being in someone else's body.] (*Radar*, trans. Jaworska, 51)

If writing and reading are considered as reciprocal transfusions, then both the donor and the recipient appear to benefit. Nonetheless, as "B+" also suggests, in reading a poem perhaps the reader also usurps, for a moment, the poet's own self-reflective identity as his or her own—"tomar sin merecer"—thereby further contributing to another possible erosion of personal being:

> mientras yo me pregunto
> a qué parte de mí he renunciado
>
> o si habrá algún recuerdo que ya no fluirá más . . .

[while I wonder
what part of me I have given up

or whether some memory will not be flowing anymore . . .]

As a vital metaphoric construct, poetry is the lifeblood of this poet and his reader recipient. Both gain new knowledge concerning human existence and self-identity. Essentially, poet and poem endure because of the many "hermanos de sangre."

Arquitectura yo is poetry as ontology, epistemology, and epiphany. It incarnates and articulates the construction of personal being in poetry and, as such, it establishes profound awareness of the nature of being human. In this exceptional 2012 collection, Josep M. Rodríguez explores reflective self-consciousness as essential to comprehending the nature of the self. His is a probing inspection where the expertly crafted image illuminates the immersion into self-identity. This thematic matter manifests a superlative example of the poetics of epiphany in Spanish poetry today. In this collection, Rodríguez demonstrates what Wallace Stevens calls, "The poem of the mind in the act of finding / What will suffice."[40] With original imagery, the absence of a confessional tone, and avid introspection, *Arquitectura yo* offers enlightening self-portraits realizing various aspects of subjective identity. This masterful work, as Andújar asserts, "es uno de esos poquísimos libros que llegará a convertirse en seña de identidad de toda una generación poética" ("*Arquitectura yo*," 29) [is one of those very few books that will become the identifying hallmark of an entire poetic generation].

AN ECOSYSTEM

In 2015, Rodríguez published *Ecosistema. Antología poética* [*Ecosystem: Poetry Anthology*], a unique gathering of selections from his poetry since 2002.[41] A prevalent feature in his poetry is that he conceives his collections within a specific framework. The initial poem highlights many of the central themes and images that are to be developed throughout the course of the book, and the final poem offers both conclusions regarding this process and imaged promises of what is yet to come in his future work. In this way, Josep M. Rodríguez skillfully suggests, even requests, a reflective reading and rereading of the collection at hand, a rereading that will prove to be instructive and illuminative. In *Ecosistema,* he now presents his own thoughtfully selected poems in this same structural framework.

This is not a gathering of what Rodríguez might consider to be his favorite poems. Instead, in this work, he exhibits a perceptive and self-reflexive thematic and stylistic reconsideration of his own poetry. He carefully chooses works he wishes to include and in what order. He also extends an open invitation to his reader to look forward to his next book of poetry, *Sangre seca* [*Dried Blood*], by gathering five new works incorporated throughout the 2015 anthology. *Sangre seca* would be published in 2017. His method is original and pioneering. Another novel feature of this anthology is that the poetry selections do not appear in a chronological ordering, and they also do not adhere to the specific ordering as originally presented in the collection in which they first were published. This too is a groundbreaking approach. Each chosen poem interacts with the other poems selections within his *Ecosistema*. Each also becomes a new opportunity for reconsidering a poem in the context of the earlier collection from which it originated.

The reader of this anthology discovers that, true to its metaphoric title, this work discloses the poetry of Josep M. Rodríguez as vitally integrative. The poems divulge their potential to interact with one another as imaged organisms. As an organic entity, the anthology discloses the dynamic intertextual configurations and reconfigurations of his vibrantly poetic *Ecosistema* and its numerous interdependent parts. Because Josep M. Rodríguez has elected not to organize this work chronologically, various thoughtful and thought-provoking interconnections gradually emerge in the evolution of his poetic trajectory. Interwoven thematic concerns and refreshing imaged innovations guide the reader to the most striking features of his work. A bonus is that the anthology collects in one place evident manifestations of the poetics of epiphany in the work of Josep M. Rodríguez.

For Rodríguez, the image embodies the immediate and radiant moment of intellectual, emotional, and epistemic discovery. The reader, when entering this, his "ecosystem," witnesses an invaluable and representative compendium of Rodríguez's work. The reader also comes to understand that Josep M. Rodríguez excels at pondering and integrating what is essential to the nature of poetry, of being, of being in the world and of constructing self-identity as a poet and as a human being. He conveys his scrutiny of each with condensed and imaginative imagistic eloquence leading to articulated discoveries.

Ecosistema, like his other works, artfully suggests a reflective rereading of the anthology at hand and a pensive reexamination of the past collections from which the selections were drawn. At the same time, it presents invitations to look forward to Rodríguez's next work. The five interwoven poems that are new to the reader in 2015, one of which is enticingly placed at the end of the anthology, are portals to his recent 2017 publication of *Sangre seca*. His Janus-like approach offers inspiring opportunities for continual interaction with his poetry.[42] Excitingly innovative, *Ecosistema* highlights a synthetic view of the poetry of Josep M. Rodríguez, one in which the reader can both appreciate what he has written and anticipate what he will write.

MEMORY

The poet establishes the underlying characteristics of *Sangre seca* earlier in his 2008 poetics when he comments, "Entiendo el yo como el punto de llegada de todo lector, del mismo modo que entiendo ese yo biográfico como el punto de partida de todo poeta" ("Memorias de un lector," 197). [I understand the I as the point of arrival for every reader; at the same time, I understand the biographical I as the point of departure for every poet.] In this same poetics, he also conveys, "Todo poema exige un margen. Y ese margen empieza en el propio poeta: en sus vivencias, en sus lecturas, en su estado de ánimo, en sus sensaciones o en el momento histórico que le he tocado vivir" (197). [Every poem requires a range. And this range begins with the poet himself: his experiences, his readings, his frame of mind, his perceptions, or the historical context in which he lives.] *Sangre seca* adds another distinguishing dimension to aspects of this 2008 poetics and to his work. In his newest collection, Rodríguez explores different features of human memory and the epiphanic nature of remembering. It is not that memories suddenly emerge in this 2017 book. In constructing self-reflexive human identity, Rodríguez investigates the activity of recollecting in various poems from *Raíz*. For example, the poetic protagonist of "Erosión II" (31) asks, "¿Acaso la memoria / es algo más que el eco de lo que ya hemos sido?" [Is memory anything else / other than an echo of what we were?] The poetic voice in "Las nubes. *Versión segunda*" (50) discovers, "Todo nace de contemplación, / incluso la memoria." [Everything originates in contemplation, / including memory.]

In *Sangre seca,* various speakers engage in remembering as an existential mode for recognizing, recovering, and coming to understand the essence of personal being in time. "Pequeña digresión. *Versión segunda*" (22–23) [A Small Digression: *Second Version*], serves as an example, as the following lines reveal:

> Lo mismo que la lluvia busca el mar,
> me regreso al origen:
>
> hay estatuas de sal cuando miro el pasado.
> ¿O acaso la memoria no es estática?
>
> Lo que antes fue principio ahora es final,
> como un extraño árbol
> que por ramas
> tuviera la raíz.

[It's the same as the rain seeking the sea
I return to my origin:

there are statues of salt when I look back at the past.
Or perchance memory isn't static?

What before was the beginning is now the end,
as if a strange tree
instead of branches
had roots.]

Rodríguez's refined expressivity voices remembrances of a past event from childhood now intermingled with an acquired knowledge of human finitude in the stellar poem "Hipódromo" (33) [Racetrack]. The pulsing tempo, combining hendecasyllabic and heptasyllabic lines, accentuates the ongoing movement between past and present temporal planes. This poetic speaker, when recalling a personalized experience, now comprehends more fully the ephemeral nature of being:

Mi padre me explicó que los caballos
llevaban anteojeras
para que vieran solo hacia adelante.

Sin distracción posible,
también mi cuerpo avanza hacia un final.

[My father told me once that horses
wear blinders
so that they can only see forward.

With no chance to get distracted,
My body also is moving forward towards the end.] (*Radar*, trans. Boldú, 67)

In other poems, sterling imagery melds self-recognition occurring in an instant. It is in the instantaneous when time always already is marked by passage. This compressed perspective is evident in "A este lado del río" (29–30) [On This Side of the River] where figurative outer and inner worlds meet when conjoining the initial and the final lines of this revelatory poem:

Crecen flores silvestres
en las vías de tren abandonadas.

Se percibe el pasado a cada instante.

. . .

Me reconozco en lo que está incompleto.
¿Qué más puedo decir?

Mi corazón
es una cuenta atrás.

[Wild flowers grow
by the abandoned railway tracks.

The past is noticed at every moment.

. . .

I recognize myself in the incomplete.
What else can I say?

My heart
is a countdown.] (*Radar*, trans. Boldú, 29)

The contemporary Macedonian poet Nikola Madzirov observes, "'No hay dos oscuridades que duelan lo mismo', así la poesía de Josep M. Rodríguez duele con su latente luz y corta con su quietud ponderosa."[43] ["There are no two darknesses / that hurt us in the same way," thus the poetry of Josep M. Rodríguez hurts with its latent light and cuts with its powerful quietness.] In citing two lines from the four-part poem "Cuaderno del desierto" [Desert Notebook] from *Sangre seca* (IV, 47), Madzirov's perspective presents invaluable insight into this newest collection by Rodríguez. Joan Margarit, himself a notable Catalan poet in his own right, provides additional views. In his excellent "Epilogue" to *Sangre seca* he explains, "Leer este libro ha significado para mí la constatación de una vieja sospecha, la de que Josep M. Rodríguez piensa cada vez más sus poemas desde la propia poesía. No es posible escribir como si uno fuera el primer poeta"[44] (69). [For me, reading this book meant verifying an old suspicion of mine—that is, that Josep M. Rodríguez more and more sees his poems from the perspective of poetry itself. It is not possible to write as if one were the first poet.] His observations underscore Rodríguez's own self-identity as a poet and his "biographical self" in his work ("Memorias de un lector," 197). This aspect of his personal and poetic identity includes various memories from his past including his remembering events, situations, and responses to being and having been in the world.

It is, however, important to keep in mind, as Margarit does, that another profound inspiration for memory in *Sangre seca* resides in Rodríguez's recollections of poets with whom he shares an affinity. Literary memory pulsates throughout his 2017 work in poems such as "Hora prima" (19) [First Hour], "Mi Tierra baldía" (31) [My Waste Land], "Casi variación Lowell" (51) [Nearly a Lowell Variation], and "Desempleo" (57–58) [Unemployment]. These poems, and there are others as well, visit the corners of a mind displaying that writing poetry is a mode of his. Recollected poetic works and poets interrelate many of the texts that highlight Rodríguez's "ancestry" in his creation of his "own family tree" ("Memorias de un lector," 199). Margarit points out that it is in the poetic tradition where "estos poemas encuentran y desenvuelven su razón de ser más profunda y, por tanto, el camino de su propia verdad" (69) [these poems encounter and develop their most profound reason for being and, therefore, the road to their own truth]. Josep M. Rodríguez cultivates a richly diverse poetics in *Sangre seca,* one that continues to foreground the self-construction of personal identity.

In 2017, Rodríguez also published selections from his poems in a unique work titled *Radar. Antología bilingüe*[45] [*Radar: Bilingual Anthology*]. All his collections are represented from *Frío,* published in 2002, through *Sangre seca,* published in 2017. His choices are quintessential. The result is an artistic cluster of his poetry in Spanish and in English translation.[46] Rodríguez has an eye for detail and *Radar* includes two sensational photographs by Luis Vioque. As in *Ecosistema,* the poems are not gathered in a chronological ordering according to their original publication in his other works. Rather, this book exhibits his meticulous selection of his representative works for introducing his poetry to an international audience. This bilingual anthology also includes one unpublished poem, "Lunula" (77), pointing to his future work. *Radar,* appropriately named, transmits Rodríguez's own considerations and reconsiderations of his poetry. As a collection, it serves to synthesize his past work and to anticipate its future directions. This book richly enhances the poetry, the multicultural audience, and the range of influence of his exemplary work. At the same time, *Radar* signals the distinctive contributions and the estimable role of Josep M. Rodríguez in the evolution of Spain's twenty-first-century poetry.

POEM AND POEM ANALYSIS BY JOSEP M. RODRÍGUEZ

What follows is a recent poem by Josep M. Rodríguez and his original analysis of this poem. He wrote his study at the request of the author for inclusion in this chapter of the book. In this poem, Rodríguez divulges the epiphanic nature of his writing. In many ways, this poem offers, by pure coincidence, a compendium of several of the features of his poetry brought to light in the present chapter. The sudden acquisition of new knowledge is imaged to perfection in this poem. His search for "the Poem" yields effective results. There is much to anticipate in his future work.

ESCRIBIR

Vuelvo a mirar al cielo:
no conozco otra forma de escapismo.

El sol
        de hoy
                parece una ruleta.
Hay un hámster de fuego
girando en su interior.

Todo tiene un adentro.
El mío,
        una Venecia
con canales de sangre.

Las nubes
        fervorosas
dibujan su alzacuellos.

(Los adjetivos solo te distraen.)

Oscuro el corazón y el verso claro.

Si Dios existe,
escribir un poema es intentar

leer
sus labios. (*Sangre seca*, 55)

[WRITING]

[I look up at the sky again:
I do not know any other form of escapism.

The sun
today
looks like a wheel.
There is a hamster of fire
spinning around inside it.

Everything has an innermost side.
Mine,
a Venice
with blood canals.

Faithful
clouds
draw their clerical collars.

(Adjectives only get you distracted).

Dark is the heart, but the verse is clear.

If God exists,
writing a poem is like trying

to read
his lips.] (*Radar*, trans. Boldú, 73)

ANÁLISIS

Al comienzo de su *Política,* Aristóteles define al hombre como aquel de entre los animales que posee la palabra. Según el Evangelio de San Juan: "En el principio era el Verbo, y el Verbo era con Dios, y el Verbo era Dios." Aunque otras traducciones (pienso en la de Schonfield o en la de Smith & Goodspeed) cambian la última parte de la oración para que el Verbo no sea Dios, sino "divino." En cierta medida, tanto Aristóteles como San Juan están de acuerdo en una cosa: la palabra hace al hombre.

* * *

Así cierra Vicente Huidobro su "Arte poética": "El poeta es un pequeño Dios." Lejos del matiz religioso, entiendo que el autor chileno se refiere a la capacidad de la palabra para crear realidades. En cada primer verso hay un nuevo Big Bang.

No conozco a ningún poeta que no escriba desde el desacuerdo con la realidad que le ha tocado vivir. Algunos se enfrentan a ella, creen que la poesía es un arma cargada de futuro. Otros prefieren huir. Quizá el ejemplo más evidente sea el fin del siglo XIX: las sedas de la China, los muebles lacados o los biombos japoneses definen la sensibilidad de la época. De Proust a Rubén Darío. En ningún otro momento hubiese encajado mejor un libro como *À rebours,* la historia de un hombre que se retira del mundanal ruido a una realidad de ensueño, artificial, creada por él mismo. Me pregunto si todo poeta no es, en el fondo, un pequeño Des Esseintes.

* * *

Junto a la casa de mis padres había un pequeño riachuelo y, detrás, unas montañas. Aquél fue el escenario de mi infancia y lo ha sido, también, de varios de mis poemas ("Indecisión," "El corazón de bosque," . . .). Recuerdo que mis amigos y yo jugábamos a ver quién aguantaba más tiempo mirando directamente al sol. Era como ver una peonza en llamas o como la rueda que hace girar un ratón de fuego. Precisamente, uno de mis traductores convirtió el ratón de fuego en un ratón en fuego, ardiendo. Y me acordé de la vez en que Kikaku y Bashō contemplaban el vuelo de unas libélulas y el primero exclamó: "¡Rojas libélulas! / Si le quitas las alas / son vainas de pimienta." A lo que el maestro objetó: "No, así no, acabas de matar a las libélulas. Di más bien: ¡Vainas de pimienta! / Si les añades alas / se vuelven libélulas." Pues eso, mi ratón no sufre ni va a morir. Yo también escribo siempre desde el lado de la vida.

* * *

Lope de Vega escribió un soneto que termina con los siguientes versos: "Porque dejen la pluma y el castigo / oscuro el borrador y el verso claro." Es decir, más allá del esfuerzo y del papel emborronado, lo verdaderamente importante es que el poema sea nítido, preciso como los planos arquitectónicos de un edificio. Sólo así podrá soportar el paso del tiempo. Pero lo que Lope de Vega no dice es que, a veces, el estado de ánimo no es el más adecuado para escribir. Y sin embargo el poema se mueve, sí, *eppur si muove.*

* * *

Stan Lee y su *Spider-Man* popularizaron la frase: "Un gran poder conlleva una gran responsabilidad." Y eso sirve también para los escritores. Ante la encrucijada infinita del papel en blanco, son muchos los que prefieren el laberinto a la salida. Palabras, palabras, palabras. Un canto de sirenas. Un mirarse al espejo para contemplar la belleza de las formas. Truman Capote ya dijo que la herramienta más útil para el escritor son las tijeras. Bashō o Issa delimitaban una escena en las diecisiete sílabas de un *haiku*. Hemingway definía a un personaje con un adjetivo o un simple detalle. No necesitaba más. El resto es distracción o extravío. Cuando escribo suelo repetirme, como si fuera un mantra: "En un poema sólo caben las palabras necesarias."

[ANALYSIS]

[At the beginning of his *Politics*, Aristotle defines man as the only animal that possesses the word. According to Saint John the Evangelist: "In the beginning was the Word, and the Word was with God, and the Word was God." Although other translations (I am thinking about Schonfield's or the one from Smith and Goodspeed) change the last part of the sentence so that the Word isn't God but rather "divine." To some extent, both Aristotle and Saint John have one thing in common: the word is man.

* * *

Vicente Huidobro closes his *Ars Poética* in this way: "The poet is a little God." Far from the religious nuance, I understand the Chilean author to be referring to the capacity of the word to create realities. In every first line, there is a new Big Bang. I don't know of any poet that doesn't write from a position of disagreeing with the reality in which he lives. Some confront it, they believe that poetry is a loaded weapon for the future. Others prefer to flee. Perhaps the most evident example is from the end of the nineteenth century: silk from China, lacquered furniture or Japanese screens define the sensibility of the times. From Proust to Rubén Darío. In no other moment would a book like *À rebours* better fit, the story of a man who retreats from the worldly hustle and bustle to an artificial fantasy that he creates. I wonder if every poet is not, at heart, a little Des Esseintes.

* * *

Next to my parents' house there was a small stream and, behind, some mountains. That was the setting of my childhood and has been, also, for various poems of mine ("Indecision," "The Heart of the Forest," etc.). I remember that one of my friends and I would play a game about seeing who could last the longest when looking directly at the sun. It was like seeing a flaming top or like a hamster of fire spinning its wheel. Indeed, one of my translators turned the hamster of fire into a hamster on fire, burning. And I recalled the time that Kikaku and Bashō were pondering the flights of some dragonflies and the former exclaimed: "Red dragonflies! / If you remove their wings / they are red pepper pods." To which the master objected: "No, not that way, you have just killed the dragonflies. Say rather: Red pepper pods! / If you add wings / they are dragonflies." Thus, my hamster does not suffer nor is it going to die. I too always write from the standpoint of life.

* * *

Lope de Vega wrote a sonnet ending in this way: "Because pen and punishment show / dark is the draft, but the verse is clear." That is to say, beyond the effort and the smudged paper, what is truly important is that the poem be clear, precise like architectural blueprints of a building. This is the only way it will withstand the passage of time. But what Lope de Vega doesn't say is that, at times, the mood is less than ideal for writing. And yet the poem moves, yes, *eppur si muove.*

* * *

Stan Lee and his Spider-Man popularized the phrase: "With great power comes great responsibility." And that also applies to writers. At the infinite crossroads of the blank piece of paper, many are they who prefer the labyrinth to the exit. Word, words, words. A song of the sirens. Looking in the mirror, appreciating the beauty of form. Truman Capote said that the most useful tool for the writer is scissors. Bashō or Issa would delineate a scene in seventeen syllables in the haiku. Hemingway would define a character with an adjective or a simple detail. He didn't need more. The rest is distraction or deviation. When I write I often repeat to myself, as if it were a mantra: "Only the necessary words fit in a poem."]

POEMS BY JOSEP M. RODRÍGUEZ

The complete text and translation of the poems examined in chapter 3 include the following:

"Indecisión," *Raíz* (2008).
"Mantra," *Raíz* (2008).
"Mediodía," *La caja negra* (2004).
"Reflejo," *La caja negra* (2004).
"Ramas," *Frío* (2002).
"Erosión I–II," *Raíz* (2008).
"La charca," *Raíz* (2008).
"Inicio," *La caja negra* (2004).
"Yo, o mi idea de yo," *Arquitectura yo* (2012).
"Ecuación," *La caja negra* (2004).
"Crudo," *Arquitectura yo* (2012).
"Morgue," *Arquitectura yo* (2012).
"B+," *Arquitectura yo* (2012).
"Hipódromo," *Sangre seca* (2017).

INDECISIÓN

Dura pocos segundos.
                    Tras la lluvia,
el pájaro está atento
y le arranca a la tierra una lombriz

y vuela hasta que ya no puede verse.

Aún hay nubes.
Nacen del agua y en el agua mueren.

También en su fluir se esconde un río.

Es curioso,
la vida
     se reinventa a cada instante:
Lo sabe el caracol
que ha perdido su punta de peonza

y la savia
que nadie puede ver, pero que existe.

La vida se reinventa a cada instante:

Aprende su lección
                y sé valiente.

[INDECISION]

[Lasting a few seconds.
                After the rain,
the bird is attentive
snatching an earthworm from the soil

and flying away no longer to be seen.

There are still clouds.
Born of water and vanishing in vapor.

In their course a river is hidden as well.

It is curious
life
        is reinvented every second:
The snail knows it
a spin top that has lost its tip

and the sap
that no one can see, but it is there.

Life reinvents itself every second.

Learn its lesson
                            and be brave.]

MANTRA

La ropa pierde lustre
si se tiende
cuando más arde el día.
Es verano.

He esperado a que el aire refrescara,
y el tiempo
se ha hecho imagen:
Mira cómo gotea.

Fijar la realidad
me ayuda a comprender lo que sucede,

pero qué significan los recuerdos.
Son un eco invisible de pisadas:

"No hay que bajar los ojos —me decía mi padre—,
quien sólo mira el suelo
se acaba lastimando con las ramas."

Me he lastimado demasiadas veces.
El tendedero es un reloj de agua.

Mira cómo gotea:
Deja un rastro en el suelo
que poco a poco secará la noche.

También existe noche en la memoria.
Es verano.

Fijar la realidad
me ayuda a estar donde una vez estuve,
me devuelve a mi sitio.

(El coral, sin el agua, es sólo arbusto.)

No hay que bajar los ojos:
Estar atento a lo que me rodea
como una forma de conocimiento.

Es verano.

El tendedero es un reloj de agua
que detendrá la noche
con su aliento.

[MANTRA]

[The wash loses its luster
if hung
during the hottest part of the day.
It is summer.

I have waited until the air cooled down
and time
becomes an image:
Watch how it drips.

Taking note of reality
helps me understand what is happening,

but what do memories mean.
They are the invisible echo of footsteps:

"Mustn't look down—my father would tell me—
whoever only looks at the ground
ends up getting hurt by the branches."

I have been hurt too many times.
The clothesline is a water clock.

Watch how it drips:
Leaving a trace on the ground
that little by little the night will dry.

The night also exists in memory.
It is summer.

Taking note of reality
helps me be where I once was,
bringing me back to where I came from.

(The coral, without water, is only a bush.)

Mustn't look down:
Be attentive to what surrounds me
as a form of knowledge.
It is summer.

The clothesline is a water wheel
that will detain the night
breeze.]

MEDIODÍA

Tiendo la ropa.
Es una cuerda más
el horizonte.

[NOON]

[I hang the wash.
Another clothesline
the horizon.]

REFLEJO

El azafrán,
tirado por el suelo
de la mañana.

[REFLECTION]

[Saffron
strewn across the terrain
morning.]

RAMAS

A contraluz,
tu pulmón al desnudo.

Y en su interior
(aunque no puedas verlas)
ramas como de almendro o de avellano

y una especie de florecillas blancas
brotando en sus extremos:

Una radiografía.
La dejas otra vez sobre la mesa
que aún conserva intacta
su memoria de ramas, tronco y árbol

(la memoria no muere,
se transforma).

Ramas en tus pulmones
y en la mesa

y en el papel de un libro.

Todo es parte de todo,
un mismo árbol.

[BRANCHES]

[Against a backlight,
your lung laid bare.

And in the inside
(even if you cannot see them)
branches like an almond or a hazelnut tree

and a type of small white flowers
sprouting from their ends:

An X-ray.
You put it back on the table
which still preserves its untouched
memory of branches, trunk and tree

(memory does not die,
it is just transformed).

Branches in your lungs
and on the table

and on the page from a book.

Everything is part of everything,
the same tree.] (Translation Ben Clark)

EROSIÓN

I
El sol es un faquir
que se ha tumbado
                              lento
sobre pinos de aguja.

Miro las montañas.

Hay algo de la piedra
que se pierde en el viento.
Erosión.

Camino por el bosque.

Hace frío
y el arroyo está helado.

En su interior,
se ha quedado atrapada una hoja de roble.

La mirada está atenta:
esa imagen resume
                              qué pasa en la memoria.

II
Sobre las montañas,
nubes
        llenas
como esas bolsas blancas de los supermercados.

Camino por el bosque.

Estoy alerta.
La mirada me explica cuanto soy.

Por eso me he negado a la elegía.

¿Acaso la memoria
es algo más que el eco de lo que ya hemos sido?

Sólo tengo interés por el instante.
El resto es erosión
o me erosiona.

[EROSION]

I
[The sun is a fakir
that has laid down
slowly
on the needles of pine trees.

I look at the mountains.

There is something in the stone
that is lost in the wind.
Erosion.

I walk through the forest.

It is cold
and the stream is frozen.
Inside it,
an oak leaf, caught.

My gaze is aware:

this image shows
what happens with memory.

II
Above the mountains,
clouds,
full
like those white bags in supermarkets.

I walk through the forest.

I am alert.
My gaze explains to me what I am.

That is why I have disallowed elegies.

Is memory anything else
other than an echo of what we were?

I am only interested in this instant.
The rest is erosion
or my own erosion.] (Translation Ben Clark)

LA CHARCA

Volver a este rincón de la memoria
no me hace más feliz.

Todo sigue en su sitio.
Los árboles, la charca, los insectos.

Si el tiempo ondula,
como escribió Deleuze,
también con la emoción debe pasar lo mismo.

No todo me emociona:
El agua de la charca sólo es agua,
el musgo,
sólo musgo,
y este poema
no es más que la corteza de lo que está pasando.

Profundiza.
Fíjate en los patos:
parece que nadar les sea fácil

y es algo muy distinto bajo el agua.

Ondulación:
Vivir la vida en círculos crecientes
que nazcan y se extiendan desde mí.

La emoción necesita de un proceso.
No olvides los anillos de los árboles.

[THE POND]

[Returning to this corner of the memory
doesn't make me happy.

Everything continues to stay in place.
The trees, the pond, the insects.

If time undulates,
                    as Deleuze wrote,
the same also should happen with emotion.

Not everything moves me:
The water in the pond only is water,
the moss,
          only moss,
and this poem
is nothing more than the surface of what is taking place.

Fathom.
          Pay attention to the ducks:
it seems that swimming is easy for them

and it is very different under the water.

Undulation:
Live life in increasing circles
originating and expanding from me.

Emotion needs a process.
Don't forget the rings of the trees.]

INICIO

La nieve del tejado se deshace
poco a poco,
igual que la belleza de la mujer que amo.

Tan oscuro es su canto a medianoche
como inmenso el silencio dentro de la piedra.

De pie,
        frente a mi casa,
el frío se convierte en armonía.

Todo es cuestión de ciclos.
Lo que ahora se va,
                después ha de volver
para irse de nuevo.

Todo es cuestión de ciclos:
yo sólo escribo círculos sobre el papel de nieve.

[THE BEGINNING]

[The snow on the roof slowly
melts,
just like the beauty of the woman I love.

At midnight its song is as dark
as vast is the silence within the stone.

Standing
        in front of the house,
cold becomes a harmony.

Everything comes down to cycles.
What now leaves,
                is sure to return
to then leave again.

Everything comes down to cycles:
I only draw circles on the paper of the snow.] (Translation Ben Clark)

YO, O MI IDEA DE YO

Tengo tendencia a generalizar:
por eso escribo "bosque"
aunque sé que no hay dos árboles iguales,

por eso escribo "yo".

Y sin embargo a ratos me construyo.
Y sin embargo a ratos me derribo.
O incluso las dos cosas:

como un niño que nace
en un barco que se hunde.

[ME, OR MY IDEA OF ME]

[I have a tendency to generalize.
This is why I write "forest"
in spite of knowing there are not two trees alike,

this is why I write "me."

And yet at times I build myself up.
And yet at times I knock myself down.
Or even both:

like a child born
on a sinking boat.] (Translation Monika Izabela Jaworska)

ECUACIÓN

De pie sobre esta peña,
acepto la mentira del paisaje.

Todo es inaccesible:
el rocío
        —que es sudor vegetal—
y el tren que pasa.

Una cigüeña vuela en blanco y negro.

Tiene su nido en lo alto de la iglesia
que hay junto al fosal.
Extraña paradoja,

la piedra testimonia lo fugaz,
la carne sólo es cauce para el tiempo.

(Cada hueso que tengo es una lápida
por los muertos que escondo en mi interior.)

¿Por qué contar el tiempo que nos queda?

Vivir es abrazar oscuridades:
de lo que no sabemos a lo que no sabemos,

desde una lejanía a otra lejanía.
Todo es inaccesible.

Quien mira un tren pasar comprende el resto.

[EQUATION]

[Standing on this large rock,
I accept the misleading landscape.

Everything is inaccessible:
the dew
        —vegetation's perspiration—
and the train that passes.

A stork flies in black and white.

Its nest is high atop the church
adjoining the cemetery.
Strange paradox,

the stone bears witness to the fleeting,
the flesh only is a channel for time.

(My every bone is a headstone
for the dead ones I hide inside of me.)

Why count the time we have left?

To live is to embrace darkness:
From what we know to what we don't know,

from one distance to another distance.
Everything is inaccessible.

Whoever watches a train pass understands the rest.]

CRUDO

De tan negra
y profunda
la tristeza parece un pozo de petróleo.

¿Se formará también de aquello que está muerto?

Nos construyen las pérdidas:
instante
tras instante
tras instante.

Así que no lo dudes,
reclama para ti
en este día
la lentitud del saurio,

la inocencia del fósil,

la oscuridad del hombre que imagina
el final de una cueva.

Deja de preocuparte por quién eres.

El árbol que no es bosque
lo anticipa.

[CRUDE]

[So black
and deep,
sadness looks like an oil well.

Is it also formed from that which is extinct?

We are constructed by our losses:
moment
after moment
after moment.

So, do not hesitate,
claim for yourself
                                        on this day
the saurian's slowness,

the fossil's innocence,

the darkness of the man who imagines
the end of a cave.

Stop worrying about who you are.

That tree which is not a forest
does anticipate it.] (Translation Ben Clark)

MORGUE

Porque todos los cuerpos
encierran una historia,

quisiste ser forense.

Así aprendiste que la soledad
es la piel fría
                de una vieja puta

y que el amor
se hace más duradero dentro de un tatuaje:

los ojos leen aquello que las palabras tocan.
Y el silencio
                anuncia la amplitud,

la vastedad de lo que no conoces.

¿Alguna vez pensaste que tu cuerpo
es sólo la envoltura
del gusano de seda de la muerte?

Su crisálida deja tras de sí,
tumbado en la camilla,

un cadáver
                abierto.

[MORGUE]

[Because all bodies
hide a story,

you wanted to be a forensic surgeon.

Thus you have learned that loneliness
is the cold skin
                of an old whore

and that love
lasts longer inside a tattoo:

eyes read what words touch.
And silence
                    announces the extent,

the immensity of what you do not know.

Have you ever thought that your body
could be nothing but the cocoon
of the silkworm of death?

Its chrysalis is left behind,
laid out on the stretcher,

an open
            corpse.] (Translation Monika Izabela Jaworska)

B+

De cerca es como el mapa de un sitio al que no has ido
pero querrías ir,
porque una aguja marca su destino concreto.

Abro y cierro la mano:
que la sangre circule hasta la bolsa
y allí espere paciente
hasta llegar a ti,

mientras yo me pregunto
a qué parte de mí he renunciado

o si habrá algún recuerdo que ya no fluirá más . . .

Tengo hermanos de sangre a los que no conozco:
¿sabrán reconocerme si se cruzan conmigo?

¿Y qué sentiré yo
al saber que mi sangre circula por sus venas?

Abro y cierro la mano
mientras pienso si eso no es también la poesía:

tomar sin merecer,

ser en el cuerpo de otro.

[B+]

[At close quarters it is like the map of a place you have never been to
but you would like to go to,
because a pin is marking its specific destination.

I open and close my hand:
let the blood flow into the bag
and wait there patiently
until it comes to you,

while I wonder
what part of me I have given up

or whether some memory will not be flowing anymore . . .

I have blood brothers whom I do not know:
Will they be able to recognize me if they come upon me?

And what will I feel
knowing that my blood is running through their veins?

I open and close my hand
while thinking if this is not poetry as well:

taking without deserving,

being in someone else's body] (Translation Monika Izabela Jaworska)

HIPÓDROMO

> Está bien copiar lo que se ve, pero aún está mejor
> dibujar lo que no se ve sino en la memoria.
> —Edgar Degas

De tan frágil, la luz
parece que está a punto de romperse.

Desde la grada observo los cajones.
Estoy dentro de un cuadro de Degas:
no importa el tema,
sino el movimiento.

Mi padre me explicó que los caballos
llevaban anteojeras
para que vieran sólo hacia adelante.

Sin distracción posible,
también mi cuerpo avanza hacia un final.

El cielo Años 70:
nubes en gotelé.

A la vuelta, mi padre
conducía en silencio.
Yo buscaba en la radio una emisora.

Al cambiar de recuerdo
hay ruido rosa.

[RACETRACK]

> [It is all very well to copy what one sees, but it is better still
> to draw what can only be seen in one's memory.
> —Edgar Degas

Fragile as it may seem, light
appears to be about to shatter.

From the grandstand I watch the starting gates.
I am inside a painting by Degas:
the theme does not matter,
the movement does.

My father told me once that horses
wear blinders
so that they can only see forward.

With no chance to get distracted,
my body also is moving forward towards the end.

The sky in the '70s:
clouds, popcorn ceiling texture.

On our way back, my father
was driving in silence.
I was trying to tune in to a radio station.

In between memories
there is pink noise.] (Translation Ester Boldú)

Ada Salas, photograph by Chema de la Peña

4 ✱ ADA SALAS: POETRY AND POETICS

PERSONAL BIOGRAPHY BY SALAS

Nací en la ciudad de Cáceres, en la región de Extremadura, en 1965. Vivo, desde hace bastantes años, en Madrid, donde me gano la vida como Profesora de Enseñanza Secundaria de Lengua y literatura españolas e imparto talleres de creación y lectura poéticas en diversas instituciones.[1] Empecé a escribir en la adolescencia, con el impulso tan natural en esa edad de "expresar" lo que sentía con gran intensidad, y con la conciencia de que solo el papel podía "comprenderme." Con el tiempo esa pulsión, la de escribir poesía, fue transformándose en algo mucho más misterioso, más inexplicable y más fascinante, algo por y para lo que merece la pena vivir. Estudié Filología española en la Universidad de Extremadura. Durante esos años universitarios ejerció una gran influencia sobre mí el ilustre profesor y poeta Juan Manuel Rozas, que contaba con una biblioteca extraordinaria, y con quien tuve la suerte de convivir estrechamente, ya que era muy amiga de uno de sus hijos. Di clases durante un tiempo en Facultad de Langues de Angers (Francia). Publiqué mi primer libro, *Arte y memoria del inocente*, en 1987. En 1994 *Variaciones en blanco* ganó el Premio de poesía Hiperión, premio que implicaba la publicación en dicha editorial. En Hiperión aparecieron después sucesivamente *La sed* (1994), *Lugar de la derrota* (2003), *Esto no es el silencio* (2008) y la recopilación *No duerme el animal* (2009). En 2013 la editoral Pre-Textos publicó *Limbo y otros poemas.*

Me interesa mucho el diálogo de la poesía con la pintura. En 2010 y 2016 se publicaron respectivamente, *Ashes to Ashes* y *Diez mandamientos*, dos libros en colaboración con el pintor Jesús Placencia. En el terreno de la reflexión ensayística sobre la poesía he publicado *Alguien aquí* (2005) y *El margen, el error, la tachadura (De la metáfora y otros asuntos más o menos poéticos)* (2010). Junto con Juan Abeleria he traducido al poeta surrealista Robert Desnos para la editorial Hiperión y espero que pronto vea la luz la traducción de *Pianissimo* del poeta italiano Camillo Sbarbaro.

[I was born in the city of Cáceres, in the region of Extremadura, in 1965. For a number of years, I have lived in Madrid where I earn my living as a professor of secondary education in Spanish language and literature, and I also direct creative writing workshops on poetry, and I give guest poetry readings at various academic institutions. I began to write in my teens, with the natural impulse at that age "to express" what I was feeling with intensity, and with the awareness that it was only on paper that I could "understand myself." In time, that drive, that of writing poetry, began changing into something much more mysterious, more incomprehensible, and more fascinating, something about which and for which it is worth living. I studied Spanish philology at the University of Extremadura. During those university years, the distinguished professor and poet Juan Manuel Rozas had a profound influence on me, he had an extraordinary library, and I was fortunate to spend time with him because I was a very close friend of one of his children. For a time, I taught at the Langues de Angers (France). I published my first book, *Arte y memoria del inocente*, in 1987. In 1994, *Variaciones en blanco* won the Hiperión Poetry Prize, an award that involved publication with this editorial press. Later, Hiperión consecutively published *La sed* (1994), *Lugar de la derrota* (2003), *Esto no es el silencio* (2008), and the collection *No duerme el animal* (2009). In 2013, Pre-Textos published *Limbo y otros poemas*.

I am very interested in the dialogue of poetry with painting. In 2010 and 2016, respectively, *Ashes to Ashes* and *Diez mandamientos* were published, two books done in collaboration with the painter Jesús Placencia. In the area of reflective essays on poetry, I have published *Alguien aquí* (2005) and *El margen, el error, la tachadura (De la metáfora y otros asuntos más o menos poéticos)* (2010). Together with Juan Abeleria, I have translated the surrealist poet Robert Desnos for Hiperión, and I hope that the translation of *Pianissimo* by the Italian poet Camillo Sbarbaro soon will appear.]

OROGENESIS

Ada Salas writes exquisite poetry. In the recent era, the mere mention of her name immediately calls to mind the carefully chiseled poem and the precision of diction. The metaphoric and transformative potential of the word is the subject of her poetry. Her style is eloquent, free of the cliché, and genuinely unique. Salas conceives each of her poems as an entryway for exhibiting a momentous discovery. In her work, only during the writing process does she encounter the extraordinary capacity of the word. Throughout her poetry, and her series of reflective poetics in which she analyzes the creative act, Ada Salas brilliantly articulates and exhibits the subject matter that is central to her work: "Orogénesis. Alteración. Complicación. Fractura. Ahí, de ahí nace el nuevo paisaje, y ahí ocurre la extrañeza, la metáfora, el poema: 'Lo inesperado emerge.'"[2] [Orogenesis.

Alteration. Complication. Fissure. There, from there a new site is born, and there the astonishment, the metaphor, the poem occurs: "Unexpectedness emerges."]

For Salas, writing is an orogenic activity. Throughout her trajectory, she explicates this process in her poetry and her series of prose poetics. The word materializes during the creative act; however, in her view, it is incumbent on the poet to engage in a sustained inquiry into verbal expression. Her ardent scrutiny of the writing process brings about a concentrated exploration of the innermost potential of the word. These are central to her lyric. When analyzing her poetry and her poetics, as this chapter exclusively demonstrates, an intertextual dialogue occurs among her poems and her prose essays. This interactive feature of her work is both fundamental to this chapter and signals an original contribution to the corpus of critical studies on recent Spanish poetry. In the case of Salas, the chapter offers a unique opportunity to engage in several elucidating moments of epiphany. Whether immersed in writing a poem or a prose poetics, Ada Salas consistently manifests her commitment to these artistic endeavors as instrumental epistemic methods for disclosing how and why she writes. The imaginative and inspired works of Ada Salas distinguish her formidable presence today.

THE GIFT

A special feature of Salas's work is her relentless pursuit of the essence of the word. As early as 1987, in *Arte y memoria del inocente* [*Art and Memory of the Innocent*], she explains, "La palabra es el don / que solicito." [The word is the gift / I request.][3] Salas, however, does not seek any word. Rather, her quest concerns "una presencia que guardaba el secreto de la palabra" [a presence that kept the secret of the word], as she indicates in her first poetics published in 1997.[4] In this quest, Salas not only exhibits an acute awareness of word but also an ardent desire to penetrate it. For her, *poiesis* involves excavation. By considering the word as a complex and densely filled site for intense exploration and painstaking examination, this poet strives to uncover its innermost features. These might have been unrecognizable or hidden before, especially when language only performs the role of expressing a superficial naming. For Salas, however, the word must expose, with lucid specificity, the knowledge she gains through her exacting mining of its essence. Here, Salas's work demonstrates her profound understanding of the inspiring role of the word as articulated by the modern Chilean poet Vicente Huidobro: "En todas las cosas hay una palabra interna, una palabra latente y que está debajo de la palabra que la designa. Ésa es la palabra que debe descubrir el poeta"[5] (*El margen*, 88). [In all things there is an internal word, a dormant word that is underneath the word it designates. That is the word the poet must discover.].

The pursuit of the word and the "secret" embedded deep within it is evident in Salas's earliest poetry. Throughout the course of her work, however, she does not seek any word. Hers is a quest for the precise word, the one that distinguishes itself from all others, the one that only emerges during the creative process. Throughout her poetic production, Salas avoids worn out expression because such language has lost meaning, has become commonplace, ordinary, tarnished, and even "dead." For Salas, language possesses and exhibits an ardent desire for its own self-expression. Her 2014 poetics "El deseo es lo mudo" [The desire is silent], appearing in *Ínsula* in the special issue on contemporary Spanish poetry, sheds substantial light on this process. She indicates, "Si algo caracteriza a la lengua es su necesidad de movimiento, su no querer estar quieta, su querer decirse. Su *querer*. Un poema es la epifanía de ese querer, de ese deseo, de esa huida de la quietud."[6] [If there is anything that characterizes language, it is its need for movement, its longing not to be immobile, its desire to speak. Its *want*. A poem is the epiphany of that want, of that desire, of that flight from being still.] During her excavation of the word, Ada Salas always is attentive to the vital undercurrent when the word reveals its own longing to elucidate its essence.

Salas approaches the word with an unparalleled alertness. Such fervent and fixed attention on evincing its underlying potential reveals her unwavering commitment to engaging in writing as a transformative method allowing language, in effect, to speak anew. Salas explains this in her indispensable *Alguien aquí. Notas acerca de la escritura poética*[7] [*Someone Here: Notes on Poetic Writing*].

> La lengua se detiene en el poeta, se mira en lo profundo de su espejo, se observa, se hurga, se embellece o se afea, juega a romper la imagen homogénea que el uso corriente le impone. El poema nace de un esfuerzo del propio lenguaje por salir de la monotonía, del cansancio. Por eso toda poesía es necesaria, vital, salutífera. Los grandes poetas han sido en cada época la espita por la que ha escapado la saturación de sí mismo que padecía el idioma. Sus obras fueron el resultado de un tremendo esfuerzo por rescatarlo de una muerte por asfixia. Aire. Otro aire. Ese que no aparece en los libros de la historia. [. . .] Depurar el libro, liberarlo de excesos, de redundancias, taparle la boca, rebajar el aspaviento, evitar hacer más evidente lo ya evidente. (67, 68)

> [Language pauses in the poet, it sees itself in the depth of its mirror, self-observing, probing, adding embellishments or revealing ugly features; it plays at shattering the usual unvarying image ordinary usage imposes. The poem originates in the effort of language itself to escape from monotony, from being worn out. That is why all poetry is necessary, vital, beneficial. In every era, the great poets have been the conduit through which language has passed so that it can avoid the very point of the saturation that it often has endured. Their works were

> the result of a remarkable effort to rescue it from a suffocating death. Air. Fresh air. That is what does not appear in historical accounts. (. . .) Refine the collection of poems, free it from superfluities, from redundancies, use silence, reduce affectation, avoid making more evident what already is evident.]

The search for the "secret" of the word in the poetry of Ada Salas defines her creative activity. Writing poetry involves a process of composing and revising; of trial and error; of verbal precision and approximation; of corrections, cross-outs, deletions, erasures; of reducing excess to exactness; and of painstaking deliberation that culminates in illuminating discovery.

WRITING

In one of her earliest poetics, she discloses, "Quizá nada me ha despertado, alzado, hundido, sacudido tanto como la escritura" (*Ellas tienen la palabra*, 583). [Perhaps nothing has awakened, lifted, engulfed, and shaken me as much as writing.] Why? Salas offers one significant response early in her twenty-first-century trajectory, "Escribir es vivir en el vivir, en otra capa, dentro de nuestra propia existencia: socavando —madriguera, hormiguero, entraña—, o alzándose por encima del horizonte de lo visible, en un intento de ensanchar la estrechez de la percepción del mundo, de nosotros mismos" (*Alguien aquí*, 94). [To write is to live in living, in another layer, within our own existence: excavating—burrow, anthill, entrails—or rising above what is visible on the horizon, by trying to expand our narrow perception of the world, of ourselves.]

This poet further observes, "La escritura nace de un deseo de deslumbramiento y afirmación propios, de una infinita curiosidad, de un deseo infinito" (*Alguien aquí*, 27). [Writing originates in its very desire to bedazzle and to affirm, to have endless curiosity and a limitless want.] Her quest also entails an inquiry where, throughout the course of her poetry and poetics, she actively engages in concentrated inspection and introspection, as she articulates also in 2005:

> La escritura crea (¿es?) un estado permanente de carencia. Su lugar es el hueco. El poeta no enuncia: llama, convoca. Desanda el camino de la elipsis diaria. Busca, en la palabra, la faz de lo real que lo real elude. No rehúye la realidad, intenta complementarla, acrecentarla. No transmuta, desvela. Su mirada no es parcial, sino totalizadora. Son fragmentos los poemas, sí: esas piezas que faltan en el puzzle ilusorio de nuestra existencia. (*Alguien aquí*, 50)

> [Writing creates (is?) a state of permanent lack. Its place is the gap. The poet does not speak but rather calls out, summons. Retracing the road of daily ellipsis. Seeking, in the word, the surface of the real that the real evades. Not

> avoiding reality, rather the intention is to complement it, to enhance it. Not transforming, revealing. One whose gaze is not partial but comprehensive. Poems are fragments, yes—those pieces that are missing in the illusive puzzle of our existence.]

This perspective, importantly, is central to her exploration and disclosure in her poetry of the epiphanic experience of writing:

> A lo largo del proceso de escritura el momento creador suele ser muy breve, muy fugaz. Concibo este proceso como un prolongado acto de escucha (de mis propias sensaciones, de recuerdos redivivos, del silencio, de la luz, del río subterráneo del pensamiento) al cabo del cual recojo el fruto de unos versos que siento como intensos y que resumen un mensaje que, sin forzar en exceso, va tomado una forma precisa —generalmente por exclusión—, y constituye un poema. Entre esa fase de búsqueda, indagación y escucha, y aquélla en que surge, aunque titubeante, el poema, está el fulgor del advenimiento del verso, idea o motivo generador del texto. (*Alguien aquí*, 28)

> [Throughout the writing process the creative moment often is very brief, very fleeting. I consider this process as a prolonged act of listening (to my own sensations, resurrected memories, silence, illumination, the undercurrent of once hidden thought) after which I gather the fruit of some lines I intensely experience and that summarize a message, without being overly forced; this begins to take shape in a precise form—in general, by means of exclusion—and constitute a poem. In between that earlier stage of search, inquiry, and listening, and that later stage from which the poem emerges, albeit with some hesitation, exists the luminous advent of engendering the line, idea, or reason for the text.]

Two significant poems, both published originally in 2003 in *Lugar de la derrota*[8] [*The Site of Defeat*], exhibit mainstays of her work. These are the acute awareness of self-reflectively participating in the creative act, and the intense desire to seek the requisite precision of only the most essential word.[9] The remarkable poem beginning with the line "No duerme el animal que busca" [The animal does not sleep seeking], published later in her 2009 anthology (*No duerme el animal*, 203) metaphorically captures this poet's never-ending quest for the poetic word. Significantly, the initial line of this poem also is, in part, the title of Salas's anthology recompiling her poetry. She elucidates the intriguing title applicable to the aforementioned works by stating, "Hay un hambre en él [el poeta] que solo puede saciar la palabra, pero la palabra es esquiva, no se da. Sólo permite, a veces, rozarla. Luego queda, de nuevo, el ansia" (*Alguien aquí*, 71). [There is a hunger in the poet that only the word can satiate, but the word is evasive, uncertain. At times, the word only permits brief contact. Afterward, once again, the craving remains.] The poet's "hunger" for the word, imaginatively imaged in this poem as a voracious animal instinctively in need of food during its incessant hunt for prey, never is fully satisfied. Still ravenous, its figurative appetite returns, and Salas here metaphorically molds this hunger into her own figurative yearning for the word:[10]

> Y vagará en la noche.
> Con la sola certeza de su hambre.
> Ciego
>
> porque una vez ya supo
>
> de ese breve temblor
> bajo su zarpa.
>
> [And it will wander in the night.
> Only certain of its hunger.
> Blinded
>
> because it already had discovered once
>
> that short-lived trembling sensation
> under its paw.]

Other self-reflexive observations provide additional insight into this poet's relentless quest as she explains in *Alguien aquí* (93):

> Las palabras del poema dibujos-testimonio sobre el papel, son las huellas del camino recorrido en la búsqueda incansable de lo que no nos pertenece —o que nos pertenece, ignorándolo—, de aquello que es objeto de nuestra conquista y que, aunque apenas lo intuimos, a veces nos visita, dejándonos la estupefacción, el temblor, el miedo incluso, porque es parte esencial nuestra, que ciegamente ignoramos.

> [The words of the poem, testimonial-drawings on paper, are the tracks left behind on the well-trodden road of our persistent search for what is not ours—or what is ours, but we ignore it—that which is the object of our achievement and that, even though we hardly intuit its presence, even when it visits us, leaves us amazed, trembling, even fearful because it is an integral part of us, that which we blindly ignore.]

The poem beginning "Y para qué esta herida" (*No duerme el animal*, 233) [And for what is this wound] underscores the process of poetry as epiphany. In this excellent work, Salas convincingly presents the creation of the poem as an acutely attentive activity always in search of the word. By foregrounding the instant in which the perceptive poet encounters the "secret" of the word, Salas elucidates both the inception of the creative act and the gestation of the poem. The vital clarity of her discovery reveals the essential nature of her quest, "El hallazgo es la búsqueda cuyo fin es el hallazgo que conducirá a la búsqueda" (*Alguien aquí*, 54). [The discovery is the search whose purpose is finding what will lead to the quest.] This effort, on the part of the poet, is not without pain principally when she probes and penetrates the metaphoric "wound" in which poetic expression originates:

> Y para que esta herida
>
> esta abertura umbilical
> por donde entra y sale
> la claridad del mundo
>
> [And for what is this wound
>
> this umbilical opening
> through which comes and goes
> the clarity of the world]

She superbly images the defining characteristics of her own writing in this poem: brevity, rigorous diction, no superfluous words. By mining the language of the poem, she exhibits in twenty-six words, in six perfectly constructed heptasyllabic lines, in seven lines uninterrupted by punctuation until the final moment, and in a single monosyllabic poetic line consisting of the perfected word "ya" [already], Ada Salas masterfully underscores that the once immediate moment of poetic inspiration now has passed. The elucidating word might be elusive; nonetheless, she pursues it throughout the course of her work. Ironically, in the poem beginning "Para qué esta herida" [And for what is this wound], Ada Salas not only reveals the essence of the object of her quest but also excels at disclosing an essential quality characteristic of her poetry: the meticulously constructed poem. Her aims are clear, as she affirms in her 2010 poetics, "No escribo para cantar, sino para indagar: plomada, sonda, rama de zahorí. Notas de campo de esa indagación, el texto."[11] [I do not write to sing, but to inquire with a plumb line, probe, dowsing rod. The field notes from that investigation, the text].

This chapter on Ada Salas's poetry and poetics does not adhere to a chronological ordering. Because her works present an informed and intertextual dialogue, this important interactive exchange of ideas among her texts is lost when superimposing a sequential and linear arrangement onto her poems and poetics. In both, Salas undertakes a thought-provoking and precise analysis of what she metaphorically refers to as "la materia poética, del barro con el que se crean los poemas"[12] [the poetic material, the clay with which poems are created]. Salas is a poet-sculptor who carefully images the word through her conceptual process of molding "la materia poética" while fully engaged in the creative act. She is concerned with where and when "sucede el poema" [the poem happens] and is ardently attentive to "the word" because within it "respira una manera de entender y expresar el mundo" ("Lo no reconocible" 15, 14) [breathes a way to understand and express the world]. Her work is amazingly self-reflective and self-attentive, and here, Ada Salas demonstrates that her poetry and her poetics are authentic methods for discovery: "Quienes escriben, [. . .] no inventan nada; si acaso, lo descubren" (*El margen*, 100). [Those who write . . . invent nothing; if at all, they discover something.]

THE POETIC EVENT

A paradigmatic quality of the poetry of Ada Salas is the revelatory capacity of the word in her unique sculpting of metaphor. She maintains a distinguished position in recent Spanish poetry because of her ability to enhance this fundamental trope. With her focused concentration on divulging the "secret" of the word, she quarries its expressive strata and the resulting diction is metamorphic. In Salas's poetry, the potential of metaphor originates in her concept of language:

> La lengua sucede. En ese sentido, todo poema es un escenario (vital) en el que la lengua acontece; sería eso, entonces, un poema: un acontecimiento de la lengua.[13] Y no existe tal cosa (poema) si no se produce en el lector (y en el autor), la sensación de que uno asiste, está asistiendo, en su escritura, en su lectura, a un acontecimiento, en el sentido también resumidamente hiperbólico que la expresión tiene en español: la ocasión única de participar, como contemplador, o como actor, en un "suceso" extraordinario, único, irrepetible. Ésa es justo la doble condición del acontecimiento poético: que es único, que puede ser tal como es —cualquier intervención en él daría al traste con su naturaleza—, y que es, además, constantemente otro: otro en cada lectura. Único, por tanto, e irrepetible. Y cada vez que un poema es leído ese acontecimiento se re-produce con la misma condición de presente, de contingente, de acontecido, con que fue formulado: todo lector asiste y participa en una encarnación que ocurre en el momento mismo en que el texto se dice.[14]

> [Language happens. In that sense, every poem is a stage (vital) on which language takes place; that would be, then, a poem, a language event. And such a thing (poem) does not exist if it does not produce in the reader (and in the author) the feeling that one attends, is attending, in writing, in reading, an event, also in the unmistakable exaggerated sense that the word has in Spanish: the unique opportunity to participate, as an observer, or as an actor, in an extraordinary, singular, unrepeatable "happening." That is exactly the twofold situation of the poetic event: that it is unique, just as it is—any interference would jeopardize its nature—and, moreover, that it constantly is something else, something different in each reading. Unique, thus, unrepeatable. And every time a poem is read, that event is re-produced in the same present, possible circumstance in which it came about, with which it was expressed, every reader attends and participates in an incarnation taking place at the very moment in which the text speaks.]

Salas's noteworthy metaphors originate in her indisputable ability to allow the poem "to speak." This original perspective prompts her strong belief in the "movement" within language when it displays its own innermost volition to seek expression in the poem ("El deseo es lo mudo," 40). The poet, thus, must be in the position to listen to what language must say. Salas presents her poems as exceptional linguistic events, as remarkable, refined, and intriguing invitations always to be attentive to the exceptional capacity of language during its self-realization in the poem. In this sense, her creative work further beckons additional rereadings allowing for other opportunities for the reader and the author to be mindful of the experience of participating in the poetic event.

How does this poet encounter the word she longingly pursues? Salas does not stumble upon the word during poetic creation. She does not merely happen to find it during the writing process. In her work, this is not a meeting by chance. Instead, hers is an arduous and focused quest in which she remains steadfast. At first, disruption occurs. Ordinary language does not satisfy. This poet "craves" the word, *the* word residing in the object of her search. The desire to express rumbles deep within her. She must concentrate on listening to what this muddled intellectual upheaval might offer. The creation of the poem is an explosive moment. In silence, the desire of language to express awaits its own eruption. In silence, the poet heeds the words as they arise because she is intent on locating "the word that the poet must discover," as Vicente Huidobro instructs (*El margen*, 88). She must prepare herself to attend to the transformative activity of language during the poetic process. With sincere honesty and lucent insight, Ada Salas describes one such "occasion" for discovery in the brilliant poem "El desorden trabaja como crece una herida"[15] (*Limbo*, 50) [Disruption acts like an open wound]. Here, she further lays bare her own individual method for discerning how the word voices its unique "song." Orogeny is the metaphoric mechanism underlying this remarkable poem. It is in this striking metapoem where Salas explicates the subject matter central to her work: "Orogénesis. Alteración. Complicación. Fractura. Ahí, de ahí nace el nuevo paisaje, y ahí ocurre la extrañeza, la metáfora, el poema: 'Lo inesperado emerge'" (*El margen*, 19). [Orogenesis. Alteration. Complication. Fissure. There, from there a new site is born, and there the astonishment, the metaphor, the poem occurs: "Unexpectedness emerges."]

The opening moments capture the formation of the poem as a process of creation and as a linguistic locale exhibiting dynamic alteration:

El desorden trabaja como crece una herida
hacia
adentro y hacia
afuera.
El deseo es lo mudo.
En lo mudo fermenta lo que
descuartiza un cerebro.

[Disruption acts like an open wound
growing inward
and growing
outward.
Desire is silent.
Silently fermenting what
mental matter fractures.]

By transforming the intense desire of language to burst forth, as if it were metaphoric magma in active motion, Salas stages this exceptional poem as if it were a geological "event." Here, *the* word exhibits self-revelation as it pushes upward, as if it were a molten underground force in movement. When it surfaces in this poem, it does so with the intensity of an explosive volcanic eruption effectuating epistemic discovery. The essence of the word, "su querer decirse" ("El deseo es lo mudo," 40) [its desire to speak], is potent, and it displays long-lasting results:

En el borde del cráter alguien
canta
y su canto remueve la pólvora.

[On the edge of the crater someone
sings
and the song stirs up the ash.]

This is not metaphor imaged through hyperbole, nor is it metaphor as a decorative trope. Rather, this is metaphor shaped with rigor, conceptual exactness, layers of significance, and cognitive eruption and disruption. As a metapoem, Salas presents the creation of metaphor during the transformation of language. For Salas, as this poem exemplifies, the "internal movement" underlying language, together with its extraordinary expressive vitality, has tectonic effects in their realization in the poem. Only by probing the word during the metamorphosis of metaphor will the unexpected emerge. By entering the language of this poem by means of Salas's symbolic (e)vent, this incomparable work activates her poetics of epiphany.[16]

THE NOT RECOGNIZABLE

Two of Salas's recent articles are exemplary poetics. "Lo no reconocible que vive en lo real" [The not recognizable that dwells in the real] appeared in 2009, and "Brechas" [Openings] followed in 2010. They are companion works because together they illumine her penetrating inspection of the metaphoric capacity of language. Additionally, these prose poetics are invaluable to a study of her poetry. Each offers points of departure for entering her work from unique yet complementary perspectives. During the intertextual dialogue with her poetry, these two poetics advance various features of Ada Salas's quest for the word. Most especially, they display her intensifying desire to come to know the linguistic identity of the poem as well as that of the writer. Undeniably, they hold a privileged place within her creative trajectory because, in both, Salas plants the seed ideas that she soon would develop in her outstanding 2010 book on metaphor.[17]

"Lo no reconocible que vive en lo real" further highlights an evolving theme in her poetry. The title of this poetics originates in a specific line in a poem appearing in her 2008 *Esto no es el silencio*[18] [*This Is Not Silence*]. She introduces her essay by quoting this poem in its entirety. The initial lines are provocative and unexpected:

> Lo que duerme en los pliegues lo no
> visto no oído lo nunca
> pronunciado.
>
> [What sleeps in the folds the not
> seen not heard not ever
> pronounced.]

They establish, at the outset, her keen examination of aspects of the creative process and the recessed potential of the word to be unearthed while writing the poem. The closing lines masterfully condense the illuminative moment of the poetics of epiphany:

> Lo no reconocible
>
> que vive en lo real
>
> y lo fulmina a veces
>
> y queda boqueando como un pez en sequía. (*Esto no es el silencio,* 34–35)
>
> [The not recognizable
>
> that dwells in the real
>
> and fulminates it at times
>
> and it is left gasping like a drought-stricken fish.]

One year after publishing this poem, she self-reflectively observes in her 2009 poetics: "Al leerlo ahora tengo la certeza —si es que, en lo que respecta a la poesía, cualquier certeza exegética es posible— de que intenta hablar acerca de la materia poética, del barro con el que se crean los poemas, del plancton que los alimenta" ("Lo no reconocible," 13–14). [Now as I read it, I am certain—if, with respect to poetry, any interpretive certainty is possible—that it intends to speak about the poetic material, the clay with which poems are created, the plankton that nourishes them].

Ada Salas is unique in her ability to probe and disclose the multiple facets of "el objeto lingüístico-poema" [the linguistic-poem object] that, as she posits, "nació plegado" (*El margen,* 20) [is born folded]. In conceptualizing a poem in this way, she illustrates central features applicable to both the metapoetic text under examination and this poet's role in the writing process. She observes in her book:

> Un poema, entonces, puede ser un "objeto lingüístico" comprimido, doblado sobre sí, como si el largo hilo de un discurso hubiera sido presionado desde sus extremos hacia el centro, a la manera de un acordeón. [. . .] El poeta no trabaja así [. . .], es absolutamente imposible desenredar el hilo, desplegar el acordeón, porque el objeto lingüístico-poema "nació" plegado. Y sin embargo los pliegues existen, existen metáforas, sentido 'condensado,' por eso es honda, inagotable y rica la "oferta de lectura" (las posibilidades de lectura) de un poema. (*El margen,* 20–21)

> [A poem, then, can be a compressed "linguistic object," folded over on itself, as if the long thread of discourse had been pressed from one of its ends toward the center, in the manner of an accordion. (. . .) The poet does not work that way (. . .), it is impossible to unravel the thread, to unfold the accordion, because the linguistic-object poem "is born" folded. And nonetheless, the folds exist, metaphors exist; "condensed" meaning, therefore, the "offer of reading" (the possibilities of reading), is profound, endless, and rich.]

In both her 2008 poem and her 2010 observations just cited, the word "pliegue" points to the exactness of diction in the work of Ada Salas. This word has extraordinary "secret" potential upon examination. When considering the figurative use of "pliegue" within the context of the metaphoric accordion, this fold, this crease, this pleat conceals sonorous access up until the act of unfolding takes place. For Salas, this occurs when overlapping concepts individually make themselves known during the process of the creative act. The precision of this image features another "secret" recessed within the word "pliegue," a secret unfolding that is not noticed but that, nevertheless, "dwells in the real." When considered in its geological sense, as Salas also employs "pliegue" in this poem, it metaphorically leads to the process of rock formation undergoing compressional stress in time, "lo hendido en la hendidura / de la roca" [the buried in the crack / of the rock]. Here, Salas articulates "lo nunca / pronunciado" [the not ever / pronounced] in a poem that is a stellar metapoetic epiphany.

"Lo que duerme en lo pliegues lo no" divulges moments of profound self-knowledge of the poet engaged in the creative process. In Salas's view, poetry is an "indagación extática entre las palabras: el de 'lo no reconocible / que vive en lo real'" [ecstatic inquiry among the words: that of "the not recognizable / that dwells in the real"]. For Salas, writing is a process leading to discovery: "A través de la hendidura dejar que se descubra lo que está en la hendidura: un lenguaje que vive debajo del lenguaje [. . .] un lenguaje que en verdad nombra" ("Lo no reconocible," 14, 15) [Through the crack what is in the crack is discovered: a language living beneath the language (. . .) a language that in truth names]. This poem displays the act of excavating the word and its potential to reveal what is first unknown and then becomes illuminated during the writing process:

> Lo que duerme en lo los pliegues lo no
> visto no oído lo nunca
> pronunciado
> lo hundido en la hendidura
> de la roca
> el punto donde empieza
> silencioso incendio. . . . (*Esto no es el silencio*, 34)

> [What sleeps in the folds the not
> seen not heard not ever
> pronounced
> buried in the crack
> of the rock
> the point where silently
> the blaze begins. . . .]

In both the 2009 poetics and the 2008 poem, Salas probes the "secret" of the word in order to manifest what lies "beneath" it (Huidobro) and "behind" it (Rilke) as she attempts to comprehend the essence of verbal expression anticipating its own awakening during the realization of the poem ("Lo no reconocible," 15, 16).[19]

Her 2009 poetics is especially noteworthy for other central reasons in Salas's trajectory. Here, she unveils metaphoric constructs that are intertextually integral to the entirety of her work. This is evident when the poet explains facets of the diction of her poetry and her poetics:

> Palabras como "margen," "error," "tachadura." Todas tienen que ver con lo que está pero no está, con lo que "esconde" algo que parece no estar pero que también es real pero, como ocurre con la fusca que se oculta en un pliegue, invisible, no tiene presencia hasta que la realidad se despliega, hasta que se lee lo que estaba escrito o dibujado bajo la tachadura, hasta que aflora, por una "hendidura" lo que está bajo "la superficie del lenguaje ordinario." Cito estos versos del poema de Anne Carson "Ensayo sobre aquello en lo que más pienso," extraña y magnífica divagación sobre el concepto aristotélico de la "metáfora":
>
> Él[20] se imagina la mente moviéndose sobre una superficie
> plana
> de lenguaje ordinario
> cuando de pronto
> esta superficie se rompe o se complica.
> Lo inesperado emerge. ("Lo no reconocible," 15–16)
>
> [Words such as "margin," "error," "crossing-out." These all pertain to what is there but not there, what "hides" something that seems not to be there but also is real, but just like what happens with something obscure hidden in a fold, invisible, it has no presence until reality unfolds, until reading what was written or drawn beneath the crossing-out, until what is beneath "the surface of ordinary language" emerges through a crack. I quote these lines from the Anne Carson poem "Essay on What I Think About Most," a surprising and magnificent digression on the Aristotelian concept of "metaphor":

He pictures the mind moving along a plane surface
of ordinary language
when suddenly
that surface breaks or complicates.
Unexpectedness emerges]

Pondering the expressive capacity of metaphor in this poetics, Salas draws on the fine translation into Spanish of a portion of Anne Carson's 2000 poem "Essay on What I Think About Most," as rendered by fellow poet Jordi Doce, published in 2007. It is Carson's poem that begins to set in motion Salas's own investigation of metaphor first in this 2009 poetics and then, importantly, one year later in her 2010 book. In addition, Carson's clever title of her own poem subtly suggests the same subject matter and figurative trope about which Ada Salas also "thinks about most." This poem by Anne Carson is a fundamental point of departure and a structural device that Salas begins to develop in her 2009 poetics. One year later, it evolves more fully and in more detail in her elucidating study of the metamorphosis of metaphor in her 2010 book.

In Salas's view, "lo no reconocible que vive en lo real" always is on display. Often, however, it goes unnoticed because it is not attentively "recognized." For Salas, ordinary natural objects incarnate unique opportunities for recognizing what previously had been "not recognizable." The poem beginning "Es una piedra y mira" [It is a rock and it watches] is an instructive example (*No duerme el animal*, 207). The poem originally appeared in *Lugar de la derrota* published in 2003. This poem explicates time as "passage," from the ingenious perspective of a wise and aged "rock." This metaphoric "twist" in point of view permits an unusual witness to concentrate on its activity of being in a natural landscape and on observing what is taking place. Salas further endows her personified poetic protagonist with the capacity both to visualize the invisible and to hear the muted presence of the essence of natural change in time, "el tránsito ligero" [the subtle passing]. Each of its immediate companions, "nubes" [clouds], "ramas" [branches], "pájaro" [bird], exhibits the ephemeral. Only the vigilant personified rock, however, comprehends what is transitory. Although this inanimate natural object might appear to embody longevity and endurance, Salas's knowledgeable protagonist discloses that permanence is but a ruse when witnessing the ever-changing presence of time.

The poem also exhibits another important aspect of Salas's poetics, one she articulates as early as 1998: "Escribir es escuchar." [To write is to listen.] She explains that in her poetry, "hay un diálogo hondo —un diálogo que es en realidad monólogo— con una presencia que yo intuía en mí. Una presencia que guardaba el secreto de la palabra" (*Ellas tienen la palabra*, 582) [there is a profound dialogue—a dialogue that really is a monologue—with a presence that I intuit in me. A presence that has kept the secret of the word]. One decade later, her 2009 poetics further would illuminate this prevalent feature in her work: "Así ante la página en blanco, ante el vacío de las palabras. Escribir no hablando, escuchando. Escuchando 'lo no reconocible que vive en lo real.' Absolutamente hermoso, y digno, y extraño, y vivo, y tembloroso" ("Lo no reconocible," 22). [Thus in front of the white page, in front of the blank page without words. To write not speaking, listening. Listening to "the not recognizable that dwells in the real." Absolutely beautiful and dignified and strange and alive and quivering.]

The selection of "una piedra" [a rock] as a lead character in this poem may seem to be odd at first. In Salas's poetry, however, it demonstrates a personal response to her own "autobiographical attraction" to "las cosas mudas y quietas" [silent and still things] that she often underscores in her work. She also indicates that elements such as "la luz, la piedra, el desierto, las ruinas" [the light, the rock, the desert, the ruins] reoccur in her poems because "el poema acaba siendo en parte una expresión de quien lo escribe" [the poem ultimately is, in part, an expression of who writes it]. Salas further observes in her 2009 poetics:

> Quietas están (¿son?) las piedras. Mineral = Muerto. Muerto = callado. Por supuesto, mineral = insensible. [. . .] Y sin embargo experimento siempre una honda afinidad (comunicación, diría) con ellas, con las piedras. Por su carácter duradero se me antoja que han escuchado y han guardado memoria de todo lo supuestamente vivo, y por lo tanto efímero: animales, plantas, hombres. Memoria: vida. Memoria: sabiduría. Una sabiduría estoica la suya me parece: ancianas (no ancianas "humanizadas," ancianas minerales) llenas de vigor dispuestas a contar, largas e incansables narradoras que han pensado y repensado el mundo, que lo han inventado, quizá. ("Lo no reconocible," 17, 18)
>
> [Rocks stay (are) still. Mineral = Dead. Dead = silent. Of course, mineral = unfeeling. (. . .) However, I always experience a deep affinity (communication, I would say) with them, with the rocks. In my opinion, due to their lasting nature, they have listened to and kept the memory of all that supposedly is alive and thus ephemeral: animals, plants, humans. Memory: life. Memory: wisdom. Theirs is a stoic wisdom it seems to me: old rocks (not "humanly" old, aged minerals), full of energy ready to share long and endless tales as the storytellers who have thought about and reflected on the world, and their invention of it, perhaps.]

This inquiry leads to epiphanic discovery in the poetry and poetics of Ada Salas: "Lo que se hace con las palabras se hace con aquello que designa. Al trabajar con las palabras el poeta trabaja *con el mundo*. [. . .] El poema nos hace ver lo visto, lo vivido, como si fuera nuevo [. . .] aun habiéndolo experimentado, no lo habíamos *conocido*. Ése es el verdadero poder de la imaginación creadora" (*El margen*, 55).

[What you do with words you do with that which designates. When working with words, the poet works *with the world.* (. . .) The poem makes us see the seen, the lived, as if it were new (. . .) even though we have experienced it, we have not *known* it. That is the real power of the creative imagination].

LISTENING

Salas's recent poetry discloses the alluring presence of everyday objects that reveal interconnected conversations to which she must be attentive. This is evident in one of her remarkable poems from *Esto no es el silencio* (25) when she writes:

> Yo sé que tienes algo que decirme
> mundo. Voy a limpiarlo todo para que todo
> sea
> aún más transparente
> y pueda oír aquello que murmuras
> sin esfuerzo y sin miedo.
> Ya puedes acercarte hasta mi oído.
>
> [I know that you have something to tell me
> world. I am going to clean up everything so that everything
> might be
> even more transparent
> and I might be able to listen to your whispers
> without effort and without fear.
> Now you can come closer to my ear.]

For Salas, ordinary things both manifest and realize their extraordinary communicative capacity. This poem divulges the fundamental activity of the poet as well as the indispensable attitude that Salas develops throughout her own creative trajectory: listening attentively. When commonplace objects figuratively speak, it is incumbent on this poet to listen because quotidian conversations always present opportunities for discovery.

She makes this clear in the superlative poem beginning with the heptasyllabic line "Solidez de esta jarra" (*Esto no es el silencio,* 31) [This solid pitcher]. The poet first presents a visualization from the unexpected specular perspective of a poetic observer possessing a heightened sense of perception. With almost photographic clarity and precision, this observer inspects, as if in a close-up, the details of specific domestic objects. For Salas, "la lengua es un ojo" (*El margen,* 118) [the tongue is an eye]. The opening section of this poem displays how and why:

Solidez de esta jarra
piel
erizada del kiwi
larguísimas tijeras
más humanas
que esta mano que escribe.

[This solid pitcher
prickly
skin of the kiwi
very long scissors
more human
than this hand that writes.]

In this poem, she not only gives voice to the objects composing her metaphoric "extraño bodegón" [strange still life] but also, she attends to the auditory essence of "la vida interior" ("Lo no reconocible," 19) [the inner life] emanating from the commonplace things she linguistically depicts:

Yo escucho desde un centro más lejos que mis ojos
vuestro limpio discurso.
Sé cómo resonáis.
Cómo hacéis del silencio un débil fondo
plano

apenas perceptible.

[I listen from a center further than my eyes
to your crisp discourse.
I know how you resonate.
How you create a faint backdrop of silence
smooth

only just perceptible.]

The closing section of the poem discloses the poetic speaker eavesdropping on the (un)usual conversations occurring among daily objects. Visual and auditory perceptions coalesce in the transformative moment of imaging the imaginary in this "extraño bodegón." Keen awareness of the everyday reveals the untold potential of ordinary objects. Even the commonplace "scissors," like the hand engaging in the familiar activity of writing the poem, presents its own capacity to "open" the scene depicted and delineate "the not recognizable that dwells in the real."

Being ever alert to what occurs in the everyday contributes to both the subject matter and the attitude underlying much of the recent poetry and poetics of Ada Salas. In her exemplary "Solidez de esta jarra," she learns that unremarkable day-to-day objects often afford unique occasions for acute observation. This, in turn, might frequently result in extraordinary epiphanic encounters with what "dwells in the real." In this poem, an improbable scene emerges when the poetic voice scrutinizes the vital constituents of the specular and acoustic aspects of the "strange still life" under scrutiny. The unexpected metaphor "piel erizada del kiwi" [prickly skin of the kiwi] serves as a noteworthy example of the metamorphosis of language in the hands of Ada Salas. Highlighting the visual, the tactile, and the gustatory, the poet de-contextualizes this fruit in such a way that the tiny hair-like fuzz on its skin figuratively becomes something else—a sheath of stiff fibers encasing a stubbly and now seemingly inedible oddity. Such a peculiar object contributes to the imaged and imaginary poem canvas. Here, Salas creates her "strange still life" of which the (un)familiar kiwi forms merely one part. This poem embodies the essence of metaphor in her poetry. In her 2010 book, she reveals that metaphor does not mask one object with another, but rather it leads to that object. She explains this process, "Nos conduce al original ofreciéndonos una faceta de él que *está en él*. Cuando el poeta nos la hace ver nos ofrece el objeto acrecentado en su realidad: lo comprendemos más intensamente, más *realmente*. [. . .] Como he dicho en otro lugar (no recuerdo dónde) 'la poesía no se aleja de la realidad, sino que se dirige a ella con ansia de filo, le busca la entraña para evidenciarla'" (*El margen*, 85–86). [It leads us to the original, offering us a facet of it that *is in it*. When the poet makes us see it, the poet offers us the object heightened: we understand it more intensely, more *genuinely*. (. . .) As I have said in another place (I do not remember where), "poetry doesn't distance itself from reality, but rather it heads toward it with sharpened eagerness, seeking its inner essence in order to reveal it."]

The poetic "bodegón" she depicts in "Solidez de esta jarra," conveys an unusual space where the objects that first appeal to the sense of sight also soon manifest an auditory charm. These perceptual perspectives not only modify reality in Salas's poem but also, and importantly, first juxtapose and then fuse the senses of sight and sound emanating from the scene and the dynamic conversational exchange she records. In her 2009 poetics, Salas offers insight into how this poem came about, "El día en que lo escribí, unos objetos agrupados al azar sobre la mesa: unas tijeras, una jarra, un kiwi. Al leerlo mucho después he pensado que este texto es una especie de homenaje a un género pictórico que me atrae particularmente: el de las 'Naturalezas muertas.' Cerámica, cristal, barro, pan, frutas, vino, agua . . . cosas 'mudas y quietas'" ("Lo no reconocible," 19).

[The day I wrote it, a few objects grouped by chance on the table: a scissors, a pitcher, a kiwi. Upon reading it afterward, I thought that this text is a type of homage to the pictorial genre that particularly attracts me: that of the "Still life." Pottery, glass, clay, bread, fruit, wine, water . . . "silent and still" things].

The acoustic conversations among such domestic objects disclose that these ordinary "things" *still* have life and *still* express their own vitality when they undergo metaphoric metamorphosis. The skin of a kiwi fruit and other habitual household items, such as a pitcher and scissors, objects that, at times, hardly merit a glance, do often escape notice. For Salas, intensely focused inspection together with an acute sense of hearing are necessary for perceiving the unique inner essence that is ever-present in elements of the everyday. The underlying imperative of this illustrative poem conveys the foundation of the creative act in her work.

FISSURE

The publication of her poetics titled "Brechas" [Openings] in 2010 establishes an illuminating interaction between her poetry and the visual arts. Salas's own pursuit of the "secret" of the word activates a thought-provoking and inventive dialogue between her poetry and the paintings of the modern Argentine-Italian artist and sculptor, Lucio Fontana. "Brechas" is a remarkable and original presentation of the conceptual foundations of her poetry. These entail Salas's ardent desire to divulge the essence of the word, her relentless inspection of the real, and the subsequent revelation of what, perhaps, previously might have escaped notice. By engaging in a compelling and inspiring exchange of ideas with Fontana's canvases, "Brechas" portrays Salas's attentive vigilance to the creative act as a mode of discovery. She explains, "Entiendo la poesía y la pintura no como una visión que se superpone a lo real, sino como una *brecha que se abre en lo real*, por la que, tal vez, *pasar al otro lado*"[21] ("Brechas," 87). [I understand poetry and painting not as a view superimposed on the real but rather as an *opening into the real*, so as, perhaps, to *pass through to the other side*.]

Why Lucio Fontana? This artist (1899–1968) used a variety of mediums and methods in his paintings and sculptural works. As a renowned painter, he "attempted to transcend the confines of the two-dimensional surface" when in his "*buchi* (holes) cycle, begun in 1949, he punctured the surface of his canvases, breaking the membrane of two-dimensionality in order to highlight the space behind the picture," as Jennifer Blessing of the Solomon R. Guggenheim Museum observes.[22] His works, both paintings and sculptures, are gathered under the title *Concetto spaziale*, or *Spatial Concept*. She further indicates, "Paintings such as *Concetto spaziale, Attese* (*Spatial concept, waiting*, 1959)" present what this artist refers to as "*tagli*" where "violent jags enforce the idea that the painting is an object, not solely a surface" ("Lucio Fontana *Concetto spaziale, Attese*," n.p.). These forceful slits in the canvas serve to place Fontana's gestural aesthetic at the core of Salas's own razor-sharp penetrations into the word and her efforts to be ever attentive to what lies beneath, beyond, within the expressivity of her art. Salas refers directly to the works of Fontana indicating the following:

> Lienzos perforados para crear otra realidad, sobre, encima, a través del lienzo, en una proyección metapictórica: el lienzo plano como destrucción de esa lectura de lo real que construye otra nueva. Destrucción que construye. [. . .] A "este otro lado" quería, quizá, acceder Fontana, multiplicando el espacio en un gesto de rebelión activa contra una lectura unívoca. [. . .] Fontana. Cuadros agujereados. Agresiones, heridas, brechas. Lienzos rasgados: poemas. No todo está aquí, desde donde miramos. ("Brechas," 89–90)
>
> [Punctured canvases to create another reality, on, on top of, through, in a designed metapainting, the flat canvas as a destruction of that reading of the real to construct another new one. Destruction that constructs. (. . .) On "this other side," Fontana wanted, perhaps, to access a multiple space in a gesture of active rebellion against an unequivocal reading. (. . .) Fontana. Pierced paintings. Attacks, wounds, openings. Slashed canvases, poems. Not everything is here, from where we look.]

With this striking analogy, Ada Salas "opens" the word, the poem, and the writing of the poem. She breaks through, as it were, to the vital expressivity for which she, as a poet, longs. In both of her outstanding poetics from 2009 and 2010, Salas approaches her own work from the enlightening perspective of the visual artist. This enriching viewpoint will augment her meticulous portrayal of the experience of writing with words and her excavation into the hidden potential dwelling within the word itself. The reader, in turn, will gain fresh insights into Salas's poetry and poetics. The viewer of Fontana's highly experimental *Concetto spaziale* enters an imaged frontier inviting access to a newly created space and time. This is a conceptual dimension where the viewer interrogates the artwork asking what lies behind the canvas and/or what lies deep within the sculpted object. Fontana's spectator, thus, must engage in active inquiry concerning what lies in front of, behind, and within the artwork. Salas invites her reader to participate in a similar inquisition. Her poetry and poetics, in this way, become unique opportunities for scrutinizing the word in order to inspect, with the same meticulous attention that she herself demonstrates in her own work, the imaged layers in metaphoric language. Salas, like Fontana, seeks to penetrate the essence of truly transformative expression defying a single, unequivocal act of interpretation. Her original contribution to the Spanish lyric of today stems from the activity of this exceptional poet to be readily observant to the revelatory, intrinsic, and epistemic "brechas" in language.

It is in her 2009 poetics where Ada Salas introduces her metaphoric construct of "fissure," affirming: "Y me asalta 'fractura'" ("Lo no reconocible," 15). [And "fissure" attacks me.] One year later, this concept would take on further significance in her probing analysis of both Fontana's work and her own. "Fissure" is a transformative process in Salas's poetry. It becomes her unique metaphoric method for identifying and explicating her own concentrated effort to be fully attentive to the innermost essence of the word.

Salas examines closely in her 2009 "Lo no reconocible que vive en lo real" a few exemplary selections from her work. Self-reflectively, the poet reviews her past and present activity of detecting and revealing the "secret" of the word during the creative process. She explicates,

> "Fractura," "hendidura," "hueco": lugares (tiempo) donde "sucede" el poema; un tiempo y un lugar de suspensión y de apertura. [. . .] Insisto en que "la fractura" se produce de un modo natural, como cuando se abre la corteza de la tierra.
>
> No abrir, estar atenta a la apertura.
> No formar. Prestarse a que la forma se haga forma.
> Y que, entonces, tenga lugar la escritura, el poema. ("Lo no reconocible," 15)
>
> ["Fissure," "crack," "gap": places (time) where the poem "happens"; a suspended time and place an aperture (. . .); I reiterate "the fissure" comes about in a natural way, like when the earth's crust opens.
>
> Do not open, be attentive to the opening.
> Do not form. Allow the form to take shape.
> Then, writing might take place, the poem.]

In her work, "fissure" becomes her optimal metaphoric strategy for facilitating access to the underlying essence of the word: "su querer decirse" [its desire to speak] ("El deseo es lo mudo," 40). Salas's 2010 "Brechas," with its revelatory title, advances her efforts to break through to an intensely concentrated examination of the realization of poetic expression during composition. This attentive creative activity allows her to penetrate and expose "the not recognizable that dwells in the real." All three of these poetics underscore exciting epistemic methods for her conscientious inspection and explication concerning the unobservable she soon will bring to light. The ingenious dialogue in which she engages with the art works of Fontana is one way in which Salas richly enhances her thematic matter of "the not recognizable that dwells in the real." At the same time, this interchange of ideas, visual as well as poetic, presents her works in a stunning new way. Most especially, her 2009 and 2010 companion poetics foster unique access to a wealth of excitingly fresh understandings of the creative and liberated expressivity that both Salas and Fontana creatively seek.

THE SEED

Ada Salas's poem beginning "En la almendra"[23] (*Limbo*, 81) [In the almond] serves as a splendid example of the interactive dialogue taking place when the precisely formed poem and a molded sculptural artwork interconnect as transformative interpretive events. Specifically, this poem suggests a stunning series of large sculpted spheres created by Lucio Fontana as part of his *Concetto spaziale, natura* (1959–1960) works. These shaped objects begin as large terra cotta forms that were later cast in bronze.[24] Fontana's *Natura* sculptures are visual metaphors where holes, perforations, incisions, made by a wooden implement into the formed clay, appear "to reach deep into the interior of the sphere."[25] The natural sculptures in this series resemble huge fruits where variously shaped and intriguing apertures metaphorically incarnate the possibilities emanating from the creative act. By opening these spherical sculptures, Fontana beckons entry into the innermost essence of these forms.

Art historian, curator, and museum director Jan van der Marck observes that in 1959 Fontana "found yet another implementation of his spatial concept, the intentional laceration. It appeared first in fired clay sculpture, then in the surfaces of lushly painted pictures. The effect is most dramatic in the *Nature* series, bronzes cast in elementary spherical forms that appear to have been ripped open by earth forces. They allude to processes of gestation and birth."[26] Art historian Sarah Whitfield further remarks, "the roundness of the large terracotta spheres of 1959" are like "vast seeds splitting open, ready to propagate."[27] Ada Salas's "En la almendra" re-presents the confluence of these sculptural and pictorial enactments in an exemplary poem. Through her analytic construct of "fissure," rendered figuratively in the lines, "Hendir en la dureza / de su cáscara" [Split open the hard / shell], Salas conveys her attentive and ongoing quest to expose the essence of the word and to allow for its own self-expression. Like Fontana, Salas too rejects the limitations of established formulas and timeworn manifestations in art and in poetry. Instead, she innovatively approaches language, "la materia poética, del barro con el que se crean los poemas" ("Lo no reconocible," 13–14) [the poetic material, the clay with which poems are created], in adroitly formed and convincingly imaginative ways. Van der Marck maintains that Fontana "considers his works not as objects to be treasured but rather as provisional results of a continuing search" ("Lucio Fontana," 39). The same is true for Salas's 2013 poem and for her poetry and poetics, in general. The figurative propagation of new ideas, new perceptions, and new interpretations originating in the seemingly simple "almond" in this poem lead to poetry as epiphany when her metaphoric transformations engage in lucid dialogues with modern sculpture.

In one sense, "En la almendra" activates the transmission of an indispensable description of the poetic process in Salas's lyric. At the same time, this poet presents a distinctive metapoetic text reflecting and revealing the activity of writing: "atender a su apertura; entonces, la 'semilla' del poema" ("Lo no reconocible," 17) [attend to its aperture; then, the "seed" of the poem]. Here too, Salas continues the conversation with the visual arts that earlier she initiated in both her 2009 and 2010 poetics.[28] At the outset of her "En la almendra," however, she gives a pointedly temporal dimension to the creative act and the essential word: "En la almendra / del tiempo" [In the almond / of time]. At first, writing appears to be an activity disclosing a relatively conventional perspective concerning the structure of time: "la sucesión" [the sequence], "el orden" [the order], "el ahora" [the now], "después" [after], "más adelante" [later]. Nevertheless, such clocklike precision does not expose the vital nature of either writing or time. Rather, the poet must heed the figurative imperatives guiding the quest for the potential of the word and the genesis of the poem:

> . . . Hendir en la dureza
> de su cáscara
> Desbaratar
> la sucesión.
> . . . Entrar
> en la semilla. Pisar en el vacío
> verdadero. En la región
> del no.
>
> [. . . Split open the hard
> shell. Disrupt
> the sequence.
> . . . Enter
> into the seed. Step onto real
> nothingness. Into the region
> of the no.]

By following these directives, Salas discloses the fundamental mandate inherent in her conception of the creative activity in which she engages: "Escribir *como voluntad*" ("Brechas," 88) [Write *with will*]. This poem is an example of the conceptual concision and impeccable artistry she exhibits in her work throughout her creative trajectory. "En la almendra," however, also is as unique as it is exemplary in that in a mere thirty-six words Salas both condenses and portrays the linguistic exactness characteristic of her meticulous diction. She masterfully compresses the nature of time into a single metaphoric instant engendering the word.

"En la almendra" exemplifies the epistemic and epiphanic quality of the poetry and the poetics of Ada Salas. Here, she positions herself to be mindful of divulging "the not recognizable that dwells in the real." This poem, thus, further underscores one of the most significant themes in her poetry and poetics. Furthermore, "En la almendra" is a compendium of all the themes of the poetry of Ada Salas examined in the present chapter. In addition, this work significantly intertwines the exchange of ideas occurring between her 2009 and 2010 poetics, as well as among all her ars poetica when considered as an organic whole. On the one hand, this poem presents an almost botanical examination of the fruit of the almond tree. At the same time, however, it also concerns a fundamental imperative that both the author and the reader must follow in order to be attentive to the "internal movement" of language during the experience of metaphoric metamorphosis ("Lo no reconocible," 15). Finally, and most especially when revisualized and reconceptualized considering Lucio Fontana's magnificent *Natura* sculptures, this poem exhibits, in surprisingly fresh and extraordinary ways, the birth of the self-expression of language during the process of writing in the works of Ada Salas.

THE SPECIAL OBSERVER

The lyric of Ada Salas demonstrates layer after layer of intriguing deposits of meaningful cognitive matter that she mines and exposes during the writing process. Her metaphoric construct of "fissure" discloses her most advantageous stratagem for discovery during the creative act: "Insisto en que 'la fractura' se produce de un modo natural, como cuando se abre la corteza de la tierra. No abrir, estar atenta a la apertura" ("Lo no reconocible," 15). [I reiterate "the fissure" comes about in a natural way, like when the earth's crust opens. Do not open, be attentive to the opening]. In her exemplary 2010 book, Salas adds another feature to the analytic of "fissure" and the insights that she provides there sustain the intertextual exchange characteristic of her poetry and poetics. She explains,

> La poesía surge de la ruptura de lo rígido. Está en el agua que aflora cuando se quiebra la superficie del hielo. Está en el agua bajo el hielo: no la vemos. El poeta rompe el hielo para verla. O lo traspasa. O ve el hielo y ve el agua. O ve en el hielo

el agua, quizá por algo tan simple como que el hielo es una forma del agua, es originariamente agua, pero lo hemos olvidado, dejándonos llevar por su apariencia dura, blanca. [. . .] Supimos que era agua, pero lo hemos olvidado. El poeta nombra el agua y se produce la revelación: despierta lo que una vez supimos. Todo poema es "metáfora" en este sentido, y no es preciso que contenga siquiera una sola de lo que la retórica nos enseña que es "metáfora." Un poema, como una metáfora, no es necesariamente ambiguo, ni polisémico, sino fusionador, integrador. Nos lleva a la vez a lo aparente y a lo esencialmente real, contiene ambas entidades, como la última onda del círculo concéntrico sobre el agua lleva en sí el primero que generó el impacto de la piedra; lleva, incluso, a la piedra misma. (*El margen*, 135)

[Poetry emerges from a break in what is rigid. It is in the water that appears when the surface of the ice splits. It is the water beneath the ice; we do not see it. The poet breaks the ice to see it. Or penetrates it. Or sees the ice and sees the water. Or sees in the ice the water, perhaps because something as simple as ice is a form of water; it originally is water, but we have forgotten it, letting ourselves be carried away by its solid, white appearance. (. . .) We knew it was water, but we have forgotten. The poet names water and a revelation takes place, awakening what we once knew. Every poem is a "metaphor" in this sense, and it is not essential that it includes even one "metaphor" about which rhetoric has taught us. A poem, like a metaphor, is not necessarily ambiguous, nor polysemic, but melded, integrated. At once it leads us to the apparent and to the essentially real, it includes both, just like the very last ripple in the series of concentric circles on the surface of the water leads to the very first created by the impact of the stone; it even leads to the stone itself.]

This passage captures the essence of Salas's poetry and poetics, and the most salient themes of her current work as the present chapter illustrates. These same observations disclose the fundamental premise of her poetic enterprise: "La escritura exige un estado de alerta, una conciencia despierta . . ." (*El margen*, 108). [Writing demands a state of alertness, an awakened awareness. . . .] As a poet, Salas elects to "see" the objects in her surroundings in new ways. This she achieves by honing her unique skill of intense inspection, especially during her continuing inquiry into "the not recognizable that dwells in the real." Her sense of visual perception is keen. As a poet, thus, Salas observes objects by scrutinizing them, their details, facets, outlines, volume, color, shape, texture, and so on. She is, indeed, a "very special observer" who has practiced the art of conscientious examination. This "art" has become a distinguishing technique that she perfects throughout her creative trajectory. Salas notes, "Es un observador muy especial, pues, el poeta. Se fija en cosas, toma nota de ellas, y crea un objeto artístico a partir de esa experiencia de percepción de la realidad con la materia común a todos —y tan compleja, sin embargo— de las palabras" (*El margen*, 121). [The poet is, then, a very special observer. Focusing on things, taking note of them, and creating an artistic object from that perceptual experience of reality with the common—and yet very complex—matter of words]. She herself identifies special characteristics of this "observer" explaining the following:

> Estamos más bien ante un trabajador atento, atentísimo, casi un notario extremo de lo real que, por añadidura, ha de esforzarse en mantener su ¿espíritu? (su lenguaje) limpio de la sedimentación del tiempo, de lo vivido, de lo que se nos ha enseñado y/o impuesto; que ha de desconfiar de lo que ve para ver realmente; que debe permanecer en entrenamiento constante para el asombro. (*El margen*, 125)

> [We have before us a rather attentive worker, most attentive, almost the ultimate notary of the real who, in addition, must endeavor to maintain the essence (language) of poetry as free of the sedimentation of time, of experience, of what we have been taught and/or what has been forced on us; the poet must doubt seeing so as actually to see; the poet should constantly prepare for astonishment.]

Salas fully understands that people often overlook "things" in their surroundings because they are distracted or inattentive. The poet, however, does otherwise: "Percibirá el milagro en lo cotidiano, verá lo que solo miramos, tocará lo que tocamos sin tocar, escuchará lo que, aparentemente, no se capta con el oído. No porque esas cosas formen parte de lo 'maravilloso,' sino porque 'lo maravilloso' [. . .] forma parte de lo real: es lo real. Un poeta no es ningún tipo de 'superhombre,' como se desprendía de algunos textos románticos; es, simplemente, un hombre que escribe, como un panadero hace pan, y escribir implica un compromiso [. . .] con lo real" (*El margen*, 107–108). [(The poet) will perceive the miracle in the everyday; will see what we only look at; will touch what we touch but without really touching it; will listen to what, apparently, our hearing does not record, not because those things pertain to "the marvelous," but rather because "the marvelous" forms part of the real; it is the real. A poet is in no way a kind of "super person," as some romantic texts have noted; a poet is, simply, a human being who writes, like a baker makes bread, and writing implies a commitment (. . .) to the real.]

SEEING

Ada Salas possesses and exhibits an astounding sense of perception. This is evident when, as a poet, she responds to sensory stimuli and interprets them in original and masterful ways. Salas demonstrates a heightened sense of sight, which permits an astute examination of the many different features of "the not recognizable that dwells in the real." Hers is an incisive inspection where, as a poet, she adheres to one of the most significant imperatives underlying both her poetry and her poetics: "*ver* con los primeros ojos" [*see* for the first time]. This "visión limpia" [clear vision] permits access to new discoveries because, as Salas maintains, "vivir, ver, como se ve y se vive lo que no ha sido conocido nunca: anular el tiempo, traicionarlo. Trabajar la mirada" (*El margen,* 124) [live, see, as though what is seen and what is lived never before have been known: annul time, fool it. Work on looking].

"Seeing" for Salas is a way in which to detain the flow of time so that she can study carefully the object under scrutiny. Never in a hurry, never thwarted by progression in time, Salas often pauses to see anew. This is particularly apparent in two recent collections of her poetry when she collaborates with the Spanish painter, graphic artist, and architect Jesús Placencia. In *Ashes to Ashes: Catorce poemas a partir de catorce dibujos a partir de T. S. Eliot* [*Ashes to Ashes: Fourteen Poems Emanating from Fourteen Drawings Emanating from T. S. Eliot*], published in 2010, and *Diez mandamientos* [*Ten Commandments*], published in 2016, Salas engages her poetry in an interactive synesthetic visual dialogue with the artworks of one of her contemporaries. In both collections, Salas employs a fresh sense of sight by fully comprehending, "No todo está aquí, desde donde miramos" ("Brechas," 90). [Not everything is here, from where we look.]

Placencia began to develop an innovative approach to his graphic illustrations in 2009. He created what he refers to as "Dibujos escritos" [Written Drawings]. These were more than experiments with new techniques in rendering black and white works using charcoal, crayon, pencil, and erasures. Placencia was initiating a new genre in Spanish graphic art, one that persists today in his ingenious contributions. By utilizing exclusively "writing as a graphic form," he was experimenting with new inventive expressive possibilities. His compositions are original verbal visualizations of "writing and erasing without 'drawing,'" and this is evident in his first series in this new genre, *Time* (2009). These depictions consist of fourteen works (each 20 x 20 cm) originating from his close reading of the *Four Quartets* by T. S. Eliot, a work that always had captivated him. He translated these poems into Spanish where his newly conceived "Written Drawings" displayed aspects of the *Four Quartets.* The results are a stunning combination of rendering themes, concepts, and wording as articulated by both Eliot and this Spanish graphic artist.[29] Placencia invited Salas to accompany each of his fourteen graphic presentations with a poem. The results are not reactions to Placencia's graphic forms but rather Salas's poems prove to be novel opportunities for her to render in poetry what she "sees" with new eyes as if "for the first time." It is critical to understand that Salas's poems are not restatements of Placencia's "Written Drawings." What is of utmost importance is that Salas "sees" in them catalysts for her own writing. Her poems, however, offer her more than this. She explains this added bonus in this way: "Escribir 'sobre' el trabajo de otro (de otros, Eliot, siempre, al fondo) me proporciona una libertad que me exonera de una responsabilidad, a veces paralizante. La escritura, entonces, como en este caso, es puro, profundísimo placer" (*Ashes to Ashes*). [Writing "about" the work of others (among them, Eliot, always in the background) gives me a freedom that exempts me from a responsibility, at times, paralyzing. Writing then, as in this case, is purely a very profound pleasure.]

The year 2016 signals a significant year in the creative trajectories of both Placencia and Salas. It marks the publication of his graphic artworks and her poetry in the intriguing and illuminating intertextual dialogue occurring in *Diez mandamientos*. This collection highlights writing as an epistemic process of discovery by featuring ten astonishing "Written Drawings" by Placencia and ten superlative poems by Salas. Always inspired by visual artworks, the poet assimilates aspects of these as unique points of entry for expanding her own poetics. Placencia's works provide Salas with a unique opportunity to ponder her own creative activity not as an extension of his work but rather as poetry written in conversation with graphic art. This collection also manifests additional "openings" through which Salas positions herself to access the activity and the results of writing, both hers and his, as a means for attentively bearing witness to "ten commandments" that are necessary for both artistic creativity and human existence.[30]

Before discussing any of Salas's exemplary poems, Placencia's outstanding artworks deserve special consideration. In his *Diez mandamientos,* each work is unique and offers imaginative innovations in aspects of graphic design. When inspected closely, and with the aid of a magnifying glass, in each of his ten works (20 x 20 cm), Placencia inscribes and erases, with painstaking detail, minute letters as writing assumes a plastic form in formulating the titles of each work. Innately visual and highly original, his compositions are intricate, and they reveal an almost miniscule assemblage of writing without drawing. All his *Ten Commandments* are superb examples of the new expressivity evident in his graphic art today.

Each poem by Ada Salas is exquisite in its precision, clarity, and piercing excavation into the word, not any word but rather "the word that the poet must discover" (*El margen,* 88). Her ten poems offer enlightening moments where she demonstrates full awareness of the need, the want, the desire, and the "hunger" for her own vital participation in the activity of writing. Her first work in the collection is a poem in three parts titled "*Vivir*" [*Live*]. This is a fitting opening command for this collection and for its initial poem (*Diez mandamientos*, 9–11). At the outset, Salas penetrates the word "vivir," in the artwork and in the poetic work, and magnificently shapes and sharpens her own investigative analyses of the creative and existential thematic matters she elucidates.

Salas's "*Vivir*" is a model poem and it serves as a metaphoric cross section representative of her work, both in this collection and throughout her creative trajectory. For Salas, "la poesía surge de la ruptura de lo rígido" (*El margen*, 135) [poetry emerges from a break in what is rigid]. In "*Vivir*," the poetic voice inspects a scene in nature by focusing on aspects of a felled tree, its bark, the carvings on and in its outer layers, and the cut exhibiting its cross section. By probing its concentric growth rings, the poet gains access to the necessity for and the essence of her writing: "Nos importa curar / con las palabras. Árbol" (*Diez mandamientos*, 10). [What matters to us is healing / with words. Tree.] This extraordinary and eloquent poem embodies the poetics of epiphany in Salas's work.

Ada Salas is a definitive and distinguished poetic voice. Throughout her creative trajectory, she privileges her reader as a direct witness to her art of poetic creation during her search for the "secret" of the word. In turn, she divulges what she encounters along the way: the essential nature of poetic writing. For Salas, "el buen poema es el que vuelve, el que produce ecos en el tiempo y nos visita una y otra vez, como una música perfecta y plena en su simpleza: imprescindible melodía, de sentido y procedencia secretos" (*Alguien aquí*, 83). [The good poem is the one that returns, the one that produces echoes in time and that visits us repeatedly, like music that is perfect and full in its simplicity, an indispensable melody, with secret meaning and origin]. "*Vivir*" is one such poem. Here, Salas inspects the overlooked recognizing in it the imperative essential to sustaining natural and human existence: "*vivir*." The ongoing quest of Ada Salas for the word is instructive, and "*Vivir*" is exemplary in this respect. Her scrutiny of what is necessary to her creative activity reveals why she writes. Salas indicates, "Escribir me hace digna de la vida y de los otros, porque me los aprende, conduciéndome secretamente a ellos" (*Alguien aquí*, 38). [Writing makes me worthy of life and of others because it helps me understand them, secretly taking me to them.]

THE LIVE CURRENT

In her intertextual exchange with the "Written Drawings" of Jesús Placencia, and in her reconceptualization of Lucio Fontana's *buchi* and *tagli* canvases, Ada Salas demonstrates that visual art presents numerous opportunities for interpenetrative conversations with her poetry and poetics. Her newest work promises further advancements regarding this innovative interactive approach. The inspiration for her current project (as of the writing of the present chapter) resides in the magnificent fifteenth century masterpiece by Rogier van der Weyden titled *Descent from the Cross*, which is part of the collection of the Prado Museum in Madrid.[31]

Salas's most recent 2016 work appears as an epilogue to *Escribir y borrar. Antología esencial (1994–2016) Ada Salas* [*Writing and Erasing. An Essential Anthology (1994–2016) Ada Salas*] compiled by José Luis Rozas Bravo.[32] The volume includes a retrospective introduction highlighting the evolution of Salas's lyric during the period indicated in the title (9–23). It also presents selected examples of Salas's poetry, along with a convenient regathering of portions of her prose poetics published from 2005 to 2014. It is an invaluable testament to her productive creative activity encompassing this last decade.

In many ways, this literary anthological compilation complements the current chapter on Ada Salas. What is especially noteworthy about the Rozas work, however, is the inclusion of Salas's newest poetics as the epilogue to this volume. Her work features an intriguing title, "Sin sentido."[33] Normally, an epilogue brings some type of closure to a work. Its placement at the end of this anthology suggests, especially when paired with Rozas's introduction, that it could function as a conclusion. At the same time, however, the process of writing in the work of Salas, as the current book chapter discloses, does not reach an endpoint. It never is complete, and it never is "without meaning," as her clever title might seem, at first, to suggest. For this poet, engaging in the creative activity of writing is an ongoing mode of being and, importantly, a continuing mode of discovery. It is "senseless" to consider her ongoing poetic enterprise otherwise. As has been demonstrated, the works of Ada Salas fundamentally concern her sustained request for the "gift" of the word and her never-ending quest for uncovering its "secret" essence.

"Sin sentido," as she expresses at the outset, establishes the aim of her creative activity. Furthermore, it adds another dimension to the dialogue that is evident in the intertextual weave of her poetry and poetics. Ada Salas's recent essay, notably, also serves as an appropriate prelude to her future work where she will continue to affirm the purpose, the need, the want, and the hunger she experiences as a poet who engages fully in creative endeavor:

> Y qué sentido tiene escribir no como una forma de decir el mundo, sino de intentar de penetrarlo [. . .] para desnudarlo. No para una lección aprendida, sino para internarse en lo que no se conoce. Sin conseguir probablemente nada más que dar cuenta, tan solo —y si acaso— de una, cada vez más oscura, perplejidad. Así que escribir sirve más bien para poco, y sin embargo responde a una necesidad —¿puede uno no atender a sus necesidades? [. . .] De momento, no sé

por cuánto tiempo, no escribir sería renunciar a estar viva. La escritura es una de las no muchas posibles formas de encuentro. Una de las no muchas posibles formas de comunicación. ¿Con qué? ¿con quién? No importa. Sabemos que hemos tocado una corriente eléctrica cuando sentimos una descarga; esa descarga es el signo de que hemos entrado en algo —a veces, también, en alguien. ¿Puedo llamar a eso "comunicación", por tanto? Es éste el tipo de comunicación al que me refiero: a través de la escritura entramos, tocamos una corriente, formamos, aunque sea por muy breve espacio de tiempo, parte de algo; dejamos, por un instante, por lo tanto, de estar completamente solos. A cambio, o, en consecuencia, recibimos una sacudida: somos sacudidos por ella; por algo tan inaprehensible, y sin embargo tan supuestamente a nuestro alcance, como esto: vida. ("Sin sentido," 203, 204)

[In addition, what sense does it make that writing is not a way to speak about the world but rather an attempt to penetrate it (. . .) to lay it bare. Not to recite a learned lesson but rather to plunge into what is not known. Probably without achieving anything more than accounting for, only—if at all—some type of uncertainty that increasingly becomes more and more obscure. Therefore, writing serves but little purpose, and yet it responds to a need—can you not address your basic needs? (. . .) For the time being, I do not know for how long not writing would be to renounce being alive. Writing is one of the few possible forms of encounter. One of the few possible forms of communication. With what? With whom? It does not matter. We know we have touched an electric current when we feel a shock; that shock is the signal that we have entered something—at times, also, someone. Could I thus call that "communication"? It is *this* kind of communication to which I am referring: by means of writing we enter, we touch a live current, we take part in something, even if it might be for only a brief period; for an instant, we therefore stop being completely alone. In return, or consequently, we receive a shock, we are jolted by it, by something so inapprehensible and yet so apparently within our reach, like this life.]

This "epilogue" really is an intriguing, inviting, and meaningful introduction to the future poetry and poetics of Ada Salas. There is much to anticipate.

POEM AND POEM ANALYSIS BY ADA SALAS

What follows is a poem by Ada Salas and her original analysis of this poem. She wrote her study at the request of the author for inclusion in this chapter of the book. Here she reveals her own stunning insights into the epiphanic nature of her work. At the same time, this poem provides an "opening" through which to enter the new and forthcoming creative endeavors of Ada Salas.[34]

Pain—has an Element of Blank—
(Se parece el dolor a un gran espacio)

—Emily Dickinson

I

Una inmensa granada.
Romperla.
Desgranarla.
Un poco de ese rojo.
Un puñado incontable de rubíes
que sangran. Una playa
de sangre
que el agua va enjuagando haciéndola
brillar —un brillo
que deslumbra y que hiere—.

II

Esa playa. Qué hacer con esa playa
que no sea
dejar que te acribille.

III

Hueles.
Oyes el mar y observas
su trabajo. Un día y otro día y una
eternidad
cerniendo en su molleja digiriendo
devolviendo a la playa lo que
—más bello cada vez—
está llamado
a
su desaparición.

IV

Pulir. Pulirlo. Hacer
con el dolor
lo que el mar hace con las piedras.
Pulirlo hasta volverlo trasparente hacerlo

joya.

[I

An immense pomegranate.
Break it open.
Remove the seeds.
A little of that red.
A handful of countless rubies
bleeding. A beach
of blood
that the water washes away making it
glisten—a brilliance
that dazzles and wounds—.

II

That beach. What to do with that beach
other than
allow that it wound you.

III

You smell.
You hear the sea and you watch
it at work. One day and another day and an
eternity
sifting through its gizzard digesting
restoring to the beach that which
—ever more beautiful—
is summoned

to
its disappearance.

IV

Polish. Polish it. Do
with pain
what the sea does with stones.
Polish it until it becomes transparent make it

jewel.]

ANÁLISIS

El inmenso poema "La pietá" de Giuseppe Ungaretti comienza con este verso: "Sono un uomo ferito": Soy un hombre herido. Unos versos del "Poema del fin" de Marina Tsvietáieva dicen: "(. . .) que yo no soy sino/un animal herido en el vientre." Al parecer (no conozco la referencia exacta) Gil de Biedma afirmó que "no hay poeta sin herida." Mujer, hombre, animal herido, el poeta. Quitémosle a este enunciado toda connotación trágica, y quedémonos con lo literal, con la pura denotación, que no supone llanto, sino conciencia; los seres humanos nacemos heridos de muerte, porque nacemos heridos de tiempo y, por tanto, estamos condenados a la pérdida: de lo otro, de los otros, de nosotros mismos. Con ese material (con esa conciencia), de un modo u otro, trabaja el poeta. Y de esa conciencia hace canto. Para huir de ella (poesía de la exaltación, de la celebración de la vida) o para enfrentarse, sumergirse en ella y darle voz: poesía que podríamos calificar de "elegíaca" ("Se canta lo que se pierde," escribió Antonio Machado). Ahora bien, la conciencia poética labora como un cedazo que separa el oro de la ganga; la suya es una labor de selección muy lenta, muy lenta: las experiencias, lo que uno vive, van dejando huellas profundas (¿heridas?), incisiones, impresiones, en la cera blanda del ¿alma? del poeta. Huellas tales que son apenas advertidas por el "hombre" poeta, pero son celosamente "almacenadas" por el poeta que es ese hombre casi a sus espaldas, sin su control, sin su consentimiento —el poeta trabaja en secreto. Tiempo después —años, toda una vida, tantas veces— esas incisiones afloran en forma de poemas. El "tiempo del poeta" ha trabajado moviendo pacientemente ese cedazo sin que el hombre tuviera noticia de ello, como si de una búsqueda de oro se tratara; ha trabajado como trabaja el mar puliendo las piedras de la orilla, poco a poco, pacientemente, "digiriendo" la experiencia, para extraer de ella la "piedra preciosa" (el poema) que la "resume," trascendiéndola, la que poética —y quizá por lo tanto incomprensiblemente— habla de lo que no podía ser nombrado, da voz a una verdad que es la verdad subyacente, y real, la verdad real de un suceso, una experiencia, un sentimiento . . . la verdad real del estar en la vida de ese hombre. Verdad cruda, sin adherencias, sin medias palabras, sin: el centro puro de lo que se vive. Esa es la epifanía, esa es la revelación: ese es el conocer que nos regala el poema.

[ANALYSIS]

[The very long poem "The Pietà" by Giuseppe Ungaretti begins with this line: "I am a wounded man." A few lines from "The Poem of the End" by Marina Tsvietáieva indicate "I am just / a wounded animal in the womb." Apparently, Gil de Biedma (I do not know the exact reference) affirmed, "There is no poet without a wound." Woman, man, wounded animal, the poet. Let's remove from this statement all connotation of the tragic, and let's consider the literal, the pure denotation, that does not imply lament but rather awareness; as human beings, we are born mortally wounded because we are born wounded by time and therefore we are condemned to a sense of loss, of another, of others, of ourselves. With that material (with that awareness), somehow or other, the poet works. Moreover, from that awareness the song originates. To escape it (there is poetry that exalts, celebrates life) or to face it, to delve into it and to give it a voice, the poetry we would qualify as "elegiac" ("You sing what you lose," wrote Antonio Machado). Well, in poetry, awareness works like a sieve that separates the gold from the gangue; its task is one of very slow, very slow selection: experiences, what one lives, leaving behind deep marks (wounds?), incisions, impressions in the soft wax of the soul of the poet. The poet as a "man" hardly notices such marks, but they are possessively "stored" by the poet who is that man at his back, free from his control, without his consent—the poet works in secret. Long thereafter—years, an entire lifetime, often—those incisions emerge in the form of poems. In "the labor stage," the poet has worked patiently moving the sieve without being noticed, as if a search for gold were completed, having worked like the sea works at polishing the stones on the seashore, little by little, patiently, "digesting" the experience, in order to extract from it the "precious stone" (the poem), condensing, transcending, that which poetics—and perhaps thus inexplicably—speaks about as that which cannot be named, giving voice to a truth that is the underlying truth, and genuine, the real truth about an event, an experience, an emotion . . . the authentic truth about being in the life of that man. Stark truth, without adhesions, without mincing words, without, the pure center of what lives. That is the epiphany, which is the revelation; that is the knowledge the poem gives us.]

POEMS BY ADA SALAS

The complete text and translation of the poems examined in chapter 4 include the following:

"No duerme el animal que busca," *Lugar de la derrota* (2003).
"Y para qué esta herida," *Lugar de la derrota* (2003).
"El desorden trabaja como crece una herida," *Limbo y otros poemas* (2013).
"Lo que duerme en los pliegues lo no," *Esto no es el silencio* (2008).
"Es una piedra y mira," *Lugar de la derrota* (2003).
"Yo sé que tienes algo que decirme," *Esto no es el silencio* (2008).
"Solidez de esta jarra," *Esto no es el silencio* (2008).
"En la almendra," *Limbo y otros poemas* (2013).
"*Vivir*," *Diez mandamientos* (2016).

No duerme el animal que busca
su alimento. Huele
y está tan lejos todavía
el aire de su presa.
Y vagará en la noche.
Con la sola certeza de su hambre.
Ciego

porque una vez ya supo

de ese breve temblor
bajo su zarpa.

[The animal does not sleep seeking
food. It sniffs
and yet far away is
the scent of its prey.
And it will wander in the night.
Only certain of its hunger.
Blinded

because it already had discovered once

that short-lived trembling sensation
under its paw.]

Y para qué esta herida

esta abertura umbilical
por donde entra y sale
la claridad del mundo

si no me quedan nombres
ya

de tanta transparencia.

[And for what is this wound

this umbilical opening
through which comes and goes
the clarity of the world

if I have run out of names
already

from such transparency.] (I thank Manuel Martín Barros for his assistance in the translation of this poem)

El desorden trabaja como crece una herida
hacia
adentro y hacia
afuera.
El deseo es lo mudo.
En lo mudo fermenta lo que
descuartiza un cerebro.
Un extraño jardín un extraño mercado.
En el borde del cráter alguien
canta
y su canto remueve la pólvora.

[Disruption acts like an open wound
growing inward
and growing
outward.
Desire is silent.
Silently fermenting what
mental matter fractures.
A strange terrain a strange marketplace.
On the edge of the crater someone
sings
and the song stirs up the ash.]

Lo que duerme en los pliegues lo no
visto no oído lo nunca
pronunciado
lo hundido en la hendidura
de la roca
el punto donde empieza
silencioso el incendio
—el cine
esa pantalla
ardida en un segundo
primer aprendizaje
de la aniquilación—.

Allí
donde no llega
la yema de los dedos.

Lo no reconocible

que vive en lo real

y lo fulmina a veces

y queda boqueando como un pez en sequía.

[What sleeps in the folds the not
seen not heard not ever
pronounced
buried in the crack
of the rock
the point where silently
the blaze begins
—the cinema
that screen
burned in an instant
the first lesson
in annihilation—.

There
where it is just out of reach
of the fingertips.

The not recognizable

that dwells in the real

and fulminates it at times

and it is left gasping like a drought-stricken fish.]

Es una piedra y mira
el tránsito ligero de las nubes
la curva de las ramas
la imposible
geometría del pájaro.

Es una piedra y muda
mira

la secreta impostura de todo movimiento.

[It is a rock and it watches
the subtle passing of the clouds
the curve of the branches
the impossible
geometry of the bird.

It is a rock and silent
it watches

the secret deception of movement.]

Yo sé que tienes algo que decirme
mundo. Voy a limpiarlo todo para que todo
sea
aún más transparente
y pueda oír aquello que murmuras
sin esfuerzo y sin miedo.
Ya puedes acercarte hasta mi oído.
Vamos a hablar despacio.
Muy despacio.
Sin prisa.

Como si nunca
mundo

nos llegara la muerte.

[I know that you have something to tell me
world. I am going to clean up everything so that everything
might be
even more transparent
and I might be able to listen to your whispers
without effort and without fear.
Now you can come closer to my ear.
Let's talk slowly.
Very slowly.
Unhurried.

As if never
world

death were to reach us.]

Solidez de esta jarra
piel
erizada del kiwi
larguísimas tijeras
más humanas
que esta mano que escribe.

Extraño bodegón.

Yo escucho desde un centro más lejos que mis ojos
vuestro limpio discurso.
Sé cómo resonáis.
Cómo hacéis del silencio un débil fondo
plano

apenas perceptible.

[This solid pitcher
prickly
skin of the kiwi
very long scissors
more human
than this hand that writes.

Strange still life.

I listen from a center further than my eyes
to your crisp discourse.
I know how you resonate.
How you create a faint backdrop of silence
smooth

only just perceptible.]

En la almendra
del tiempo. Hendir en la dureza
de su cáscara. Desbaratar
la sucesión.
El orden.
El ahora después
más adelante. Entrar
en la semilla. Pisar en el vacío
verdadero. En la región
del no.

[In the almond
of time. Split open the hard
shell. Disrupt
the sequence.
The order.
The now after
later. Enter
into the seed. Step onto real
nothingness. Into the region
of the no.]

VIVIR

I
Podemos empezar
desde el principio
                    una piedra
en el centro una expansión
muy lenta
un extenderse hacia
lo que parece vida —los signos
del amor
con un trazo muy torpe tal vez
mas decidido. Una inscripción
muy pura—. Este era el principio —todo era
tal vez
solo el principio—. Luego
el hacha. Luego el hacha
si no
cómo podría
ver
cómo poder narrar
todo el proceso.

II
Mira. Así se representa un movimiento
sísmico
pero no
se dibujan
la destrucción la conmoción el grito
el silencio y la ruina. Bueno. Y qué. Eso no
nos importa. Nos importa que el árbol
acuda
para dar otro anillo.
—reparación
resurrección
sutura—.
Nos importa curar
con las palabras. Árbol. Una vez
y otra vez
sobre el tocón
alzándose

la memoria visible
—no fantasma—
de lo que en otro tiempo fuera un
árbol.

III
Muy
ordenadamente algo crece
adentro
de la herida
hace carne de la carne
corteza
muy
desprendidamente
muy amorosamente
—lo de fuera
cuidando alimentado
a lo de dentro—
para crecer
se ensidevora
da
de sí.

[*LIVE*]

[I
We can start
from the beginning
a stone
in the center an expansion
very slowly
extending toward
what seems like life—the signs
of love
with an awkward line perhaps
but resolute. A very pure
inscription—. This was the beginning—everything was
perhaps
only just the beginning—. Then
the ax. Then the ax

otherwise
how would it
see
how could it express
the entire process.

II
Look. This portrays a movement
seismic
but not
making visible
the destruction the shock the scream
the silence and the ruin. Fine. And what. That
does not matter to us.
What matters to us is that the tree
grows
and produces another ring
—reparation
resurrection
suture—.
What matters to us is healing
with words. Tree. Again
and again
from the stump
rising up
the visible memory
—not a ghost—
of what in another time was once a
tree.

III
Very
neatly something grows
within
the wound
making flesh of flesh
bark
very
unselfishly
very lovingly
—what is outside

protecting nourishing
what is inside—
                    in order to grow
self-consuming
                    giving
of itself.] (I thank Brigette Walters for her assistance, review, and insights concerning the translations of these Salas poems.)

AFTERWORD

The subject of this book is the epistemic poetry in the twenty-first-century works of Luis Muñoz, Abraham Gragera, Josep M. Rodríguez, and Ada Salas, four premier poets currently publishing in Spain. My careful examination of the creative activity of each of these poets demonstrates that writing is a process of discovery and a fundamental method for exploring and manifesting moments of exceptional new insights into the nature of poetry and knowledge. Each of these poets exhibits an individual voice and a distinctive style. Each artistically shapes their probing inquiries and elucidating findings in the epiphanic poem. This study concerns discovery both as a mode of investigation and as an outcome. How do these poets approach discovery and image the results in exemplary poems disclosing the emergence and development of what I refer to as the poetics of epiphany? Each chapter, one on the work of each of the four poets, divulges my findings.

Each chapter examines the methodologies of discovery for the poets engaged in the activity of epistemic inquiry in their works. For Luis Muñoz, time is of the essence. Each componential moment within the temporal interval known as the "present" has strategic importance for him. Exquisitely distilled and inventive analogies disclose ways in which to examine the present and to extract from it the multilayered features of its essence—the instant. Keen awareness of the sensorial and deliberate attentiveness to ordinary objects, events, and activities in daily life yield extraordinary participatory opportunities for his poetic protagonists. His underlying imperatives: Apprehend the instant. Be in the moment. Discover what is fresh before it spoils. Abraham Gragera expands and revitalizes the referential capacity of the word. For him, the poet's task is not only to say anew but also to say in ways that never have been said. His works uncover that once familiar language can, indeed, become unfamiliar when the word undergoes enlightening metaphoric transformation. Gragera's continuing imperatives: Rid the word of excess. Empower the word. Speak now for the future. Josep M. Rodríguez exploits the image as his indispensable epistemic instrument for disclosing lifelong lessons concerning how to be in the world. His poetry also underscores another important mode of being when his poetic voices examine fundamental features of the nature of the subjective self. His fundamental imperatives: Be alert. Take note of reality. Be self-aware. Construct personal identity. The poetry and the prose poetics of Ada Salas are intimately interconnected in a discourse of discovery. Salas seeks the word—not just any word but rather

her word. She seeks to comprehend that word by penetrating it with an intense analysis of her own metaphoric construct of "fissure." In her poetry, these pursuits only occur during the elucidating activity of writing. Impeccable linguistic expressivity, painstaking attention to detail, and the refined extraction of the essence of the word converge in her carefully crafted poems and poetics. Her imperatives: Inspect. Listen. Write. Live.

Poetry as a process for attaining knowledge did not suddenly emerge in my own work with this book. It has piqued my interest, has been the subject of graduate student courses that I have taught, and has resulted in the publications of several of my findings over the years. The 1984 pioneering *Poetry of Discovery* by Andrew P. Debicki has had a lasting effect on my approach to poetry, my research, and my teaching, and it has influenced my thinking on the act of writing as an act of discovery. It also has had an impact on my discerning the participatory role of the reader during the process of discovery. Poets such as Josep M. Rodríguez and Ada Salas are cognizant of the reader and summon him or her, at times, to engage in encountering the poem as a method for attaining new knowledge. Ada Salas views the reader as the poet's "accomplice," and Josep M. Rodríguez conveys "respect" for the reader by recognizing her or his role in the poetic act. The interconnected activities of reading and writing as epistemic encounters are highlighted in several of my analyses in the book.

The strategies for discovery vary. The gateways through which each poet enters the activity of writing as a process of knowledge are different as well as unique. The poets do share a common goal: epistemological inquiry. Yet they find their own methodology for disclosing their newly acquired insights into poetry, reality, and being. The imperatives they each follow guide the chapter concerning their unique works. When following their urgings, the reader becomes an integral part of the process of the poem as the means to acquire a better understanding of the poetics of epiphany central to this book.

Their own approaches may differ, but they also point to the variety of voices expressing multiple instructive methods of discovery. The current Spanish lyric is vibrant and bountiful because of these differences. Luis Muñoz, Abraham Gragera, Josep M. Rodríguez, and Ada Salas each practice the poetic enterprise in specific ways. Although the lyric examined in this study articulates a common thematic concept, the stimulating points of access, the innovative artistic effects, the individual styles, the expressive capacity of language, and the several moments of elucidation are fascinating as well as diverse.

Looking to the future, there is much to anticipate. Muñoz, Gragera, Rodríguez, and Salas remain fully engaged in the poetic enterprise. Ada Salas published *Descendimiento* with the superb Spanish press Pre-Textos in the fall of 2018, after having written this collection during her very productive

2017–2018 sabbatical year. Luis Muñoz published his guest work titled *Vecindad* in December 2018 with the distinguished editorial Visor. I have read an earlier draft, and the poetry is superb. Josep M. Rodríguez published his guest poem, intriguingly titled "Diagrama de Venn," in *La Razón* in July 2018. In June 2018, he provided me with a copy of this poem, and it whetted my poetry appetite for what he will be publishing in the next few years. Given his expertise, Rodríguez has been asked to coordinate a special issue on the haiku for the prestigious Spanish poetry magazine *Ínsula*. Currently, Abraham Gragera is working on a book of prose poetics that will be published in 2019 by the Editora Regional de Extremadura. At present, he also is engaged in developing the themes and perspectives for his next poetry collection now under construction. As he has mentioned to me, he never is quite certain of the ultimate direction his books will take. At this point, however, the impetus originates in what he refers to as an "autobiographical and anthropological" approach, one that he began to articulate in his 2017 *O Futuro*.

In September 2018, as I was putting the finishing touches on my final book manuscript, Spain's leading literary critic on recent Spanish poetry, José Andújar Almansa, published his long-awaited work with Pre-Textos, *Centros de gravedad. Poesía española en el siglo XXI (Una antología)*. Eight years in the making, the book is the most significant contribution to investigative research on and the literary criticism of the recent lyric poetry published in Spain since 2000. His subject matter, the meticulous nature of his research, and his own exacting style most certainly promise that the book will become *the* reference point for examining the poetry of the current era. The critic provides a substantial prologue, almost sixty pages, that could and should be considered as a decisive scholarly article or investigative monographic study. This superb and original prologue unmistakably conveys that this distinguished book is a triumph. By publishing this work as an anthology, it will be better disseminated in bookstores and, thus, readily available to a wider readership. I note with pride that two of the poets whose works I examine in my book are included, Abraham Gragera and Josep M. Rodríguez.

The publication of Andújar's book is a literary landmark for the twenty-first-century lyric in Spain. By including, in a singular publication, the various voices of many of the most important poets currently writing today, Andújar opens avenues both for further study and for different pathways for coming to know and appreciate the recent lyric. He begins his anthology in 1971, with the birthdate of the first poet included in this work, Mariano Peyrou. The penultimate poet, Juan Andrés García Román, was born in 1979, and the final poet whose works he includes is Elena Medel, whose birthdate is 1985. However, the poems he includes in his anthology surpass dates of birth, thereby extending his work to the present day. He features selections of poems from collections appearing in 2018 and 2017, for example. The earliest published poetry of the anthologized poets begins with the year 2000.

José Andújar Almansa received the recognition that he deserves in the public presentation of his book on October 30, 2018, in Madrid. The twelve poets represented in his groundbreaking work were all to be in attendance, and I name each in the order in which they appear in Andújar's collection: Mariano Peyrou, Abraham Gragera, Miriam Reyes, Juan Carlos Abril, Juan Manuel Romero, Rafael Espejo, Carlos Pardo, Antonio Lucas, Josep M. Rodríguez, Erika Martínez, Juan Andrés García Román, and Elena Medel. Some of these poets I have mentioned in the introduction to my book, and some of these, as well as others from this grouping, are cited in my chapters for their literary criticism and essays. Andújar's book and mine, although different in approach, coincide in shining a light on Spain's current lyric production. I could not have asked for more.

The future of the lyric of other poets writing today is bright. Promising poets such as Paula Bozalongo, Laura Casielles, and Ben Clark merit attention. Bozalongo's *Diciembre y nos besamos*, published by Hiperión in 2014, won the XXIX Premio de Poesía Hiperión in March of that same year. Casielles's *Los idiomas comunes*, published by Hiperión in 2010, won the XIII Premio de Poesía Joven "Antonio Carvajal" in September 2010. Clark's *La policía celeste*, published by Visor in 2018, won the XXX Premio Internacional de Poesía Fundación Loewe for that year of the annual competition. Readers of my book might recognize Ben Clark's name because of his translations into English of specific poems that I use in my chapter on the poetry of Josep M. Rodríguez. There are other poets deserving mention. For further exploration, I suggest *Nacer en otro tiempo. Antología de la joven poesía española*, published by Renacimiento in 2016. The three poets I acknowledge here are included. I thank Abraham Gragera for alerting me to this work. I found this anthology to be very helpful in anticipating where Spain's current lyric written in Spanish possibly could be heading. It is hoped that other scholars will delve into exploring aspects of today's lyric by poets writing in other languages in Spain.

The photograph on the cover of my book images discovery. Intense scrutiny of the night sky. Immediate exploration. The powerful optics of an astronomical observatory telescope. A visible representation of the process of successful scientific inquiry. An instant captured and enhanced by the interpretive artistry of photoastronomy. A stellar manifestation of epiphany.

ACKNOWLEDGMENTS

This book is about discovery, and the photograph on the front cover serves as a fitting metaphor and point of entry. I express my deepest gratitude to Adam Block of the Mount Lemon SkyCenter, University of Arizona, for permitting me to introduce my book with his stellar astrophotography and his image M29. My most grateful acknowledgment goes to each one of the singular poets featured in my study. My book could not have been written without their own astounding contributions to the Spanish lyric of today. I extend an individual and sincere thank you to Luis Muñoz, Abraham Gragera, Josep M. Rodríguez, and Ada Salas for granting me permission to quote their own poems and for granting me the permission to translate many of these, or portions of them, into English. Most of all, I am grateful to each for infusing my book with their own unique expressive vitality. My professional life has been invigorated because of their works. Coming to know each one of them as warm and welcoming human beings led me to invite their participation in my book. I also wish to acknowledge the fine translators who granted me permission to use their works. I thank Professor Curtis Bauer for his translations of several poems that I study by Luis Muñoz. I am indebted to Juan de Dios León Gómez for his translations of the poetry and the poem analysis of Abraham Gragera. Ester Boldú, Ben Clark, and Monika Izabela Jaworska merit special thanks for permitting me to use their English translations of various poems of Josep M. Rodríguez. I extend my heartfelt gratitude to Ada Salas for allowing me to translate her poetry and poetics that I examine in my study.

My interest in this new era of Spanish poetry began a few years ago when I first encountered the work of Luis Muñoz and wrote a guest article on one of his poems. This piece, and my other guest pieces, were the earlier "seeds" that later would develop and soon flourish in this book. The idea of the poetics of epiphany, as my central theme, took time to evolve. In the spring of 2014, I taught a graduate seminar, after two years of research, on the "Recent Poetry from Spain." Two years later, after furthering my investigations, meeting several of the poets whose works I had taught, and concentrating on specific ideas emerging during my preparation for a new graduate seminar, I then experienced my own "eureka" moment. The topic of my spring 2016 graduate course was "poetry as epiphany" and by then I had narrowed my focus to the twenty-first-century works of specific poets. My "findings" began to indicate the thematic matter for what would become this book. However, without the encouragement and support of the members of each of these graduate classes, I would not have written the book. It was their idea. They planted the "seed" when some of them simply told me "you should write a book." I sincerely thank each of them. My study could not have come to fruition without our class discussions and the students' insights and keen interest. The book also could not have been written without the support of my colleague and former department head, Professor Malcolm Compitello. He made it possible for me to engage in productive research. He did not hesitate to provide his unwavering support and to acknowledge my efforts and results. I am deeply appreciative of my sabbatical semester in the fall of 2015 that was made possible by the College of Humanities. That semester jump-started the process of writing this book. At key moments when my study was taking shape, Mary Portillo and Jack Kauffman provided me with assistance for which I am greatly appreciative. I also acknowledge the generosity of Laura Goyanes for the "buddy pass" that enabled various of my discussions with the poets in Spain. During the summer of 2018, graduate student Brigette Walters, ABD, provided key commentaries on portions of the manuscript and I remain appreciative.

The referees that read my manuscript and recommended publication offered excellent and perceptive commentaries for which I am deeply thankful. Incorporating their suggestions was a pleasure because their careful reading and remarkable insights only enhanced my study. I also thank Greg Clingham and Pam Dailey of Bucknell University Press, Daryl Brower of Rutgers University Press, and Bradley Cox of Scribe Inc. for their professional guidance during the various stages involved in producing my manuscript as a book.

Lastly, my gratitude knows no bounds when it comes to the infinite support that Chris Maloney has given me during our life together. These past years, while developing and advancing my study, were ones in which he applauded my efforts and encouraged my visits to Spain in order to further my investigations and bring this book to completion. Our two beautiful daughters, Maura and Brigid, merit special and heartfelt thanks for their unwavering support not only during this book project but also throughout my career. For me, being in the world, a theme I investigate in this book, means being with them. Chris, Maura, and Brigid are my guiding stars.

NOTES

INTRODUCTION

1. A few examples, alphabetically ordered, are those works by Juan Cano Ballesta, "Introducción. Orientaciones recientes de la poesía española," in *Poesía española reciente (1980–2000)*, ed. Juan Cano Ballesta (Madrid: Cátedra, 2001); José Luis García Martín, *La generación de los ochenta* (Valencia: Mestra, 1988); José Luis García Martín, *La poesía figurativa* (Sevilla: Renacimiento, 1992); José Luis García Martín, *La generación del 99: Antología crítica de la joven poesía española* (Oviedo: Nobel, 1999); Araceli Iravedra, *Poesía de experiencia* (Madrid: Visor, 2007); Araceli Iravedra, "Prólogo," in *Hacia la democracia. La nueva poesía (1968–2000)*, ed. Araceli Iravdera (Madrid: Visor, 2016); Juan José Lanz, *La poesía durante la transición y la generación de la democracia* (Madrid: Devenir, 2007); Juan José Lanz, "Luces de cabotaje: La poesía de la transición y la generación de la democracia en los albores del nuevo milenio," *Monteagudo. Revista de literatura española, hispanoamericana y teoría de la literatura* 3, no. 13 (2008): 25–48; and José-Carlos Mainer, *En el último tercio del siglo 1968–1998. Antología consultada de la poesía española*, ed. José-Carlos Mainer (Madrid: Visor, 1999).
2. Some of the poetry and prose poetics by Luis Muñoz have been published in an English translation. The pioneering bilingual edition by Muñoz titled *From behind What Landscape: New and Selected Poems* (Madrid: Vaso Roto, 2015) brought to the attention of a much larger audience the works of this important poet. The translations of the selected poems and the portion of the prose poetics included in this work are by Curtis Bauer. Both he and the poet graciously have allowed me to use the English translations in my book as applicable to works I study. In 2017, Josep M. Rodríguez published *Radar. Antología bilingüe* (Lucena: El Orden del Mundo, 2017). This bilingual collection offers selected exemplary poems of his in Spanish with English translations. The work features twenty-five poems. In my monograph, I use selected English translations of the poems that I examine with the gracious permission of the poet and specific translators—Ester Boldú, Ben Clark, and Monika Izabela Jaworska. Much of the poetry of Abraham Gragera that I analyze has been translated into English by Juan de Dios León Gómez at my request. Earlier, he had translated some of Gragera's poems into English for a poetry reading given by the poet in London. Since the poet had granted me permission to use those translations in my book, I made my request of the professional translator. The selected poems I study are used with the kind permission of the poet and Juan de Dios León Gómez. The English translations appearing in my book for the poetry and prose poetics of Ada Salas are my own. Her works have not been translated into English before their publication in my book, although several of her poems have been translated into other languages. The poet kindly granted me permission to translate the works I examine in my study. Throughout my book, I cite, where applicable, the relevant translator. Otherwise, the English translations are my own.
3. Luis Muñoz, "Transición," in *Limpiar pescado. Poesía reunida (1991–2005)* (Madrid: Visor, 2005), 11–12. His *Septiembre* (Madrid: Hiperión, 1991) was published at this time.
4. Muñoz is referring to a very complex period in Spanish poetry, the closing two decades of the twentieth century. It was an era of debates, slogans, and opposing schools of thought. In

2005, Muñoz writes with the benefit of hindsight and looks back with his personal perspective on the era in which he was a budding poet, in this contentious atmosphere, and beginning to publish his own works. His insights are invaluable. Without any attempt on my part to oversimplify the period to which Muñoz refers, I note that it has received the critical attention of and has been the object of historical accounts by several authors. In retrospect, the evolution of late twentieth-century contemporary Spanish poetry demonstrates two modes—one advocating and practicing the dominant trend of "poetry of experience" and the other in favor of what came to be known as "poetry of difference." Reactive in nature, these "trends," together with subcomponents of them, have been the object of substantial study. I mention influential and informative views assisting me in my understandings of the 1980s and 1990s in Spanish poetry. See, for example, Luis Antonio de Villena, "Tradición y renovación en la poesía española última. Un breve panorama," in *10 menos 30 la ruptura interior en la "poesía de la experiencia,"* ed. Luis Antonio de Villena (Valencia: Pre-Textos, 1997), 9–42; Juan Cano Ballesta, "Introducción. Orientaciones recientes de la poesía española," in *Poesía española reciente (1980–2000),* ed. Juan Cano Ballesta (Madrid: Cátedra, 2001), 21–72; Diana Cullell, "Preface" and "Introduction," in *Spanish Contemporary Poetry: An Anthology,* ed. Diana Cullel (Manchester, U.K.: Manchester University Press, 2014), vii–ix, 1–33; Diana Cullell, *La poesía de la experiencia a finales del siglo XX y al XXI* (Madrid: Devenir, 2010); Araceli Iravedra, *Poesía de experiencia* (Madrid: Visor, 2007); José-Carlos Mainer, *En el último tercio del siglo 1968–1998. Antología consultada de la poesía española,* ed. José-Carlos Mainer (Madrid: Visor, 1999); Ángel L. Prieto de Paula, "Poesía en la era de la perplejidad," in *Las moradas del verbo. Poetas españoles de la democracia. Antología,* ed. Ángel L. Prieto de Paula (Madrid: Calambur Poesía, 2010), 9–58; Antonio Rodríguez Jiménez, "Diferencia 'versus' experiencia: la poesía heterodoxa frente a la tendencia oficial," *Claves de razón práctica* 60 (1996): 77–78; Domingo Sánchez-Mesa Martínez, "Prólogo," in *Cambio de siglo: Antología de poesía española 1990–2007,* ed. Domingo Sánchez-Mesa Martínez (Madrid: Hiperión, 2007), 9–28; Sylvia Sherno, "Poetry Wars," in "Defining Differences," guest ed., special issue, *Studies in Twentieth and Twenty-First-Century Literature,* 36, no. 2 (Summer 2012): 189–203. I have kept in mind throughout my book that my study is not to tell a tale of what came before. My aim, rather, is to focus on a thematic matter that has reinvigorated my own efforts to come to know, to appreciate, to publish on, and to teach a poetry of the here and now that is outstanding. My book demonstrates why.

5. Luis Muñoz has translated to Spanish the famous work of the modern Italian poet Giuseppe Ungaretti, *Il Taccuino del Vecchio (1952–1960).* Luis Muñoz, *El cuaderno del viejo (1952–1960)* (Valencia: Pre-Textos, 2000).

6. Ignacio Elguero, "El siglo de las individualidades," in *Íneditos 11 poetas,* ed. Ignacio Elguero (Madrid: Huerga and Fierro Editores, 2002), 11.

7. José Andújar Almansa, "Paisaje de la poesía última," *El maquinista de la generación* 15 (July 2008): 32.

8. Luis Antonio de Villena, *La lógica de Orfeo: Antología. Un camino de renovación y encuentro en la última poesía española,* ed. Luis Antonio de Villena (Madrid: Visor, 2003); Luis Antonio de Villena, *La inteligencia y el hacha. Un panorama de la generación poética de 2000,* ed. Luis Antonio de Villena (Madrid: Visor, 2010); Rafael Morales Barba, *Última poesía española (1990–2005). Antología,* ed. Rafael Morales Barba (Madrid: Marenostrum, 2006); María Rosal, *Con voz propia. Estudio y antología comentada de la poesía española escrita por mujeres (1970–2005),* ed. María Rosal (Sevilla. Renacimiento, 2006); Domingo Sánchez-Mesa Martínez, *Cambio de siglo: Antología de poesía española 1990–2007,* ed. Domingo Sánchez-Mesa Martínez (Madrid: Hiperión, 2007); Juan Carlos Abril, *Deshabitados. Antología,* ed. Juan

Carlos Abril (Granada: Diputación de Granada, 2008); Ángel L. Prieto de Paula, *Las moradas del verbo. Poetas españoles de la democracia. Antología,* ed. Ángel L. Prieto de Paula (Madrid: Calambur, 2010); Luis Bagué Quílez, *Quien lo probó lo sabe: 36 poetas para el tercer milenio,* ed. Luis Bagué Quílez (Zaragoza: Instituto Fernando el Católico, 2012); Remedios Sánchez García and Anthony Geist, *El canon abierto: Última poesía en español 1970–1985,* ed. Remedios Sánchez García (Madrid: Visor, 2015).

9. Antonio Jiménez Millán, *Poesía hispánica peninsular (1980–2005)* (Sevilla: Renacimiento, 2006); Alberto Santamaría, "Nuevos territorios poéticos. Apuntes para una lectura abierta de la joven poesía española," *El maquinista de la generación* 11 (2006): 96–106; José Andújar Almansa, "Retrato robot de la poesía reciente," *Paraíso: Revista de poesía* 2 (2007): 23–38; José Andújar Almansa, "El paisaje de la poesía última," *El maquinista de la generación* 15 (July 2008): 32–42; Juan Carlos Abril, "Introducción. Afinidades discursivas," in *Deshabitados. Antología,* ed. Juan Carlos Abril (Granada: Diputación de Granada, 2008), 11–40; Juan Carlos Abril, *Campos magnéticos. Veinte poetas españoles para el siglo XXI,* ed. Juan Carlos de Abril (Ciudad de México-Monterrey: La Otra Libros-Universidad Autónoma de Nuevo León, 2011); Juan Carlos Abril, "Hacia otra caracterización de la poesía española actual," in *Malos tiempos para la épica. Última poesía española (2001–2012),* ed. Luis Bagué Quílez and Alberto Santamaría (Madrid: Visor, 2013), 35–48; Luis Bagué Quílez, "La Poesía después de la poesía. Cartografías estéticas para el tercer milenio." *Monteagudo. Revista de literatura española, hispanoamericana y teoría de la literatura* 13 (2008): 49–72; Luis Bagué Quílez, "Introducción. Los poetas zurdos," in *Quien lo probó lo sabe: 36 poetas para el tercer milenio,* ed. Luis Bagué Quílez (Zaragoza: Instituto Fernando el Católico, 2012), 15–45; Luis Bagué Quílez and Alberto Santamaría, "Introducción: 2001–2012: Una odisea en el tiempo," in *Malos tiempos para la épica. Última poesía española (2001–2012),* ed. Luis Bagué Quílez and Alberto Santamaría (Madrid: Visor, 2013), 11–32; Ángel L. Prieto de Paula, "El medio lírico. Antologías, revistas, poéticas, poetas," in *Literatura y bellas artes,* ed. Francisco Rico, Jordi Gracia, and Antonio Bonet, vol. 5 (Madrid: Biblioteca Nueva, 2009), 109–133; Ángel L. Prieto de Paula, "Poesía en la era de la perplejidad," in *Las moradas del verbo. Poetas españoles de la democracia. Antología, ed. Ángel L. Prieto de Paula* (Madrid: Calambur, 2010), 9–58; and Diana Cullell, "Introduction," in *Spanish Contemporary Poetry: An Anthology,* ed. Diana Cullell (Manchester, U.K.: Manchester University Press, 2014), 1–33.

10. "Poesía española contemporánea," ed. Ángel L. Prieto de Paula and Luis Bagué, special issue, *Ínsula. Revista de letras y ciencias humanas,* no. 805–806 (January–February 2014): 2–48.

11. Josep M. Rodríguez, "Presentación," in *Yo es otro* (Barcelona: DVD Ediciones, 2001), 13.

12. Josep M. Rodríguez, "El grito," in *Veinticinco poetas españoles jóvenes. Antología,* ed. Adriana García, Guillermo López Gallego, and Álvaro Tato (Madrid: Hiperión, 2003), 178.

13. Josep M. Rodríguez, "Memorias de un lector," in *Deshabitados. Antología,* ed. Juan Carlos Abril (Granada: Diputación de Granada, 2008), 199.

14. Martín López-Vega, "Se debe escoger entre la cultura y el mercado," Cafe Babel, last modified April 15, 2011, http://www.cafebabel.es/cultura/articulo/el-poeta-martin-lopez-vega-se-debe-escoger-entre-la-cultura-y-el-mercado.html (accessed July 26, 2013).

15. Luis Muñoz, "Un nuevo simbolismo," in *Clarín. Revista de nueva literatura* 3, no. 18 (1998): 18–21.

16. "Luis Muñoz y Ana Gorría. Diálogos," *Años diez revista de poesía* 3 (Spring 2016): 83.

17. Araceli Iravedra, "Luis Muñoz," in *Hacia la democracia. La nueva poesía (1968–2000),* ed. Araceli Iravdera (Madrid: Visor, 2016), 779.

CHAPTER 1 LUIS MUÑOZ: THE INSTANT

1. Luis Muñoz wrote this personal biography at my request for inclusion in this chapter and provided his recent photo. Since 2000, Muñoz's works include poetry such as *Correspondencias* (Madrid: Visor, 2001), which won the III Premio de Poesía Generación del 27 (2000) and the Premio El Ojo Crítico de Poesía (2001); *Limpiar pescado. Poesía reunida (1991–2005)* (Madrid: Visor, 2005); and *Querido silencio* (Barcelona: Tusquets, 2006), which won the Premio Público (2006), and a poetry anthology, *From behind What Landscape: New and Selected Poems*, trans. Curtis Bauer (Madrid: Vaso Roto Poetry, 2015). He published his most recent collection, *Vecindad*, in December 2018 with Visor.

2. Luis Muñoz, "Atracción de los opuestos," in *Poesía con norte (Los poetas y sus poéticas)*, ed. Lorenzo Oliván (Valencia: Pre-Textos, 2012), 81.

3. Luis Muñoz, *Limpiar pescado. Poesía reunida (1991–2005)* (Madrid: Visor 2005).

4. Luis Muñoz, *From behind What Landscape: New and Selected Poems*, trans. Curtis Bauer (Madrid: Vaso Roto Ediciones, 2015), 142. Both Professors Muñoz and Bauer graciously granted permission to use the translations from this 2015 work in my book. Unless otherwise indicated, the other English translations in this chapter are my own.

5. Some of my ideas in this chapter were at a much earlier stage of development when I published my guest article for the special issue on Luis Muñoz in *Arquitrave* in 2015.

6. "Luis Muñoz," *Deriva. Revista digital literatura cine*, last modified August 8, 2005, http://www.deriva.org/entrevistas/entrevistas.php?ID-10 (accessed July 24, 2010).

7. Luis Muñoz, "Poética," in *La generación del 99: Antología crítica de la joven poesía española*, ed. José Luis García Martín (Madrid: Ediciones Nobel, 1999), 254.

8. Luis Muñoz, "Muñoz por Muñoz," elmundolibro.com, last modified March 25, 2003, http://www.elmundo.es/elmundolibro/especiales/2003/03/poetas/luismunoz.html (accessed April 19, 2011).

9. Luis Muñoz, "Poética," in *Última poesía española (1990–2005). Antología*, ed. Rafael Morales Barba (Madrid: Marenostrum, 2006), 129–130.

10. Luis Muñoz, "Luis Muñoz," in *Cambio de siglo: Antología de poesía española 1990–2007*, ed. Domingo Sánchez-Mesa Martínez (Madrid: Hiperión, 2007), 405.

11. Luis Muñoz, *Querido silencio* (Barcelona: Tusquets, 2006), 93.

12. Rafael Morales Barba, "Introducción," in *Última poesía española (1990–2005). Antología*, ed. Rafael Morales Barba (Madrid: Marenostrum, 2006), 41.

13. José-Carlos Mainer, "Literatura: entre el canon y el mercado," in *Literatura y bellas artes*, ed. Francisco Rico, Jordi Gracia, and Antonio Bonet, vol. 5, *España siglo XXI* (Madrid: Editorial Biblioteca Nueva, 2009), 36.

14. José María Brucart and Jonathan MacDonald, "Empty Categories and Ellipsis," in *Handbook of Hispanic Linguistics*, ed. José Ignacio Hualde, Antxon Olarrea, and Erin O'Rourke (Cambridge, Mass.: Blackwell, 2011), 579–590. Their discussion of "empty (pro)nominal categories" was invaluable. José María Brucart, *La elisión sintáctica en español* (Bellaterra: Servei de Publicaciones de la Universitat Autònoma de Barcelona, 1987), 215–220. This work also assisted me in my analysis. I thank my colleague Professor Antxon Olarrea for bringing to my attention Brucart's fundamental work on ellipsis in Spanish syntax and for his own insightful explanations concerning "empty subjects" and the use of the "impersonal you."

15. My 2012 article analyzes in detail the use of syntactic ellipsis in this poem. In this chapter of my book, I offer other perspectives. For example, in my earlier article, I did not consider the poetics of epiphany in this poem. I also did not address the condensed present instant in

which the creative activity of writing occurs. Finally, Muñoz's poetics "Atracción de opuestos" offers significant and self-reflective observations on the origin of this poem. This poetics also appeared in 2012 but after the publication of my article. I incorporate enlightening aspects of this poetics in my current study of the poem "Dejar la poesía."

16. One might be tempted to argue that the "you" is the reader, should the reader wish to identify with what he or she might assume to be her or his textual counterpart, or even the author, should the reader imagine that the poet might be engaged in a conversation with himself. However, the salient and impersonal nature of the second person singular "you" must be considered. I thank Professor Olarrea for illuminating this matter.

17. Octavio Paz, *El arco y la lira. El poema. La relevación poética. Poesía e historia* (Mexico: Fondo de Cultura Económica, 2003), 53. This fundamental work first appeared in 1956 and was republished in 1967. All translations to English of this book are from Octavio Paz, *The Bow and the Lyre. The Poem, the Poetic Revelation, Poetry and History*, trans. Ruth L. C. Simms (Austin: University of Texas Press, 2009), 42.

18. Francisco Brines, "Entrevista: Francisco Brines XIX Premio Reina Sofía de Poesía: 'Los que leen la poesía la necesitan como drogadictos,'" *El país*, April 29, 2010, https://elpais.com/diario/2010/04/29/cultura/1272492002_850215.html (accessed December 20, 2010).

19. Luis Muñoz, *Correspondencias* (Madrid: Visor, 2001). This collection is out of print. In 2005, Muñoz included the poetry from this earlier work in *Limpiar pescado*. The pages I reference are from his 2005 collected poems. Regarding the title *Correspondencias*, critic and poet Luis Antonio de Villena comments, "El Baudelaire al que puede sonar el título está tan asimilado que nada directo debe esperar hallarse." Luis Antonio de Villena, "Luis Muñoz," *Arquitrave. Revista colombiana de poesía* 61 (October–December, 2015): 7.

20. José Andújar Almansa, "Correspondencias de poesía y vida (Sobre *Limpiar pescado*, de Luis Muñoz)," *Ínsula. Revista de letras y ciencias humanas* 753 (September 2009): 29.

21. Domingo Sánchez-Mesa Martínez, "Sin foto de familia. Ensayo de radiografía de la poesía del cambio de siglo," in *Cambio de siglo: Antología de poesía española 1990–2007*, ed. Domingo Sánchez-Mesa Martínez (Madrid: Hiperión, 2007), 47.

22. Luis Muñoz, "Un nuevo simbolismo," *Clarín. Revista de nueva literatura* 3, no. 18 (1998): 21.

23. Luis Muñoz, "Luis Muñoz, la realidad a través de los sentidos," interview by Javier Díaz Gil, *Javier Díaz Gil* (blog), August 17, 2007, http://javierdiazgil.blogspot.com/2007/08/luis-muoz-la-realidad-travs-de-los.html (accessed November 27, 2013, and December 5, 2017).

24. He examines these subjects in the following poems from *Querido silencio*: "Raíces" (21), "Uña nueva" (37), "Cepillos de dientes" (39), "Continuidad" (47), "Moscas pegadas al cristal de la ventana" (57), "Paréntesis" (95), and "Los asientos traseros del autobús" (99).

25. Luis Muñoz, "El poema no escrito," in "Poesía española contemporánea," ed. Ángel L. Prieto de Paula and Luis Bagué, special issue, *Ínsula. Revista de letras y ciencias humanas*, no. 805–806 (January–February 2014): 41.

26. "Sierra de Guadarrama National Park," Tourist Office of Spain, https://www.spain.info/en_US/que-quieres/naturaleza/espacios-naturales/parque-nacional-sierra-de-guadarrama.html (accessed June 28, 2017).

27. On March 6, 2014, Luis Muñoz gave a guest poetry reading of selections from his works, published and unpublished. It was a bilingual reading (Spanish and English) attended by students, professors, and community members. The reading was sponsored by the Department of Spanish and Portuguese at the University of Arizona. The poem "El bocadillo que vuelve de excursión" was included. During the department's Hispanic Cultural Day in April 2014, one of the students participating in that event told our associate head professor, Katia

Bezerra, that Muñoz's poem about the "sandwich" was his favorite cultural event during the 2013–2014 academic year.

CHAPTER 2 ABRAHAM GRAGERA: THE WORD

1. Abraham Gragera wrote this personal biography at my request for inclusion in this chapter and provided his recent photo. Gragera's poetry works include: *Adiós a la época de los grandes caracteres* (Valencia: Pre-Textos, 2005); *El tiempo menos solo* (Valencia: Pre-Textos, 2012), which won the Premio El Ojo Crítico de Poesía (2013); and *O Futuro* (Valencia: Pre-Textos, 2017), which won the Premio Mejor Libro de Poesía de 2017 awarded by El Gremio de Libreros de Madrid.
2. Edward Hirsch, "Metaphor: A Poet Is a Nightingale," in *How to Read a Poem and Fall in Love with Poetry* (New York: Harvest Books, 1999), 13.
3. "Metaphor," in *The New Princeton Encyclopedia of Poetry and Poetics*, 3rd ed. (Princeton: Princeton University Press, 1993), 761.
4. Abraham Gragera, *Adiós a la época de los grandes caracteres* (Valencia: Pre-Textos, 2005); Abraham Gragera, *El tiempo menos solo* (Valencia: Pre-Textos, 2012); and Abraham Gragera, *O Futuro* (Valencia: Pre-Textos, 2017). The translations of these titles are my own. A further word on the translations in this chapter, I have translated to English the critical and scholarly works that I cite. I use an endnote when indicating the selections from Gragera's poems that I translated into English.
5. The poems in the series "Siete presentes" have been translated into English by Juan de Dios León Gómez. Unless otherwise noted, all the specific poems that I study in this chapter have been translated into English by him. I use his translations with his permission and with the permission of the poet. None of these translations have been published before. A few years ago, he had translated "Siete presentes" along with four other of Gragera's poems for a public reading that the poet gave in London. Gragera confirmed this in my conversation with him in Madrid on June 18, 2018. After having read these, I asked the translator to address four other of Gragera's poems that I study in my chapter. The full text of the nine poems, in Spanish and in English, appear in the "Poems by Abraham Gragera" section of my book.
6. José Andújar Almansa, "Retrato robot de la poesía reciente," *Paraíso: Revista de poesía* 2 (2007): 37.
7. Abraham Gragera, "Poética, I," in "Poesía española contemporánea," ed. Ángel L. Prieto de Paula and Luis Bagué, special issue, *Ínsula. Revista de letras y ciencias humanas*, no. 805–806 (January–February 2014): 44.
8. Manuel Borrás, "Abraham Gragera: Adiós a la época de los grandes caracteres," Editorial Pre-Textos, last modified October 14, 2006, https://www.pre-textos.com/prensa/?p=1035 (accessed December 12, 2015).
9. Octavio Paz, *El arco y la lira. El poema. La relevación poética. Poesía e historia* (Mexico: Fondo de Cultura Económica, 2003), 45. His work first appeared in 1956 and was republished in 1967. All translations of this book into English are from Octavio Paz, *The Bow and the Lyre. The Poem, the Poetic Revelation, Poetry and History*, trans. Ruth L. C. Simms (Austin: University of Texas Press, 2009), 35.
10. The translations are mine for the lines and images from this poem.
11. Some of my earlier ideas on Gragera's work were in seminal form in my "The Poetics of Epiphany: Recent Works by Abraham Gragera and Josep M. Rodríguez," *Poéticas. Revista*

de estudios literarios 2, no. 2 (September 2016): 63–87. At that time, *O Futuro* had not been published.

12. Martín López-Vega, "El tiempo menos solo," *Clarín. Revista de nueva literatura* 104 (April 22, 2013), http://abrahamgragera.blogspot.com/2013/04/el-tiempo-menos-solo-revista-clarin-n_22.html (accessed August 19, 2014).

13. Túa Blesa, "Adiós a la época de los grandes caracteres," *El cultural*, last modified January 5, 2006, https://elcultural.com/Adios-a-la-epoca-de-los-grandes-caracteres (accessed August 11, 2015).

14. Abraham Gragera, "Abraham Gragera," in *La lógica de Orfeo: Antología. Un camino de renovación y encuentro en la última poesía española*, ed. Luis Antonio de Villena (Madrid: Visor, 2003), 219.

15. José Andújar Almansa, "Paisaje de la poesía última," *El maquinista de la generación* 15 (July 2008): 34.

16. Federico García Lorca, "La imagen poética de Don Luis de Góngora," in *Obras completas* (Madrid: Aguilar, 1971), 67.

17. I thank my graduate student Brigette Walters for her insight into this image during our spring 2016 seminar.

18. José Andújar Almansa, "El signo borrado: Poéticas simbolistas para un nuevo siglo," in "Poesía española contemporánea," ed. Ángel L. Prieto de Paula and Luis Bagué, special issue, *Ínsula. Revista de letras y ciencias humanas*, no. 805–806 (January–February 2014): 13.

19. When we studied "El susurro del polvo" in my spring 2016 graduate class, my student Manuel Martín Barros said that after having read this poem he would never "see" a coat hanger in the same way again.

20. Rafael Espejo, "Encuentro con la poesía de Abraham Gragera," *Biblioteca Palma del Rio* (blog), January 18, 2012, http://bibliotecadepalmadelrio.blogspot.com/2012/01/los-secretarios-de-la-luna-nos-invitan.html (accessed May 27, 2015).

21. Rafael Espejo, "Adiós a la época de los grandes caracteres de Abraham Gragera," *Paraíso: Revista de poesía* 2 (2007): 108, 109. He indicates that a few of the poems from this work were dispersed in published anthologies and in literary magazines earlier. He also indicates that during that time Gragera continued to work on his poems to make them better. I note that the final versions were gathered into his 2005 book later. In addition, "Estrella fugaz" and "Adiós a la época de los grandes caracteres" were included in *La lógica de Orfeo: Antología. Un camino de renovación y encuentro en la última poesía española*, ed. Luis Antonio de Villena (Madrid: Visor, 2003), 221, 226–227. I also note that when these two poems were later published in *Adiós a la época*, Gragera had altered the punctuation in the former poem and changed the spacing in the latter.

22. "Abraham Gragera, Premio El Ojo Crítico de RNE de Poesía por su obra *El tiempo menos solo*," RTVE, last modified December 12, 2013, http://www.rtve.es/radio/20131213/abraham-gragera-premio-ojo-critico-rne-poesia-su-obra-tiempo-menos-solo/820420.shtml (accessed May 15, 2015). This was the twenty-fourth awarding of the prize by Spanish National Radio (RNE).

23. Ana Corroto, "Premios Ojo Crítico 2013: Abraham Gragera, un poeta, un sophói," *La girándula*, last modified February 23, 2014, http://girandula.com/2014/02/23/premios-ojo-critico-2013-abraham-gragera-un-poeta-un-sophoi/ (accessed May 8, 2015).

24. Antonio Mochón, "El tiempo menos solo, Abraham Gragera," *La vida no existe* (blog), January 18, 2013, http://lavidanoexiste.blogspot.com.es/2013/01/el-tiempo-menos-solo-abraham-gragera.html (accessed June 30, 2017).

25. I thank Abraham Gragera for sharing his ideas on this poem with me during our conversation in Madrid on May 25, 2016.
26. Roberto Juarroz, "Desbautizar el mundo 40," in *Poesía vertical (antología)* (Madrid: Visor, 2008), 132. The poem is from his *Sexta poesía vertical*, first published in 1975.
27. Roberto Juarroz, *Poesía y realidad* (Valencia: Pre-Textos, 2000), 18–19. This collection of essays was first published in 1992.
28. Mariano Peyrou, "La soledad del tiempo y el tiempo de la soledad," *La estafeta del viento. La revista de poesía de la Casa de América Segunda Época—edición digital*, May 19, 2015, http://www.laestafetadelviento.es/resenas/la-soledad-del-tiempo-y-el-tiempo-de-la-soledad-por-mariano-peyrou (accessed June 19, 2015).
29. In his 2013 review of Gragera's 2012 work, Martín López-Vega also points out this poet's keen attentiveness to tradition—poetic, biblical, classical, and mythological—as well as his knowledge of the visual arts.
30. Ana Corroto, "Abraham Gragera, los cuerpos de la palabra," *Llanuras rutas para lectores*, last modified November 25, 2013, http://llanuras.es/protagonistas/autores/abraham-gragera-los-cuerpos-palabra/htm (accessed June 30, 2017).
31. Aldo Pellegrini, "Se llama poesía todo aquello que cierra la puerta a los imbéciles," *Revista de Poesía* 9 (August 1961), http://www.lamaquinadeltiempo.com/prosas/pellegrini.html (accessed December 8, 2016).
32. In a conversation with the poet in Madrid on June 18, 2018, when I was seeking permission to cite his poetry, we also discussed the title of his 2017 work. I thank him for his illuminating comments.
33. Unless otherwise noted, the English translations of the selected lines from Gragera's 2017 work are my own in this part of my chapter.
34. This poem appears in the "Poems by Abraham Gragera" section of my book. The translation into English of this poem is by Juan de Dios León Gómez.
35. Martín Lopez-Vega, "El futuro como presente perpetuo," *Cuadernos hispanoamericanos* 805–806 (July–August 2017): 237, https://issuu.com/publicacionesaecid/docs/ydray-web-ch-805-806-julio-agosto-2 (accessed September 15, 2017).
36. "El Gremio de Libreros de Madrid anuncia los ganadores de sus premios anuales," Librerias de Madrid, last modified October 19, 2017, https://www.libreriasdemadrid.es/gremio-libreros-madrid-anuncia-los-ganadores-premios-anuales/ (accessed June 12, 2018).
37. At my request, the translation to English of both this poem and the poet's analysis are by Juan de Dios León Gómez. He is a gifted and remarkable translator. Working with him during the poem translation process reflected in this chapter was immensely rewarding for me during our different conversations in which we exchanged several ideas. He also was in the position to discuss his translations, when/if in doubt, with Abraham Gragera, who offered important insights.

CHAPTER 3 JOSEP M. RODRÍGUEZ: THE IMAGE

1. Josep M. Rodríguez wrote this personal biography at my request for inclusion in this chapter and provided his recent photo. Rodríguez's works include poetry such as *Frío* (Valencia: Pre-Textos, 2002); *La caja negra* (Valencia: Pre-Textos, 2004), which won the V Premio Internacional de Poesía Emilio Prados (2003); *Raíz* (Madrid: Visor, 2008), which won the VII Premio Internacional de Poesía Emilio Alarcos (2008); *Arquitectura yo* (Madrid: Visor, 2012), which won the XIV Premio de Poesía Generación del 27 (2012); *Sangre seca* (Madrid:

Hiperión, 2017), which won the XXIV Premio de Poesía Ciudad de Córdoba Ricardo Molina (2017); poetry anthologies such as *Ecosistema. Antología poética* (Valencia: Pre-Textos, 2015); *Radar. Antología bilingüe* (Lucena: El Orden del Mundo, 2017); *Yo es otro. Autorretratos de la nueva poesía* (Barcelona: DVD, 2001); and literary criticisms such as *Alfileres. El haiku en la poesía española última*, ed. Josep M. Rodríguez (Lucena: 4 Estaciones, 2004); *Hana o la flor del cerezo* (Valencia: Pre-Textos, 2007), which won the V Premio Internacional de Crítica Literaria Amado Alonso (2006).

2. Wallace Stevens, "Adagia I," in *Opus Posthumous: Poems, Prose, Plays*, ed. Milton J. Bates (New York: Vintage Books, 1989), 185. The distinguished Stevens scholar Samuel French Morse published the first edition in 1957. Bates's excellent work presents revisions and corrections while also enlarging the 1957 edition with copious notes and other poetry and prose unavailable earlier.

3. Josep M. Rodríguez, "Memorias de un lector," in *Deshabitados. Antología*, ed. Juan Carlos Abril (Granada: Diputación de Granada, 2008), 203.

4. Josep M. Rodríguez, *Frío* (Valencia: Pre-Textos, 2002); Josep M. Rodríguez, *La caja negra* (Valencia: Pre-Textos, 2004); Josep M. Rodríguez, *Raíz* (Madrid: Visor, 2008); Josep M. Rodríguez, *Arquitectura yo* (Madrid: Visor, 2012); and Josep M. Rodríguez, *Sangre seca* (Madrid: Hiperión, 2017).

5. Ezra Pound, "A Few Don'ts by an Imagiste," *Poetry*, March 1913, https://www.poetry foundation.org/poetrymagazine/articles/58900/a-few-donts-by-an-imagiste (accessed October 2, 2015). This is the original spelling.

6. I examine the poetics of epiphany in my 2016 article, where I study aspects of Rodríguez's poetry from *Raíz* (2008) and *Arquitectura yo* (2012). There I sow seeds later developed in the more comprehensive analysis that I present in this chapter concerning his poetry collections published from 2002 to 2017. In that same article, as mentioned earlier, I also examine selected works by Abraham Gragera.

7. Josep M. Rodriguez, "Josep M. Rodriguez," in *La lógica de Orfeo: Antología. Un camino de renovación y encuentro en la última poesía española*, ed. Luis Antonio de Villena (Madrid: Visor, 2003), 269.

8. Josep M. Rodríguez, ed., *Radar. Antología bilingüe* (Lucena: Orden del Mundo, 2017). *Radar* is a bilingual anthology of poems selected by the poet. Each poem in Spanish is accompanied by a translation into English. The poems "Erosión I, II" have been translated into English by Ben Clark.

9. I use the term "self" in the sense of "as applied to the bearer of subjective experience" and what that experience entails, "the contents of that experience." The self, as I use it, is the "I," is the "subject," and is the "me." I use "identity" to refer to the human psychology of "personal identity, or the continuous existence of the personality despite physiological and psychological changes." In Rodríguez's poetry, the subjective experience of the self often is a pathway to knowledge of human existence, and this I refer to as "self-consciousness"—"the knowledge by the self of itself." I use the term self-awareness in this same vein. The term "being" is complex and much more difficult to encapsulate. By way of explanation, I employ "mode" in the sense of manner. Although others might disagree, I am using the term "being" in the sense of existence. I am concerned with, as is Rodríguez, human existence. My study examines the ways in which human beings interact with other things and experience the actuality in which they "are," in which they "exist" (*Dictionary of Philosophy [Ancient-Medieval-Modern]*, ed. Dagobert D. Runes, s. v. "self," "self-consciousness," "identity," and "being," http://www.ditext.com/runes/ [accessed November 6, 2015]). Further clarifications of additional terms are found in other chapter notes.

10. Josep M. Rodriguez, "El grito," in *Veinticinco poetas españoles jóvenes. Antología*, ed. Adriana G. García, Guillermo López Gallego, and Álvaro Tato (Madrid: Hiperión, 2003), 178.
11. Josep M. Rodríguez, "Dejo huecos para que el lector se cuele por ellos," interview by Paché Merayo, *El comercio*, May 30, 2009, http://www.elcomercio.es/gijon/20090530/cultura/dejo-huecos-para-lector-0090530.html (accessed April 4, 2015).
12. Josep M. Rodríguez, "Presentación," in *Yo es otro*, ed. Josep M. Rodríguez (Barcelona: DVD Ediciones, 2001), 13.
13. Pound's 1913 article later was published in 1918 as a part of the literary essay "A Retrospect." Ezra Pound, "'A Retrospect' and 'A Few Don'ts,'" Poetry Foundation, last modified October 13, 2009, https://www.poetryfoundation.org/articles/69409/a-retrospect-and-a-few-donts (accessed October 2, 2015). I make no attempt to "correct" any of his discourse.
14. Josep M. Rodríguez, ed., *Alfileres. El haiku en la poesía española última* (Lucena: 4 Estaciones, 2004). This is the first anthology on the haiku and its manifestations as a poetic form in contemporary Spain.
15. Josep M. Rodríguez, *Hana o la flor del cerezo* (Valencia: Pre-Textos, 2007). The essay concerns the haiku and its reception in the West.
16. Josep M. Rodríguez, "Un mismo cielo: Aproximación a extremo oriente," in *Malos tiempos para la épica. Última poesía española (2001–2012)*, ed. Luis Bagué Quílez and Alberto Santamaría (Madrid: Visor, 2013), 181–190.
17. Josep M. Rodríguez, ed. and trans., *Kobayashi Issa: Poemas de madurez. Edición bilingüe* (Lucena: Juan de Mairena, 2008).
18. It is evident that Rodríguez has various publications on the haiku. In his 2013 article "Un mismo cielo: Aproximación a extremo oriente," he indicates that this poetic form has become an assimilated referent for the Spanish poets writing today (189). He also told me in Madrid on June 15, 2018, that he had been invited by *Ínsula* to coordinate the special monographic issue on the haiku.
19. Josep M. Rodríguez, "Entrevista a Josep M. Rodríguez," *Hojas en la acera. Gaceta internacional de haiku* 18 (June 8, 2013): 27, https://haikunversaciones.files.wordpress.com/2014/01/hojas-en-la-acera-nro-18.pdf (accessed April 4, 2015).
20. José Andújar Almansa, "*Raíz* de Josep M. Rodríguez," *El maquinista de la generación* 17 (October 2009): 228. This literary critic is the leading authority on the Spanish lyric of today, as I discuss in my introduction and afterword. He is also the foremost critic on the poetry of Josep M. Rodríguez, having written several exceptional articles on his works. Andújar's investigations have been vital to my own research on Rodríguez's poetry, and I cite his articles, prologues, and reviews in this chapter. He richly deserves these references because his ideas have sparked new discoveries of my own when analyzing the work of this important poet.
21. Josep M. Rodríguez, "Cuaderno de viaje," in *Segunda poesía con norte (Los poetas y sus poéticas)*, ed. Lorenzo Oliván (Valencia: Pre-Textos, 2014), 89.
22. In 2016, *Fragmenta. Revista anual de poesía* published a monographic issue on the poetry of Josep M. Rodríguez. In my guest contribution, I published some of my earlier ideas concerning Rodríguez's crafting of the image that I further explicate here. In my article, however, I did not develop the thematic matter of being in the world.
23. I use the term "reality" as Andújar employs it in his exceptional critical article "Paisaje de la poesía última" (34–36).
24. Josep M. Rodríguez, "Prólogo, Círculos concéntricos," in *Alfileres. El haiku en la poesía española última*, ed. Josep M. Rodríguez (Lucena: 4 Estaciones, 2004), X–XI.

25. José Andújar Almansa, "Dos o tres cosas que yo sé de Josep M. Rodríguez," in "La poesía de Josep M. Rodríguez," ed. Rafael Morales Barba, special issue, *Fragmenta. Revista anual de poesía* 7 (2016): 51.
26. José Andújar Almansa, "Retrato robot de la poesía reciente," *Paraíso: Revista de poesía* 2 (2007): 37.
27. José Andújar Almansa, "Paisaje de la poesía última," *El maquinista de la generación* 15 (July 2008): 34.
28. José Andújar Almansa, "*Raíz* de Josep M. Rodríguez," *El maquinista de la generación* 17 (October 2009): 227.
29. Alberto Santamaría, "Nuevos territorios poéticos. Apuntes para una lectura abierta de la joven poesía española," *El maquinista de la generación* 11 (2006): 104.
30. José Andújar Almansa, "El signo borrado: Poéticas simbolistas para un nuevo siglo," in "Poesía española contemporánea," ed. Ángel L. Prieto de Paula and Luis Bagué, special issue, *Ínsula. Revista de letras y ciencias humanas*, no. 805–806 (January–February 2014): 12.
31. See the excellent review of this collection by one of Rodríguez's fellow poets. Rafael Espejo, "*Raíz*," *La estafeta del viento. La revista de poesía de la Casa de América Segunda Época—edición digital*, January 24, 2012, http://www.laestafetadelviento.es/resenas/raiz (accessed July 13, 2015).
32. The concept of "reflective self-consciousness" is explained by Shaun Gallagher and Dan Zahavi in "Phenomenological Approaches to Self-Consciousness," in *Stanford Encyclopedia of Philosophy*, winter 2016, ed. Edward N. Zalta, https://plato.stanford.edu/archives/win2016/entries/self-consciousness-phenomenological/. The authors indicate, "Reflective self-consciousness is an explicit, conceptual, and objectifying awareness that takes a lower-order consciousness as its attentional theme. I am able at any time to attend directly to the cognitive experience itself, turning my experience itself into the object of my consideration." Furthermore, they argue, "Some philosophers who are inclined to take self-consciousness to be intrinsically linked to the issue of self-reference would argue that the latter depends on a first-person *concept*. One attains self-consciousness only when one can *conceive* of oneself *as* oneself and has the linguistic ability to use the first-person pronoun to refer to oneself (Baker 200, 68; cf. Lowe 2000, 264). On this view, self-consciousness is something that emerges during a developmental process, and depends on the acquisition of concepts and language."
33. The translation of "Inicio" is by Ben Clark (*Radar*, 17).
34. Antonio Lucas, "La realidad de lo visible. Aproximación y sospechas sobre una construcción de la mirada," in *Malos tiempos para la épica. Última poesía española (2001–2012)*, ed. Luis Bagué Quílez and Alberto Santamaría (Madrid: Visor, 2013), 74.
35. "Madera" has been translated by Ester Boldú (*Radar*, 61).
36. The concept of "being becoming nonbeing" is explained by Karin Verelst and Bob Coecke in "Early Greek Thought and Perspectives for the Interpretation of Quantum Mechanics: Preliminaries to an Ontological Approach," preprint, submitted 1999, http://philsci-archive.pitt.edu/id/eprint/3028. For the present study, I use this article because I am interested in the emergence of the main paradox of early Greek thought as it relates to what these authors refer to as "the co-incidence of being and nonbeing in the world of change and motion as we experience it," most especially in the here and now. This paradox, "one of the oldest problems of human thought," is relevant, as I argue, to some aspects of *Arquitectura yo*.
37. I also use the term "instant" in my study of *Arquitectura yo* in the sense used by Verelst and Coecke. The authors place the concept of the instant in a historical context, explaining, when referencing the thought of Heraclitus of Ephesus, "Everything that is at this moment changes at the same time, therefore it is not." For Heraclitus, "flux is the characteristic of time,

by virtue of which all things change inevitably." It is he who brought the problem into prominence, "all things flow; nothing abides" (*Dictionary of Philosophy [Ancient-Medieval-Modern]*, ed. Dagobert D. Runes, s. v. "flux," http://www.ditext.com/runes/ [accessed November 6, 2015]).

38. For an additional perspective, see José Andújar Almansa, "*Arquitectura yo.* La poesía de Josep M. Rodríguez," *Ínsula. Revista de letras y ciencias humanas* 803 (November 2013): 30.

39. In his commentary on this poem, Andújar explains, "La poesía es una transfusión, aunque no exactamente una transfusión romántica" ("*Arquitectura yo*," 33). His insight is a point of departure for my analysis of the poem "B+."

40. Wallace Stevens, "Of Modern Poetry," Poetry Foundation, https://www.poetryfoundation.org/poems/43435/of-modern-poetry (accessed July 8, 2017).

41. Josep M. Rodríguez, *Ecosistema. Antología poética. De Josep M. Rodríguez,* ed. Josep M. Rodríguez (Valencia: Pre-Textos, 2015).

42. The anthology includes, as Rodríguez explains in the "Procedencia de los poemas" (95), five works that would form a part of his next collection: "Hora prima" (26), "Continuidad" (48), "Pequeña digresión. *Versión segunda"* (63), "Material infancia" (77), and "Casi variación Lowell" (92). The pagination referenced is from the 2015 anthology. These poems later appear in *Sangre seca* in the following order and where the pagination references the 2017 publication: "Hora prima" (21), "Continuidad" (18), "Pequeña digresión. *Versión segunda"* (22), "Material infancia" (36), and "Casi variación Lowell" (51).

43. Nikola Madzirov, "Nikola Madzirov," foreword to *Radar. Antología bilingüe,* by Josep M. Rodríguez (Lucena: el Orden del Mundo, 2017), 10. These observations, translated to English by Rodríguez (11), form a part of the opening remarks for his bilingual anthology, which I will discuss shortly.

44. Joan Margarit, "Epílogo," in *Sangre seca,* by Josep M. Rodríguez (Madrid: Hiperión, 2017), 69.

45. As noted in my introduction, Luis Muñoz (2015) and Josep M. Rodríguez (2017) have published selected poems in bilingual poetry anthologies presenting texts in Spanish and in English.

46. The translations to English by Ben Clark, Monika Izabela Jaworska, and Ester Boldú that I reference in my chapter for Rodríguez's poems first appeared in *Radar. Antología bilingüe.* The translators graciously gave me permission to use their works in this chapter and in the "Poems by Josep M. Rodríguez" section of my book.

CHAPTER 4 ADA SALAS: POETRY AND POETICS

1. Ada Salas wrote this personal biography at my request for inclusion in this chapter and provided her recent photo. Since 2000, Salas's works includes poetry such as *Lugar de la derrota* (Madrid: Hiperión, 2003); *Esto no es el silencio* (Madrid: Hiperión, 2008), which won the XV Premio de Poesía Ciudad de Córdoba Ricardo Molina (2007); *No duerme el animal. Poesía 1987–2003* (Madrid: Hiperión, 2009); Ada Salas and Jesús Placencia, *Ashes to Ashes: Catorce poemas a partir de catorce dibujos a partir de T. S. Eliot* (Mérida: Editora Regional de Extremadura, 2010); *Limbo y otros poemas* (Valencia: Pre-Textos, 2013); Ada Salas and Jesús Placencia, *Diez mandamientos* (Madrid: Oficina de Arte y Ediciones, 2016); *Descendimiento* (Valencia: Pre-Textos, 2018) and books such as *Alguien aquí. Notas acerca de la escritura poética* (Madrid: Hiperión, 2005); *El margen. El error. La tachadura. De la metáfora y otros asuntos más*

o menos poéticos (Badajoz: Diputación de Badajoz, 2010), which won the II Premio Literario de Ensayo Fernando Tomás Pérez González (2010).

2. Ada Salas, *El margen. El error. La tachadura. De la metáfora y otros asuntos más o menos poéticos* (Badajoz: Diputación de Badajoz, 2010), 19. Unless otherwise noted, all translations in this chapter are my own. Salas's works, either in part or in full, have not been translated into English. This is the first time that selected poems, selections from her poetics, and portions from her books on writing poetry are published along with English translations. In my conversation with her in June 2017, Salas confirmed that some of her poems have been translated to French, German, Italian, Greek, and Russian but none to English. In my translations of her poems to English, I do not attempt to capture or follow metrical or rhythmic or rhyming patterns that may be evidenced in the original. I do, however, try to maintain the special spacing she uses.

3. Ada Salas, "He vivido cien siglos con horas semejantes," in *No duerme el animal. Poesía 1987–2003* (Madrid: Hiperión, 2009), 48. A word on her poetry, Salas's poems usually do not have titles. When referring to her poems, I cite the first line in order to orient the reader. Only two of her published collections display titles for her poems. These are Ada Salas, *Limbo y otros poemas* (Valencia: Pre-Textos, 2013); and Ada Salas and Jesús Placencia, *Diez mandamientos* (Madrid: Oficina de Artes y Ediciones, 2016).

4. Ada Salas, "Poética," in *Ellas tienen la palabra (Dos décadas de poesía española). Antología*, ed. Noni Benegas and Jesús Munárriz (Madrid: Hiperión, 1997), 582–583. The revised second edition of this work appeared in 1998 and was compiled by the same editors. I note that the Spanish pronoun "ellas" in the title is gender specific, and this is lost in translation.

5. This quotation is from a presentation that Vicente Huidobro delivered at the Ateneo in Madrid in 1921. Years later, his talk appeared as an article in a 1989 special issue of *Poesía* dedicated to his work. For additional information, see Salas's note 98 (*El margen*, 88).

6. Ada Salas, "El deseo es lo mudo," in "Poesía española contemporánea," ed. Ángel L. Prieto de Paula and Luis Bagué, special issue, *Ínsula. Revista de letras y ciencias humanas*, no. 805–806 (January–February 2014): 40.

7. Ada Salas, *Alguien aquí. Notas acerca de la escritura poética* (Madrid: Hiperión, 2005).

8. Ada Salas, *Lugar de la derrota* (Madrid: Hiperión, 2003). This collection is out of print.

9. Some of the scholars addressing her stylistic precision use the term "minimalist." José María Balcells, "Introducción," in *Ilimitada voz (Antología de Poetas Españolas 1940–2002). Serie 2*, ed. José María Balcells (Cádiz: Publicaciones de la Universidad de Cádiz, 2003), 72; Rafael Morales Barba, "Introducción," in *Última poesía española (1990–2005). Antología*, ed. Rafael Morales Barba (Madrid: Mare Nostrum, 2006), 50; Domingo Sánchez-Mesa Martínez, "Sin foto de la familia. Ensayo de radiografía de la poesía del cambio de siglo," in *Cambio de siglo: Antología de poesía española 1990–2007*, ed. Domingo Sánchez-Mesa Martínez (Madrid: Hiperión, 2007), 36; Luis Bagué Quílez, "Introducción. Los poetas zurdos," in *Quien lo probó lo sabe: 36 poetas para el tercer milenio*, ed. Luis Bagué Quílez (Zaragoza: Instituto Fernando el Católico, 2012), 34. In my view, this description captures neither the exquisite manner in which Salas constructs the poem nor the exactness of her diction.

10. Salas's poems display a particularized spacing of poetic lines on the printed page. When quoting selections from her poetry in the corpus of the chapter, I have attempted to incorporate her original spacing. In the "Poems by Ada Salas" section of my book, I also attempt to duplicate her specific placement of lines, words, and spacing in the Spanish version of her texts as well as in my English translations of these.

11. Ada Salas, "Brechas," *Nayagua. Revista de poesía*, June 13, 2010: 85.

12. Ada Salas, "Lo no reconocible que vive en lo real," *Cuadernos hispanoamericanos* 709–710 (July 2009): 13–14.

13. Because Salas is a female poet, the reader might be tempted to posit a female poetic voice. This is not accurate, however, in her works. The voice speaking in the poetry and the poetics of Ada Salas is sincerely, genuinely, and unmistakably a human one. Salas does not employ a gendered voice in her work, and I have kept this in mind in my translations. In the quoted passage, she uses the term "author," and in other works, she will use the term "poet." She explains her perspective in her famous essay "¿Poesía en femenino?"; Salas presented this essay publicly on various occasions. It later was published in her *Alguien aquí* (145–150). In her view, "La poesía es, quizá, el género literario más 'asexuado.' En la mayoría de los casos escribir un poema no implica crear un personaje, masculino o femenino. . . . Se escribe desde la raíz, y en la raíz sólo reside lo humano" (*Alguien aquí*, 146). [Poetry is, perhaps, the most "asexual" of the literary genres. In most instances, the writing of a poem does not imply creating a character, masculine or feminine. . . . A poem is written starting from the root, and the human is the only source.]

14. Ada Salas, "En una lengua extranjera," in *Segunda poesía con norte (Los poetas y sus poéticas)*, ed. Lorenzo Oliván (Valencia: Pre-Textos, 2014), 56.

15. "El desorden trabaja como crece una herida III" (*Limbo*, 50) is part of the longer poem "Coda: Chanson du désir I–IV" (*Limbo*, 43–51). Salas provides an illuminating analysis of part III of her longer poem in her 2014 poetics, "El deseo es lo mudo" (40) appearing in the special issue on contemporary Spanish poetry published by *Ínsula* that same year.

16. *Encyclopedia Britannica*, s.v. "volcano," last modified July 6, 2018, https://www.britannica.com/science/volcano (accessed June 11, 2018). The authors note, "the term volcano means the vent from which magma and other substances erupt to the surface." Salas's metaphoric construct of "fissure" (*El margen*, 19) also is at work in this poem.

17. During my conversation with Ada Salas in Madrid on May 29, 2014, she explained that her poetics published in 2009 and 2010 mark the beginning of many of the concepts that she would discuss and enhance in her longer 2010 book. The poet graciously provided me with these two essays in manuscript form noting that they were "the seeds" for her book. I reference the page numbers of the published articles.

18. Ada Salas, "Lo que duerme en los pliegues lo no," in *Esto no es el silencio* (Madrid: Hiperión, 2008), 34–35.

19. Each of these poets holds a distinctive place in her overall poetics. I addressed her admiration for Vicente Huidobro earlier. Salas also is fully attentive to Rainer Maria Rilke's poetry and admires his quest for penetrating the poetic word in order to find the "meaning" that lies "behind" it ("Lo no reconocible," 16).

20. Salas indicates in note 2 of her 2009 poetics ("Lo no reconocible," 14) that the Spanish pronoun "Él" refers to Aristotle. Here she quotes a portion of part one of Anne Carson's longer poem titled "Essay on What I Think About Most." Carson published this poem in 2000. The translation to Spanish of Carson's poem is by Salas's fellow poet Jordi Doce ("Lo no reconocible," 15). Jordi Doce, trans., "Ensayo sobre aquello en lo que más pienso," in *Hombres en sus horas libres* (Valencia: Pre-Textos, 2007), 72–77. Utilizing Doce's translation, Salas quotes all of part one of Carson's poem in Spanish in the introduction to her 2010 book when she launches her larger study on metaphor (*El margen*, 14–15). I note that Doce's translation of Carson's 2000 collection is invaluable because he presents her original poem in English accompanied by his translation of it in Spanish (Anne Carson, *Hombres en sus horas libres*, trans. Jordi Doce [Valencia: Pre-Textos, 2007], 72–77). My use of portions of the first part of the Carson poem, "Essay on What I Think About Most," in English are from Doce's 2007 collection.

21. The italicized words are in the original. Salas indicates in note 9 of "Brechas" (87) that she is citing from Octavio Paz's collection *Árbol adentro* (Barcelona: Seix Barral, 1987), 33.
22. Jennifer Blessing, "Lucio Fontana: *Concetto spaziale, Attese*," Guggenheim, https://www.guggenheim.org/artwork/1334 (accessed February 1, 2016).
23. "En la almendra" (*Limbo*, 81) is the first line of part III of Salas's five-part poem titled "Pieza de exposición I–V" (*Limbo*, 79–83).
24. Barbara Hess, *Fontana* (Cologne, Germany: Taschen Basic Art Series, 2006), 45.
25. Fontana began the *Nature* sculptures in the summer of 1959. These were a series of ceramics subsequently cast in bronze (*Fontana*, 44–45). Hess comments, "At the outset, Fontana sliced small lumps of clay like fruit and marked the surfaces of the cut with incisions. Later, retaining the spherical shape, he began to deform it by means of holes made with a wooden stick or incisions that appeared to reach deep into the interior of the sphere" (*Fontana*, 45).
26. Jan van der Marck, "Lucio Fontana: The Spatial Concept of Art (1966)," in *Lucio Fontana: Sculpture* (Aspen: Aspen Art Museum, 2012), 35.
27. Sarah Whitfield, "Handling Space," in *Lucio Fontana* (London: Hayward Gallery Exhibit, 2000), 48.
28. In my study of this poem, I was inspired by Whitfield's observations concerning Fontana's *Nature* sculptures and the objects themselves: "The oval form, a universal symbol of creation and regeneration, is linked to the roundness of the large terracotta spheres of 1959, vast seeds splitting open, ready to propagate" ("Handling Space," 48).
29. To condense the quoted matters in the text, I note that the citations are from Jesús Placencia (http://www.jesusplacencia.com/index.php?/cuadr/) and Ada Salas and Jesús Placencia, *Ashes to Ashes: Catorce poemas a partir de catorce dibujos a partir de T. S. Eliot* (Mérida: Editora Regional de Extremadura, 2010). I recommend that the reader view Placencia's innovative "written drawings" online: http://www.jesusplacencia.com/index.php?/cuadr/.
30. I include the website link to encourage the reader to "see" these works: http://www.jesusplacencia.com/index.php?/dibujos/diez-mandamientos/. In 2013, Placencia exhibited eighteen of his "written drawings" from the series titled *Songlines*. At the time, the artist was also preparing ten "written drawings" for his series *Diez mandamientos*. These were to be a part of a book, *Songlines*, where he intended to gather both series (http://www.jesusplacencia.com/index.php?/dibujos/diez-mandamientos/). In the fall of 2015, he asked Ada Salas to consider accompanying his "Written Drawings" in the series *Diez mandamientos* with poems. When I met with Ada Salas in Madrid in October of 2015, while I was on sabbatical researching the present book, she informed me that she was very interested in this new collaboration.
31. In my June 12, 2017, conversation in Madrid with Ada Salas, she explained that she was currently writing a collection of poems inspired by the fifteenth-century masterpiece painting *Descent from the Cross* by Rogier van der Weyden. The formidable artwork is tempera and oil on wood, it measures 7′3″ by 8′7″, and it is part of the Prado Museum collection. On June 14, 2018, in Madrid, I met with Ada Salas and asked about this project. As I explain in the afterword of my book, Salas's *Descendimiento* was published in the fall of 2018 with Pre-Textos. This work, her newest collection of poetry, was completed during her 2017–2018 sabbatical year.
32. José Luis Rozas Bravo, *Escribir y borrar. Antología esencial (1994–2016). Ada Salas*, ed. José Luis Rozas Bravo (Madrid: Fondo de Cultura Económica, 2016).
33. Ada Salas, "Sin sentido," in *Escribir y borrar. Antología esencial (1994–2016). Ada Salas*, ed. José Luis Rozas Bravo (Madrid: Fondo de Cultura Económica, 2016), 203–204.

34. When I met with Ada Salas on June 14, 2018, in Madrid regarding permissions to cite her works in my book, she explained that this poem had appeared in *Sibila* 49 (April 2016): 13, but that it had not been published in one of her collections. She also explained that the final section of this poem, part IV, constitutes the last section (numbered III) of her poem, "*Callar y obrar*." This last portion appeared in *Diez mandamientos* (53). Her analysis has not been published before.

BIBLIOGRAPHY

Abril, Juan Carlos, ed. *Campos magnéticos. Veinte poetas españoles para el siglo XXI.* Ciudad de México-Monterrey: La Otra Libros-Universidad Autónoma de Nuevo León, 2011.

———. "Hacia otra caracterización de la poesía española actual." In *Malos tiempos para la épica. Última poesía española (2001–2012)*, edited by Luis Bagué Quílez and Alberto Santamaría, 35–48. Madrid: Visor, 2013.

———. "Introducción. Afinidades discursivas." In *Deshabitados. Antología*, edited by Juan Carlos Abril, 11–47. Granada: Diputación de Granada, 2008.

Andújar Almansa, José. "*Arquitectura yo*. La poesía de Josep M. Rodríguez." *Ínsula. Revista de letras y ciencias humanas* 803 (November 2013): 23–34.

———. *Centros de gravedad. Poesía española en el siglo XXI. Antología.* Valencia: Pre-Textos, 2018.

———. "Correspondencias de poesía y vida (Sobre *Limpiar pescado*, de Luis Muñoz)." *Ínsula. Revista de letras y ciencias humanas* 753 (September 2009): 26–29.

———. "Dos o tres cosas que yo sé de Josep M. Rodríguez." In "La poesía de Josep M. Rodríguez." Special issue, *Fragmenta. Revista anual de poesía* 7 (September 2016): 47–54.

———. "Paisaje de la poesía última." *El maquinista de la generación* 15 (July 2008): 32–42.

———. "Prólogo." In *Ecosistema. Antología poética. De Josep M. Rodríguez*, edited by Josep M. Rodríguez, 9–18. Valencia: Pre-Textos, 2015.

———. "*Raíz* de Josep M. Rodríguez." *El maquinista de la generación* 17 (October 2009): 226–229.

———. "Retrato robot de la poesía reciente." *Paraíso: Revista de poesía* 2 (2007): 23–38.

———. "El signo borrado: Poéticas simbolistas para un nuevo siglo." In "Poesía española contemporánea." Special issue, *Ínsula. Revista de letras y ciencias humanas* 805–806 (January–February 2014): 12–15.

Bagué, Luis Quílez. "Introducción. Los poetas zurdos." In *Quien lo probó lo sabe: 36 poetas para el tercer milenio*, edited by Luis Bagué Quílez, 15–49. Zaragoza: Instituto Fernando el Católico, 2012.

———. "Introducción: 2001–2012: Una odisea en el tiempo." In *Malos tiempos para la épica. Última poesía española (2001–2012)*, edited by Luis Bagué Quílez and Alberto Santamaría, 11–32. Madrid: Visor, 2013.

———. "La poesía española bajo el efecto 2000 (dos o tres cosas que sé de ella)." In "Poesía española contemporánea." Special issue, *Ínsula. Revista de letras y ciencias humanas* 805–806 (January–February 2014): 5–8.

———. "La poesía después de la poesía. Cartografías estéticas para el tercer milenio." In "Poesía española del siglo XXI." Special issue, *Monteagudo. Revista de literatura española, hispanoamericana y teoría literaria* 13 (2008): 49–72.

Balcells, José María. "Introducción." In *Ilimitada voz (Antología de poetas españolas 1940–2002). Serie 2*, edited by José María Balcells, 17–90. Cádiz: Publicaciones de la Universidad de Cádiz. 2003.

Benegas, Noni, and Jesús Munárriz. *Ellas tienen la palabra. Dos décadas de poesía española.* Edited by Noni Benegas and Jesús Munárriz. Madrid: Hiperión, 1997, 1998.

Blesa, Túa. "Adiós a la época de los grandes caracteres." *El cultural.* Last modifed January 5, 2006. https://elcultural.com/Adios-a-la-epoca-de-los-grandes-caracteres (accessed August 11, 2015).
Blessing, Jennifer. "Lucio Fontana *Concetto spaziale, Attese.*" Guggenheim. https://www.guggenheim.org/artwork/1334 (accessed February 1, 2016).
Borrás, Manuel. "Abraham Gragera: Adiós a la época de los grandes caracteres." Pre-Textos. Last modified July 14, 2006. https://www.pre-textos.com/prensa/?p=1035 (accessed December 12, 2015).
Bozalongo, Paula. *Diciembre y nos besamos.* Madrid: Hiperión, 2014.
Brines, Francisco. "Francisco Brines XIX Premio Reina Sofía de Poesía: 'Los que leen la poesía la necesitan como drogadictos.'" Interview by Elsa Fernández-Santos. *El país,* April 29, 2010. https://elpais.com/diario/2010/04/29/cultura/1272492002_850215.html (accessed December 20, 2010).
Brucart, José María. *La elisión sintáctica en español.* Bellaterra: Servei de Publicaciones de la Universitat Autònoma de Barcelona, 1987.
Brucart, José María, and Jonathan MacDonald. "Empty categories and ellipsis," In *Handbook of Hispanic Linguistics,* edited by José Ignacio Hualde, Antxon Olarrea, and Erin O'Rourke, chapter 27. Cambridge, Mass.: Blackwell, 2011.
Cano Ballesta, Juan. "Introducción. Orientaciones recientes de la poesía española." In *Poesía española reciente (1980–2000),* edited by Juan Cano Ballesta, 21–72. Madrid: Cátedra, 2001.
Carson, Anne. *Men in the Off Hours.* New York: Knopf, 2000.
———. "Ensayo sobre aquello en lo que más pienso." In *Hombres en sus horas libres,* translated by Jordi Doce, 72–73. Valencia: Pre-Textos, 2007.
Casiellas, Laura. *Los idiomas comunes.* Madrid: Hiperión, 2010.
Clark, Ben. *La policía celeste.* Madrid: Visor, 2018.
Corroto, Ana. "Abraham Gragera, los cuerpos de la palabra." *Llanuras.* Last modified July 25, 2014. http://llanuras.es/protagonistas/autores/abraham-gragera-los-cuerpos-palabra/ (accessed June 30, 2017).
———. "Premios Ojo Crítico 2013: Abraham Gragera, un poeta, un sophói." *La girándula.* Last modified February 23, 2014. http://girandula.com/2014/02/23/premios-ojo-critico-2013-abraham-gragera-un-poeta-un-sophoi/ (accessed May 8, 2015).
Cullell, Diana. "Introduction." In *Spanish Contemporary Poetry: An Anthology,* edited by Diana Cullell, 1–33. Manchester, U.K.: Manchester University Press, 2014.
———. *La poesía de la experiencia a finales del siglo XX y al XXI.* Madrid: Devenir, 2010.
———. "Preface." In *Spanish Contemporary Poetry: An Anthology,* edited by Diana Cullell, vii–ix. Manchester, U.K.: Manchester University Press, 2014.
Debicki, Andrew P. *Poetry of Discovery: The Spanish Generation of 1956–1971.* Lexington: University of Kentucky Press, 1982.
Díaz Gil, Javier. "Luis Muñoz, la realidad a través de los sentidos." *Javier Díaz Gil* (blog), August 17, 2007. http://javierdiazgil.blogspot.com/2007/08/luis-muoz-la-realidad-travs-de-los.html (accessed November 27, 2013, and December 5, 2017).
Elguero, Ignacio. "Prólogo. El siglo de las individualidades." In *Inéditos 11 poetas,* edited by Ignacio Elguero, 9–11. Murcia: Huerga y Fierro Editores, 2002.
Espejo, Rafael. "Adiós a la época de los grandes caracteres de Abraham Gragera." *Paraíso: revista de poesía* 2 (2007): 107–109.
———. "Encuentro con la poesía de Abraham Gragera." *Biblioteca Palma del Rio* (blog), January 18, 2012. http://bibliotecadepalmadelrio.blogspot.com/2012/01/los-secretarios-de-la-luna-nos-invitan.html (accessed May 27, 2015).

———. "Raíz." *La estafeta del viento. La revista de poesía de la Casa de América Segunda Época—edición digital,* January 24, 2012. http://www.laestafetadelviento.es/resenas/raiz (accessed July 13, 2015).

Floriano, Miguel, and Antonio Rivero Machina, eds. *Nacer en otro tiempo. Antología de la joven poesía española.* Sevilla: Renacimiento, 2016.

Gallagher, Shaun, and Dan Zahavi. "Phenomenological Approaches to Self-Consciousness." In *Stanford Encyclopedia of Philosophy,* winter 2016, edited by Edward N. Zalta. https://plato.stanford.edu/archives/win2016/entries/self-consciousness-phenomenological/ (accessed July 9, 2015).

García Lorca, Federico. "La imagen poética de Don Luis de Góngora." In *Obras completas,* 62–85. Madrid: Aguilar, 1971.

García Martín, José Luis. *La generación del 1999 antología crítica de la joven poesía española.* Oviedo: Nobel, 1999.

———. *La generación de los ochenta.* Valencia: Mestra, 1988.

———. *La poesía figurativa.* Sevilla: Renacimiento, 1992.

Gragera, Abraham. "Abraham Gragera." In *La lógica de Orfeo: Antología. Un camino de renovación y encuentro en la última poesía española,* edited by Luis Antonio de Villena, 219–220. Madrid: Visor, 2003.

———. *Adiós a la época de los grandes caracteres.* Valencia: Pre-Textos, 2005.

———. *O Futuro.* Valencia: Pre-Textos, 2017.

———. "Poética, I." In "Poesía española contemporánea." Special issue, *Ínsula. Revista de letras y ciencias humanas* 805–806 (January–February 2014): 44.

———. *El tiempo menos solo.* Valencia: Pre-Textos, 2012.

Hess, Barbara. *Fontana.* Cologne: Taschen Basic Art Series, 2006.

Hirsch, Edward. "Metaphor: A Poet Is a Nightingale." In *How to Read a Poem and Fall in Love with Poetry.* 13–15. New York: Harvest Books, 1999.

Huidobro, Vicente. "La Poesía." Vicente Huidobro. http://www.vicentehuidobro.uchile.cl/manifiesto2.htm.

Iravedra, Araceli, ed. *Hacia la democracia. La nueva poesía (1968–2000).* Madrid: Visor, 2016.

———. "Luis Muñoz." In *Hacia la democracia. La nueva poesía (1968–2000),* edited by Araceli Iravedra, 779–783. Madrid: Visor, 2016.

———. *Poesía de experiencia.* Madrid: Visor, 2007.

———. "Prólogo." In *Hacia la democracia. La nueva poesía (1968–2000),* edited by Araceli Iravedra, 9–170. Madrid: Visor, 2016.

Jiménez Millán, Antonio. *Poesía hispánica peninsular (1980–2005).* Sevilla: Renacimiento, 2006.

Juarroz, Roberto. "Desbautizar el mundo 40." In *Poesía vertical (antología).* Madrid: Visor, 2008.

———. *Poesía y realidad.* Valencia: Pre-Textos, 2000.

Lanz, Juan José. "Luces de cabotaje: La poesía de la transición y la generación de la democracia en los albores del nuevo milenio." *Monteagudo. Revista de literatura española, hispanoamericana y teoría de la literatura* 13 (2008): 25–47.

———. *La poesía durante la transición y la generación de la democracia.* Madrid: Devenir, 2007.

———. "Poéticas del fragmento y esquirlas dialógicas en la poesía española reciente (1992–2013)." In "Poesía española contemporánea." Special issue, *Ínsula. Revista de letras y ciencias humanas* 805–806 (January–February 2014): 15–18.

López-Vega, Martín. "El futuro como presente perpetuo." *Cuadernos hispanoamericanos* 805–806 (July–August 2017): 235–237. https://issuu.com/publicacionesaecid/docs/ydray-web-ch-805-806-julio-agosto-2 (accessed September 15, 2017).

———. "Se debe escoger entre la cultura y el mercado." Cafe Babel. Last modified April 15, 2011. http://www.cafebabel.es/cultura/articulo/el-poeta-martin-lopez-vega-se-debe-escoger-entre-la-cultura-y-el-mercado.html (accessed July 26, 2013).

———. "El tiempo menos solo." *Clarín. Revista de nueva literatura* 104 (April 22, 2013). http://abrahamgragera.blogspot.com/2013/04/el-tiempo-menos-solo-revista-clarin-n_22.html (accessed August 19, 2014).

Lucas, Antonio. "La realidad de lo visible aproximación y sospechas sobre una construcción de la mirada." In *Malos tiempos para la épica. Última poesía española (2001–2012)*, edited by Luis Bagué Quílez and Alberto Santamaría, 73–76. Madrid: Visor, 2013.

Madzirov, Nikola. "Nikola Madzirov." Foreword to *Radar. Antología bilingüe*, by Josep M. Rodríguez, 10–11. Lucena: El Orden del Mundo, 2017.

Mainer, José-Carlos, ed. *En el último tercio del siglo 1968–1998. Antología consultada de la poesía española*. Madrid: Visor, 1999.

———. "Literatura: entre el canon y el mercado." In *Literatura y bellas artes*, vol. 5, *España siglo XXI*, edited by Francisco Rico, Jordi Gracia, and Antonio Bonet, 15–41. Madrid: Editorial Biblioteca Nueva, 2009.

Margarit, Joan. "Epílogo." In *Sangre seca*, by Josep M. Rodríguez, 69–72. Madrid: Hiperión, 2017.

Merayo, Paché. "Dejo huecos para que el lector se cuele por ellos." *El comercio*, May 30, 2009. http://www.elcomercio.es/gijon/20090530/cultura/dejo-huecos-para-lector-20090530.html (accessed April 4, 2015).

Mochón, Antonio. "El tiempo menos solo, Abraham Gragera." *La vida no existe* (blog), January 18, 2013. http://lavidanoexiste.blogspot.com.es/2013/01/el-tiempo-menos-solo-abraham-gragera.html (accessed June 30, 2017).

Mora, Vicente Luis. *La cuarta persona del plural Antología de poesía española contemporánea (1978–2015)*. Madrid: Vaso Roto Ediciones, 2016.

Morales Barba, Rafael. "Introducción." In *Última poesía española (1990–2005). Antología*, edited by Rafael Morales Barba, 7–58. Madrid: Marenostrum, 2006.

Muñoz, Luis. *El apetito*. Valencia: Pre-Textos, 1998.

———. "Atracción de opuestos." In *Poesía con norte (Los poetas y sus poéticas)*, edited by Lorenzo Oliván, 77–86. Valencia: Pre-Textos, 2012.

———. *Correspondencias*. Madrid: Visor, 2001.

———. *Limpiar pescado. Poesía reunida (1991–2005)*. Madrid: Visor, 2005.

———. *From behind What Landscape: New and Selected Poems*. Translated by Curtis Bauer. Madrid: Vaso Roto Ediciones, 2015.

———. "Luis Muñoz." *Deriva. Revista digital literatura cine*, August 8, 2005. http://www.deriva.org/entrevistas/entrevistas.php?ID-10 (accessed July 24, 2010).

———. "Luis Muñoz." In *Cambio de siglo: Antología de poesía española 1990–2007*, edited by Domingo Sánchez-Mesa Martínez, 404–406. Madrid: Hiperión, 2007.

———. "Luis Muñoz." In *La lógica de Orfeo: Antología. Un camino de renovación y encuentro en la última poesía española*, edited by Luis Antonio de Villena, 93–94. Madrid: Visor, 2003.

———. "Luis Muñoz y Ana Gorría. Diálogos." *Años diez revista de poesía* 3 (Spring 2016): 78–89.

———. *Manzanas amarillas*. Madrid: Hiperión. 1995.

———. "Muñoz por Muñoz." *El mundo*, March 25, 2003. http://www.elmundo.es/elmundolibro/especiales/2003/03/poetas/luismunoz.html (accessed April 19, 2011).

———. "Un nuevo simbolismo." *Clarín. Revista de nueva literatura* 3, no. 18 (1998): 18–21.

———. "El poema no escrito." In "Poesía española contemporánea." Special issue, *Ínsula. Revista de letras y ciencias humanas* 805–806 (January–February 2014): 41.

———. "Poética." In *La generación del 99: Antología crítica de la joven poesía española*, edited by José Luis García Martín, 252–255. Madrid: Ediciones Nobel, 1999.

———. "Poética." In *Última poesía española (1990–2005). Antología*, edited by Rafael Morales Barba, 129–130. Madrid: Marenostrum, 2006.

———. *Querido silencio*. Barcelona: Tusquets, 2006.

———. *Septiembre*. Madrid: Hiperión, 1991.

———. "Transición." In *Limpiar pescado: Poesía reunida*, 7–17. Madrid: Visor Libros, 2005.

———. *Vecindad*. Madrid: Visor Libros, 2008.

Nantell, Judith. "Crafting the Image: Poetry as Epiphany in the Work of Josep M. Rodríguez." In "La poesía de Josep M. Rodríguez," edited by Rafael Morales Barba. Special issue, *Fragmenta. Revista anual de poesía* 7 (2016): 111–122.

———. "La poesía de Luis Muñoz." Special issue, *Arquitrave. Revista colombiana de poesía* 61 (October–December 2015): 11–15.

———. "The Poetics of Epiphany: Recent Works by Abraham Gragera and Josep M. Rodríguez." *Poéticas. Revista de estudios literarios* 2, no. 2 (September 2016): 63–87. http://www.poeticas.org/index.php/poeticas/issue/view/2/showToc.

———. "Syntactically Silent Subjects: Luis Muñoz and Poetry of Ellipsis." *Studies in Twentieth and Twenty-First-Century Literature* 36, no. 2 (Summer 2012): 324–339.

Paz, Octavio. *El arco y la lira. El poema. La relevación poética. Poesía e historia*. Mexico: Fondo de Cultura Económica, 2003.

———. *The Bow and the Lyre. The Poem, the Poetic Revelation, Poetry and History*. Translated by Ruth L. C. Simms. Austin: University of Texas Press, 2009.

Pellegrini, Aldo. "Se llama poesía todo aquello que cierra la puerta a los imbéciles." *Revista de Poesía* 9 (August 1961). http://www.lamaquinadeltiempo.com/prosas/pellegrini.html (accessed December 8, 2016).

Peyrou, Mariano. "La soledad del tiempo y el tiempo de la soledad." *La estafeta del viento. La revista de poesía de la Casa de América* segunda época, edición digital (December 2015). http://www.laestafetadelviento.es/resenas/la-soledad-del-tiempo-y-el-tiempo-de-la-soledad-por-mariano-peyrou (accessed February 19, 2016).

Pound, Ezra. "A Few Don'ts by an Imagiste." *Poetry*, March 1913. https://www.poetryfoundation.org/poetrymagazine/articles/58900/a-few-donts-by-an-imagiste (accessed October 2, 2015).

———. "'A Retrospect' and 'A Few Don'ts.'" Poetry Foundation. Last modified October 13, 2009. https://www.poetryfoundation.org/articles/69409/a-retrospect-and-a-few-donts (accessed October 2, 2015).

Prieto de Paula, Ángel L. "El medio lírico. Antologías, revistas, poéticas, poetas." In *Literatura y bellas artes*, vol. 5, *España siglo XXI*, edited by Francisco Rico, Jordi Gracia, and Antonio Bonet, 109–133. Madrid: Biblioteca Nueva, 2009.

———, ed. *Las moradas del verbo. Poetas españoles de la democracia. Antología*. Madrid: Calambur Poesía, 2010.

———. "Poesía en la era de la perplejidad." In *Las moradas del verbo. Poetas españoles de la democracia. Antología*, edited by Ángel L. Prieto de Paula, 9–58. Madrid: Calambur Poesía, 2010.

———, ed. "Poesía española contemporánea." Special issue, *Ínsula. Revista de letras y ciencias humanas* 805–806 (January–February 2014).

———. "Poesía y contemporaneidad: Unas cuestiones de partida." In "Poesía española contemporánea." Special issue, *Ínsula. Revista de letras y ciencias humanas* 805–806 (January–February 2014): 2–5.

Rodríguez, Josep M., ed. *Alfileres. El haiku en la poesía española última*. Lucena: 4 Estaciones, 2004.

———. *Arquitectura yo*. Madrid: Visor, 2012.

———. *La caja negra*. Valencia: Pre-Textos, 2004.

———. "Cuaderno de viaje." In *Segunda Poesía con Norte (Los poetas y sus poéticas)*, edited by Lorenzo Oliván, 80–90. Valencia: Pre-Textos, 2014.

———. *Las deudas del viajero*. Lleida: Dama Ginebra, 1998.

———. "Diagrama de Venn." *La razón*, July 8, 2018, 52.

———, ed. *Ecosistema. Antología poética. De Josep M. Rodríguez*. Valencia: Pre-Textos, 2015.

———. "Entrevista a Josep M. Rodríguez." *Hojas en la acera. Gaceta internacional de haiku*, June 8, 2013, 27–30. https://haikunversaciones.files.wordpress.com/2014/01/hojas-en-la-acera-nro-18.pdf (accessed April 4, 2015).

———. "Fractura." In "Poesía española contemporánea." Special issue, *Ínsula. Revista de letras y ciencias humanas* 805–806 (January–February 2014): 46–47.

———. *Frío*. Valencia: Pre-Textos, 2002.

———. "El grito." In *Veinticinco poetas españoles jóvenes. Antología*, edited by Adriana García, Guillermo López Gallego, and Álvaro Tato, 178. Madrid: Hiperión, 2003.

———. *Hana o la flor del cerezo*. Valencia: Pre-Textos, 2007.

———. "Josep María Rodríguez." In *La lógica de Orfeo: Antología. Un camino de renovación y encuentro en la última poesía española*, edited by Luis Antonio de Villena, 269–270. Madrid: Visor, 2003.

———. *Kobayashi Issa: Poemas de madurez*. Bilingual edition. Edited and translated by Josep M. Rodríguez. Lucena: Juan de Mairena, 2008.

———. "Memorias de un lector." In *Deshabitados. Antología*, edited by Juan Carlos Abril, 197–204. Granada: Diputación de Granada, 2008.

———. "Un mismo cielo: Aproximación a extremo oriente." In *Malos tiempos para la épica. Última poesía española (2001–2012)*, edited by Luis Bagué Quílez and Alberto Santamaría, 181–190. Madrid: Visor, 2013.

———. "Presentación." In *Yo es otro. Autorretratos de la nueva poesía*, edited by Josep M. Rodríguez, 9–15. Barcelona: DVD Ediciones, 2001.

———. "Prólogo: Círculos concéntricos." In *Alfileres. El haiku en la poesía española última*, edited by Josep M. Rodríguez, i–xxxviii. Lucena: 4 Estaciones, 2004.

———, ed. *Radar. Antología bilingüe*. Lucena: El Orden del Mundo, 2017.

———. *Raíz*. Madrid: Visor, 2008.

———. *Sangre seca*. Madrid: Hiperión, 2017.

———, ed. *Yo es otro. Autorretratos de la nueva poesía*. Barcelona: DVD Ediciones, 2001.

Rodríguez Jiménez, Antonio. "Diferencia 'versus' experiencia: la poesía heterodoxa frente a la tendencia oficial." *Claves de razón práctica* 60 (1996): 77–78.

Rosal, María, ed. *Con voz propia. Estudio y antología comentada de la poesía española escrita por mujeres (1970–2005)*. Sevilla: Renacimiento, 2006.

Rozas Bravo, José Luis, ed. *Escribir y borrar. Antología esencial (1994–2016) Ada Salas*. Madrid: Fondo de Cultura Económica, 2016.

Runes, Dagobert D., ed. *Dictionary of Philosophy (Ancient-Medieval-Modern)*. http://www.ditext.com/runes/a.html (accessed September 14, 2015).

Salas, Ada. "Ada Salas." In *Cambio de siglo Antología de poesía española 1990–2007*, edited by Domingo Sánchez-Mesa Martínez, 367–370. Madrid: Hiperión, 2007.

———. *Alguien aquí. Notas acerca de la escritura poética*. Madrid: Hiperión, 2005.

———. *Arte y memoria del inocente*. Cáceres: Universidad de Extremadura, 1988.

———. "Brechas." *Nayagua revista de poesía* 13 (June 2010): 85–90.

———. *Descendimiento*. Valencia: Pre-Textos, 2018.

———. "El deseo es lo mudo." In "Poesía española contemporánea." Special issue, *Ínsula. Revista de letras y ciencias humanas* 805–806 (January–February 2014): 40.

———. *Esto no es el silencio*. Madrid: Hiperión, 2008.

———. *Limbo y otros poemas*. Valencia: Pre-Textos, 2013.

———. "Lo no reconocible que vive en lo real." *Cuadernos hispanoamericanos* 709–710 (July 2009): 13–22.

———. *Lugar de la derrota*. Madrid: Hiperión, 2003.

———. *El margen. El error. La tachadura. De la metáfora y otros asuntos más o menos poéticos*. Badajoz: Diputación de Badajoz, 2010.

———. *No duerme el animal. Poesía 1987–2003*. Madrid: Hiperión, 2009.

———. "¿Poesía en femenino?" In *Alguien aquí. Notas acerca de la escritura poética*, by Ada Salas, 143–150. Madrid: Hiperión, 2005.

———. "Poética." In *Ellas tienen la palabra. Dos décadas de poesía española*, edited by Noni Benegas and Jesús Munárriz, 582–583. Madrid: Hiperión, 1998.

———. "Poética." In *Última poesía española (1990–2005). Antología*, edited by Rafael Morales Barba, 95–96. Madrid: Marenostrum, 2006.

———. *La sed*. Madrid: Hiperión, 1997.

———. "Sin sentido." In *Escribir y borrar. Antología esencial (1994–2016) Ada Salas*, edited by José Luis Rozas Bravo, 203–204. Madrid: Fondo de Cultura Económica, 2016.

———. "En una lengua extranjera." In *Segunda poesía con norte (Los poetas y sus poéticas)*, edited by Lorenzo Oliván, 51–58. Valencia: Pre-Textos, 2014.

———. *Variaciones en blanco*. Madrid: Hiperión, 1994.

Salas, Ada, and Jesus Placencia. *Ashes to Ashes: Catorce poemas a partir de catorce dibujos a partir de T. S. Eliot*. Mérida: Editora Regional de Extremadura, 2010.

———. *Diez mandamientos*. Madrid: Oficina de Artes y Ediciones, 2016.

Sánchez García, Remedios, ed. *El canon abierto: Última poesía en español 1970–1985. Selección de poemas de Anthony L. Geist*. Madrid: Visor, 2015.

———. "Introducción 'El canon abierto.'" In *El canon abierto: Última poesía en español 1970–1985*, edited by Remedios Sánchez García, 9–95. Madrid: Visor, 2015.

Sánchez-Mesa Martínez, Domingo, ed. *Cambio de siglo: Antología de poesía española 1990–2007*. Madrid: Hiperión, 2007.

———. "Guardianes de la diversidad: Funciones de las antologías en la era de las multitudes." In "Poesía española contemporánea." Special issue, *Ínsula. Revista de letras y ciencias humanas* 805–806 (January–February 2014): 22–25.

———. "Prólogo." In *Cambio de siglo: Antología de poesía española 1990–2007*, edited by Domingo Sánchez-Mesa Martínez, 9–28. Madrid: Hiperión, 2007.

———. "Sin foto de familia. Ensayo de radiografía de la poesía del cambio de siglo." In *Cambio de siglo: Antología de poesía española 1990–2007*, edited by Domingo Sánchez-Mesa Martínez, 29–65. Madrid: Hiperión, 2007.

Santamaría, Alberto. "Nuevos territorios poéticos. Apuntes para una lectura abierta de la joven poesía española." *El maquinista de la generación* 11 (2006): 96–106.

Sherno, Sylvia. "Poetry Wars." In "Defining Differences." Special issue, *Studies in Twentieth and Twenty-First-Century Literature* 36, no. 2 (Summer 2012): 189–203.

Stevens, Wallace. "Adagia I." In *Opus Posthumous: Poems, Prose, Plays*, edited by Milton J. Bates, 185. New York: Vintage Books, 1989.

———. "Of Modern Poetry." Poetry Foundation. https://www.poetryfoundation.org/poems/43435/of-modern-poetry (accessed July 8, 2017).

van der Marck, Jan. "Lucio Fontana: The Spatial Concept of Art (1966)." *Lucio Fontana: Sculpture*. Aspen: Aspen Art Museum, 2012.

van der Weyden, Rogier. "Descent from the Cross." Museo del Prado. https://www.museodelprado.es/en/the-collection/art-work/the-descent-from-the-cross/856d822a-dd22-4425-bebd-920a1d416aa7 (accessed June 30, 2017)

Verelst, Karin, and Bob Coecke. "Early Greek Thought and Perspectives for the Interpretation of Quantum Mechanics: Preliminaries to an Ontological Approach." Preprint, submitted 1999. http://philsci-archive.pitt.edu/id/eprint/3028 (accessed July 7, 2015).

Villena, Luis Antonio de, ed. *La inteligencia y el hacha. Un panorama de la Generación poética de 2000*. Madrid: Visor, 2010.

———. "La inteligencia y el hacha. (Un panorama de la Generación poética de 2000)." In *La inteligencia y el hacha*, edited by Luis Antonio de Villena, 7–38. Madrid: Visor, 2010.

———, ed. *La lógica de Orfeo: Antología. Un camino de renovación y encuentro en la última poesía española*. Madrid: Visor, 2003.

———. "Luis Muñoz." Special issue, *Arquitrave Revista colombiana de poesía* 61 (October–December 2015): 1–10.

———. "Tradición y renovación en la poesía española última. Un breve panorama." In *10 menos 30 la ruptura interior en la 'poesía de la experiencia*, edited by Luis Antonio de Villena, 9–42. Valencia: Pre-Textos, 1997.

Whitfield, Sarah. "Handling Space." *Lucio Fontana*. London: Hayward Gallery Exhibit, 2000.

INDEX

ABOUT THE AUTHOR

Judith Nantell is a professor in the Department of Spanish and Portuguese at the University of Arizona. She received her PhD and MA from Indiana University-Bloomington. Her publications center largely on Spanish Peninsular poetry, modern and contemporary. This book is the result of her latest research, guest articles, and graduate teaching on the Spanish lyric of today. In 1994, she published *The Poetry of Francisco Brines: The Deconstructive Effects of Language*. Her 1986 book, *Rafael Alberti's Poetry of the Thirties: The Poet's Public Voice*, received the 1984 South Atlantic Modern Language Association (SAMLA) Studies Award. Professor Nantell received the College of Humanities Distinguished Faculty Teaching Award in 2011. She served as the appointed vice dean of the College of Humanities from 1993 to 2008.

Teaching Representations of the First World War